New
Jersey
Getaways

Irina,

Every time I open this book I get excited - it is filled w/ places to go and things to do + stories - all things I had always hoped I'd get to share with you - one at a time + for a very long time. I gave it to you once - and you gave it back. Well, now you're getting it again. From when I bought it until now, unfortunately, none of what I had hoped has happened. I know now that it isn't going to. So maybe you'll look thru - find a place - go there - + think of me - think of maybe how we would have enjoyed it - + I'll be there w/ you - I'll be w/ you somehow forever - listen for me - in the wind, in your heart, in the music, in your gut.

I Love You

New Jersey Getaways

The Complete Guide to Garden State Day Trips

by Willa Speiser

New Jersey Monthly Press
Morristown, New Jersey

Manufactured in Canada

Library of Congress Control Number: 2001 130106
ISBN: 1-893787-02-8

Cover and interior design by Mayapriya Long, Bookwrights
Cover photographs by Walter Choroszewski

For Ruth Rosenblatt, who enjoyed all trips

Contents

Introduction

How long is a day trip? How many miles do you drive, when do you leave home, and when do you come back? Because New Jersey is small, each trip in this book can be done in one day from just about any part of the state. Depending upon where you live and how much you want to see in a particular place, you can spend a morning touring a living history farm, an afternoon rafting on the Delaware, or a whole day exploring a part of the state you hadn't discovered before.

It is only fair to note that I made these trips and wrote this book from the perspective of a determined traveler who once made a family day trip to Washington, D.C., from Essex County. My husband and I packed our two children into the car early one November morning, the Thursday of teacher's convention weekend, drove to the Lincoln Memorial, visited the Vietnam Memorial, stopped at the Smithsonian Institution's Air and Space Museum long enough to have very clear images of both the *Spirit of St. Louis* and lunar spacesuits in our minds (and freeze-dried ice cream in our son's hand), then drove to Mt. Vernon for a quick late-afternoon tour. We stopped at a Route 95 rest area in Maryland for dinner and were home after our children's bedtime but before our own. It wasn't an in-depth tour, but it was a surprisingly successful introduction to a city where we have since spent more time, exploring it in greater depth and seeing other sights, but always enjoying the memory of that earlier trip.

Even if you don't want to carry day-tripping to quite such an extreme, depending upon where you live, most if not all the destinations in this book are an easy trip. If you live in central New Jersey, nothing is likely to be more than a couple of hours away. If you live closer to one of the corners, some of the trips may stretch to three hours each way, or in a few cases a little longer than that, which may be longer than you'd like to spend traveling each way on a single day. It is certainly possible, and very inviting if time and money allow, to turn some of these trips into weekends or overnight trips, so that you can drive from one corner of the state to another and see several places that you might not otherwise have visited.

Each of the chapters is meant to work as a trip in its own right, but some trips can be combined, or you may decide that parts of two or three chapters would make a good trip because they focus on subjects that really appeal to you, whether it's antiquing or the Revolutionary War or the natural history and wildlife of New Jersey. You can see some of the historic sites in Morristown (chapter 11), then go for a walk along the boardwalks of the Great Swamp (chapter 12); you can ride your bike along part of the Delaware and Raritan Canal towpath (chapter 18), then go antiquing in Lambertville, or visit the living history farm in Titusville, or go to a Trenton Thunder baseball game (chapter 19).

By the same token, you don't have to do everything in one chapter in a single trip. Some places have so much to offer that they can be enjoyed on a beautiful summer day and again on a cold November day. The Shore is a world of its own, and if it's 85 degrees and sunny and you've just bought a beach pass, that's your day trip. But if you're at the Shore and the weather changes, you'll want to venture a few miles inland and indoors, perhaps to the Monmouth Museum in Lincroft (chapter 21). And if the weather isn't disappointing but you are tired of waves and feel like going swimming, you'll want to know about Lake Absegami, in Wharton State Forest (chapter 23).

This book is arranged from north to south, starting in the northeast along the Hudson and then cutting inland. Usually, places covered within the same section are close enough to each other so that you can combine them or choose different parts of two or even three trips to create an excursion especially suited to your own interests. For example, you could choose to do a Revolutionary War trip in the central part of the state, focusing on Princeton (chapter 14) and Monmouth (chapter 15). Depending upon how far you travel to get there, you might even be able to fit Washington Crossing (chapter 19) into the mix.

Some chapters are geared toward adults, but almost every place has something to make the trip a treat for children of various ages. For example, Belvidere (chapter 16) is a lovely place to walk and think, and may not seem exciting to an eight-year-old. But not far from Belvidere are two places that probably will: the Pequest Trout Hatchery and Natural Resource Education Center and the Land of Make Believe. So with a little juggling of time, everyone can enjoy a day in Warren County.

For a state that looks so small on the map, New Jersey has an amazingly diverse landscape. You can find beaches and lakes, flat land and real mountains, elegant small towns, cities with skyscrapers, and, even now, beautiful farm land. You can canoe small rivers and swim in real lakes, bicycle on boardwalks and hike on the Appalachian Trail. You can visit Revolutionary War homesteads and brand-new baseball stadiums. There's a great mix of old and new, quiet and bustling. It's amazing how easy it is to feel as though you've left home on an adventure even though you haven't left your own state.

Bon voyage.

New Jersey Getaways

Chapter One

Jersey City:
Parks, Waterfront,
and the Statue of Liberty

The eastern edge of New Jersey—Hudson County's Jersey City and adjacent waterfront areas—has had several identities over the centuries. It started as marshland, became an industrial and transportation hub, sank back into disuse after years of overuse and abuse, and has reemerged wonderfully in all its former incarnations and more. The marshes are still there, the transportation is coming back, and a state park and a museum provide recreational opportunities for everyone who ventures east across the Turnpike. There are preserved or revived urban neighborhoods to explore, and from virtually any waterside vantage point, there is a visual reward that was not there in the area's first heyday in the nineteenth century: the view of Manhattan's waterfront and skyline. The scenery sets the stage for a day's worth of activities and sightseeing, no matter what the weather or the ages and interests of your companions. Whether you are coming from Manhattan, the nearby suburbs, or points farther west or south, the view will be there, along with the interactive science center, the elegant new waterfront promenade in Jersey City, and the nature trails of Liberty State Park.

The logical place to start is **Liberty State Park** (Morris Pesin Drive, Jersey City, 201-915-3400; www.state.nj.us.dep/forestry/

1

parks/liberty; www.libertystatepark.com). It's right on New York Harbor, less than half a mile from the Statue of Liberty. The area it occupies was industrial throughout the nineteenth century, and its natural appearance is undeniably flat and marshy. It was criss-crossed by railroad tracks; the Central Rail Road of New Jersey (CRRNJ) Terminal, which is in the northern part of the park, was the heart of a busy freight and passenger transportation network.

The railroad declined and the area gradually fell into disuse over several decades. Liberty State Park was opened on June 14, 1976. About three hundred acres of its thousand-acre-plus area are developed for public recreation; the rest is open land. The park offers the usual attractions: hiking, biking, and nature trails to help you explore a sixty-acre salt marsh; an interpretive center (201-915-3409); a boat launch ramp (offering access to both the Hudson River and the Atlantic Ocean); fishing and crabbing; picnicking, and even a swimming pool. Entrance to the park is free. The daily launch ramp fee is nine dollars; annual permits cost one hundred dollars and can be used at Leonardo State Marina in Monmouth County as well as at Liberty State Park. When the swimming pool is open, it is free for senior citizens and for children five and under; the fee peaks at four dollars for adults on weekends. Given Liberty State Park's location in a densely populated part of a densely populated state, the open space and recreational opportunities are certainly appreciated. The historical and cultural extras, however, are what make Liberty State Park special and worthy of a trip from considerably farther away than the adjacent communities. They also mean that a trip to this park doesn't have to be a good-weather, warm-season excursion; if the weather is unpleasant, you can do some of your exploring indoors.

The flags of all fifty states fly at the entrance to the park, in the order that each state entered the Union. There is also a circular display of thirteen historic flags representing the original thirteen colonies. Nearby is the South Overlook, with views of New York Harbor. This is the site of sculptor Natan Rappaport's Liberation Monument, a massive figure depicting a heroic-looking soldier carrying a smaller figure to safety and security. To give you a more general sense of the park and a chance to get some mild exercise, you might want to stroll along Liberty Walk, which runs for two miles, connecting the information center, picnic area, and Central Rail Road of New Jersey Terminal. In addition to breezes and a level path, it offers dramatic views of those structures and of New York City, as well as benches where you can sit and absorb the view.

You may keep seeing tantalizing glimpses of an ornate brick building along the water. This is the old railroad terminal. For decades this majestic structure served as the beginning and end of the line for thousands of New Jersey commuters who depended on ferries to Manhattan for the rest of their journey, as New Jersey Transit riders using the Hoboken Terminal still do. The remains of the ferry piers outside the terminal and the enormous train sheds of the terminal provide impressive reminders of how bustling and vital this site used to be.

The Central Rail Road of New Jersey

In 1831 the Elizabeth and Somerville Railroad was chartered; it merged with the Somerville and Easton Railroad and became the Central Rail Road of New Jersey in 1849, with a terminus in Elizabeth. In 1864, the railroad bought land in Jersey City, bolstered the marshy terrain with ballast from oceangoing ships and other fill, and opened a terminal. The terminal served as a transportation center for troops and equipment during the Civil War. A larger terminal was designed in 1889; it covered twelve tracks and six platforms, and the complex included not only freight and passenger terminals but storage yards, power stations, ferries and sheds, barges, and other structures. When the Ellis Island Immigration Center opened in 1892, replacing Castle Garden in Manhattan as an arrival point for immigrants, even more passengers went through the Central Rail Road of New Jersey Terminal—about eight million of the twelve million immigrants who passed through Ellis Island went on to travel via the terminal to areas in the South and West, as well as to New Jersey itself.

The terminal expanded again between 1912 and 1914. In this period and the decade or two immediately preceding it, between thirty and fifty thousand people a day traveled between New Jersey and New York along this route, on up to 300 trains and 128 ferries. The construction of the Lincoln and Holland Tunnels under the Hudson River and the increased use of automobiles in general led to a decline in rail ridership. Ellis Island ceased operations in 1954, cutting off another source of passengers, and in 1967 the Central Rail Road of New Jersey declared bankruptcy. The state bought the deserted terminal and waterfront. Now restored and used for special events and exhibits, the terminal is open to the public seasonally and is on both the state and national registers of historic places.

Central Rail Road of New Jersey Terminal

James Casserly

If the antique railroad terminal hasn't caught your eye, that's probably because your attention was captured by the science-fiction castle of **Liberty Science Center** (201-200-1000; www.lsc.org). This interactive science museum is a prime choice for school trips or family outings on a rainy day. It is popular, and it can be crowded. Open daily from April through Labor Day and Tuesday through Sunday during most of the school year, Liberty Science Center (LSC) has three floors with permanent and special exhibits devoted to invention, health, and the environment. One perennial children's favorite is the hundred-foot-long, pitch-dark Touch Tunnel. LSC's Kodak Omni Theatre has the largest IMAX dome screen in the country. Exhibit tickets and IMAX theater tickets are sold separately. You can purchase tickets in advance by telephone.

The science center's moderately priced Laser Lights Café is a museum cafeteria with a great view of New York Harbor. LSC's "Science to Go" store sells a variety of innovative gifts for children, from freeze-dried ice cream to science-related books and toys.

Crossing the Water

Clearly, there is enough to keep you busy for hours at Liberty State Park, but if the sights of Ellis Island's rambling buildings and Lady Liberty's torch are too tempting to resist, you will be pleased to know that there is daily (weather permitting) year-round ferry service from Liberty State Park to the Statue of Liberty and Ellis Island, which together make up the **Statue of Liberty National Monument** (212-363-3200). One round-trip ferry ticket includes visits to both islands. For rates and boat schedules, call 201-435-9499.

The Statue of Liberty, which was dedicated on October 28, 1886, quickly became an international symbol of freedom and hope; it was designated a National Monument on October 15, 1924. Ellis Island, which had served as the processing center for millions of immigrants for more than fifty years, became part of the Statue of Liberty National Monument in 1965; the island's Main Building reopened in 1990 as a museum dedicated to the history of immigration. Both the statue and island are open daily, except for December 25, and hours vary seasonally. They can be very crowded, especially in summer, but there is a good reason for the crowds—these are exciting places to visit. Do be aware, however, that lines for the ferries both coming and going can get very long, and passengers on boats other than the first one each day may not be able to get tickets to the Statue of Liberty's crown.

The Statue of Liberty Museum is inside the pedestal; its exhibits feature the history of the Statue. Exhibits at the three-floor Ellis Island Immigration Museum cover the history of Ellis Island and the immigration process as a whole. Among the most moving is the one called "Treasures From Home," which is a collection of the belongings immigrants carried with them. The museum exhibits in the pedestal of the Statue of Liberty are wheelchair-accessible, and there is an elevator that goes to the top of the pedestal. Ellis Island is completely wheelchair accessible, with elevator access to all museum areas. There's a cafe at Ellis Island with both indoor and outdoor seating.

Views of a City with a View

If you time your trip right, the drive to Jersey City on the Turnpike from Exit 14 will seem like a Hollywood film. On a weekend morning, after breakfast but before most businesses open, there are few if any trucks between Exits 14 and 14B, and the Lower Manhattan skyline and the Statue of Liberty will keep getting bigger. The buildings are densely packed and the skyline varied—flat, pointed, gabled, terraced, turreted.

If you take Montgomery Street and head toward Exchange Place, you will pass a big church, and nice brick and brownstone row houses. Exchange Place itself reminds me of what Lower Manhattan was like on Sunday mornings in the early 1970s—empty streets, brisk winds, and the feeling of a city with endless new streets to discover. If your point of reference is more recent, it may remind you of the Toronto of the late 1990s, with tall buildings rising near a waterfront, a few pre–World War II buildings punctuating the skyline with detail instead of glass and metal lines. Some of the new buildings at Exchange Place are impressive, with limestone exteriors and fine wood trim visible in the two-story lobbies. However, the one or two regrettable buildings of green metal and glass overlooking the river, meant perhaps to resemble the color of the river, look artificial and chemical, like the New Jersey stereotype that the best of Jersey City's waterfront so clearly disproves.

At Exchange Place there's an imposing statue of a soldier, a monument to the Polish army massacred in the Katyn Forest in World War II. Inscribed in both Polish and English, it adds to the monumental feeling and sense of destination that seems to have been created so magically here.

There are graceful black tubular benches on the new promenade, and a narrow, pedestrian-friendly concrete pier juts into the river near the Exchange Place PATH entrance. One of the nice things about Jersey City is that it's accessible from several directions by public transportation. Journal Square is both a PATH hub and a bus stop, and the new light rail system, although not finished, is up and running between Jersey City and Bayonne. (Though this is a book about New Jersey day trips, it's only fair to point out that the next stop for PATH trains eastbound from Hoboken is Christopher Street, in Manhattan.) You can sit and look out at the water and the city on the other side, but be sure to glance back at the building behind the promenade, 90 Hudson Street, a wonderful, new but traditional giant with huge ground-floor windows, perhaps two or even three stories tall, that curve at the top. The first segment of the Hudson-Bergen Light Rail system opened for business in the spring of 2000. The platforms are protected by elegant glass shelters; it looks like a city planner's fantasy come to life, with a little Disney World thrown in.

The recently glamorized waterfront is only part of Jersey City's architectural display. Jersey City's nineteenth-century residential neighborhoods make for pleasant walking tours any day of the week. Their tree-lined streets feature red-brick rowhouses, some very simple and some heavily ornamented. The **Paulus Hook Historic District** (parts of Essex, Grand, Greene, and York streets, among others) is closest to the waterfront, and the elegant **Van Vorst Park** area (including Barrow, Bright, Mercer, Montgomery, and Varick streets, among others) is west of Paulus Hook. **Hamilton Park** is several blocks north, literally across the tracks, west of Manila Avenue (Grove Street) from Sixth to Tenth streets.

If you are in Jersey City during the week, it's worth going to the old **Hudson County Courthouse**, now known as the William J. Brennan Courthouse, on Newark Avenue at the fringe of Jersey

City's bustling downtown. The domed exterior is imposing, but the interior, which is open for regular county business during the week, is spectacular. Designed by local architect Hugh Roberts, who apparently used Cass Gilbert's Essex County Courthouse as a design model, the courthouse was built in 1910. It housed the county's judicial system until the 1960s and has since undergone a dazzling renovation that began in the 1970s. The multi-story central rotunda is dazzling, from its patterned marble floor to the stained-glass dome. Below the stained glass are historical and mythological murals, including one commemorating the first trip by steamship up the Hudson River in 1807. It's definitely worth walking up the flights of stairs to see the paintings close up. The courtrooms themselves are worth a look; they have soaring ceilings carefully painted in period color schemes, and massive light fixtures that match the grandeur of the rooms. This is still an active courthouse; be careful not to disturb the proceedings as you walk through the halls. You can enter the courtrooms if they are not being used or if the trials or hearings are in recess. The courthouse is open Monday through Friday, 9 AM to 5 PM, and the public is welcome. Occasionally, there are special public events on weekends (Hudson County Office of Cultural Affairs, 201-459-2070).

Food

Even if you go to Jersey City on a Saturday, when the huge Au Bon Pain in one of the glittering office buildings at Exchange Place is closed, you won't go hungry. From the cafeteria at **Liberty Science Center** to **Café Newport** (500 Washington Boulevard, 201-626-7200), there are lots of places to eat. Café Newport, open daily for lunch and dinner, is on the waterfront and therefore noted for its spectacular view of the New York skyline. Of course, you can also bring a picnic from home and feast with an equally spectacular view at Liberty State Park. Other possibilities for in-city dining include several Italian restaurants; reservations are a good idea at all of them. **Casa Dante** (737 Newark Avenue, 201-795-2750), known for good traditional food, is open daily (lunch and dinner during the week, dinner on weekends). The two **Laico's** (67 Terhune Avenue, 201-434-4115; 600 Pavonia Avenue, 201-216-1166), popular family-style spots, are open daily for lunch and dinner. **Pronto Cena Ristorante** (87 Sussex Street, 201-435-0004) is a little more formal; it's convenient to Exchange Place and is open daily (lunch and dinner during the week, dinner on weekends). If you want to stop for a substantial dinner on your way home, you won't have to go far. **Ruth's Chris Steak House** (1000 Harbor Boulevard, Lincoln Harbor, Weehawken, 201-863-5100) is an upscale steak house that's open daily for dinner. It offers children's portions as well as great views, so it could be the setting for a festive finale to a family outing.

If It Rains

If you have to take the Turnpike southbound to get home from your Liberty day trip, there is some good shopping along the way. **IKEA** (1000 Center Drive, Elizabeth, off New Jersey Turnpike Exit 13A, 908-289-4488; for information about the free shuttle from New York, call 800-BUS-IKEA/287-4532) was the first retail building to brighten the stretch of Turnpike near Newark Airport. The giant blue-and-yellow building, one of the first American branches of the Swedish chain, is clearly visible from the road. The chain is known for simple designs, bright colors, and reasonable prices, and it sells everything from napkin rings and dishcloths to sofas, bedroom sets, and cabinets for custom kitchens. The supervised child-care area, known as the ballroom for the mass of balls that children play in, is a convenience for parents who need to do some serious measuring or decision-making. The store's restaurant serves specialties such as Swedish meatballs and lingonberries as well as American food.

Jersey Gardens (651 Kapkowski Road, 908-289-9400) joined IKEA at Exit 13A in 1999. It is a mall with a difference: its stores are primarily off-price outlets of major retailers. They include Neiman

Marcus's Last Call, Off 5th—Saks Fifth Avenue Outlet, Daffy's, Foot Locker, Gap, Harry and David, and Mikasa. You won't go hungry at Jersey Gardens: it has a food court, and lots of other stores that sell some kind of food, notably pretzels (Auntie Anne's) and chocolate (Rocky Mountain).

Chapter Two

Bread and Brownstones
in Hoboken

There are so many different Hobokens, in reality and in imagination, in stereotype and in fact. There's the gritty port of the classic 1954 film *On the Waterfront*. There's the Hoboken of Frank Sinatra, a heritage impossible to miss, thanks to Sinatra Drive and the "Thank you, Mr. Sinatra" signs you see occasionally. There's the train station, whose grandeur goes back nearly a century, and the PATH station, which probably never had any grandeur but whose trains miraculously transport NJ Transit commuters to Manhattan's West Village within ten minutes (on a good day, at a good time). And then there are the streets, with their shops, both old and new, and their buildings, three, four, and five stories, mostly, with the occasional high-rise interloper, a densely packed mile-square place with views of New York and enough appeal in its own right for the views not to matter too much.

Hoboken's current fashionable image may date back only a decade or two, but it has a long and distinctive history. Well before World War II, it was the most densely populated city in the nation; its docks were home to passenger ships and freighters and its railroad terminal bustled with commuters on their way to ferries that would carry them to Manhattan. It was also, even in the nineteenth century, a place where people went to get away from the bigger city across the river; there were beer gardens, country homes, and a scenic River Walk. In 1846, the first game of organized baseball was, it is widely believed, played in Hoboken—at Elysian Fields, located at what is now Tenth and Hudson Streets.

All the things that were still are, although in different form. The city is a fine place to walk: compact, not too hilly, full of interesting buildings from another century. The streets that run east to west are numbered, which makes it easy to figure out where you are; it takes longer to master the named streets, which run north to south. Washington Street, the main commercial street, is wide and lined with a variety of stores and restaurants. Throughout the residential streets west of Washington, small Italian grocery stores and bakeries and other survivors of an earlier era provide a texture and pattern that makes a simple walk through the neighborhood appealing. The waterfront, with its park and views and Stevens Institute of Technology rising on a hill north of the railroad, is more dramatic, but it's the combination of the two moods that makes the whole city, its history and its streetscape, a place to visit.

Hoboken is still a transportation center. Its rails and buses serve thousands of commuters a day, even now that Midtown Direct has made it easier for some NJ Transit commuters to bypass Hoboken and go directly to New York's Penn Station. One of the nice things about planning a trip to Hoboken, in fact, is that you don't need to drive. You can get on a train in one of dozens of towns with NJ Transit rail service (for information, call 973-762-5100; 800-772-2222) and get off at Hoboken, arriving directly in what is probably the most spectacular building in the city. (And if you decide, once in Hoboken, that it's not where you want to be, you can take a ferry, bus, PATH train, or NJ Transit train to connect with someplace else.) The old Erie Lackawanna Terminal, built in 1907, was a rail and ferry facility, originally the terminal for the Delaware, Lackawanna, and Western Railroad. Passengers getting off trains would head directly for the ferries that took them to Manhattan. In 1967, all ferry service to Manhattan ended; PATH trains had begun to supplant the ferries in the early twentieth century. Downtown ferry service, via NY Waterways, resumed in 1989.

When I first started commuting from western Morris County to New York in the late 1970s, the station's interior was grimy, even shabby; I remember high ceilings, dull tiles—but also the feeling that visiting this wonderfully evocative place was like taking a trip back to the turn of the century. Getting there still meant a ride on the old, pre–air conditioning, pre–World War II trains, with their straw seats, windows that opened, and fans that worked but didn't cool the air. Virtually every person would head directly from the trains to the tunnel that led to the PATH, with not even a glance at the river just beyond the terminal.

The NJ Transit trains that arrive at the station now are not nearly as charming as the trains on which I first became a New Jersey commuter, but the air conditioning usually works, though the permanently sealed windows are not always sparkling clean. The seats are smooth, so you don't have to worry about getting a run in your stockings (always a risk with the old straw seats). Convenience and blandness reign. But when you get the to Erie Lackawanna Terminal, the world changes. The terminal's revival matches that of the beautiful old turn-of-the-century houses that dominate so many of the suburbs on the rail lines that lead to the station. The charm is still there, but it's a deliberate, well-cared-for charm. Recently refurbished, it looks a little like a movie set. The interior is freshly painted, with a lovely stained-glass skylight covering almost the entire waiting room and wood benches that look regularly polished. Lighting fixtures, too, are perfectly in period as well as functional, and glass-block doors and signs at one end of the waiting room direct passengers to the lunchroom. The lunchroom isn't there any more, but the sign looks great, and is another welcome if hollow reminder of the station's past. Even if you are on your way someplace else, it's worth taking a few minutes to wander through the station and admire it.

The PATH lines still carry most of the travelers going to Manhattan, but ferries provide a wonderfully scenic alternative route to the World Financial Center. Although the ride is short—about ten minutes—it's well worth taking even if you have no intention of getting off the boat and spending time in New York. The views are spectacular, the price is reasonable, and if you have small children, the voyage will seem like an adventure to them. Even for grownups, the sight of Manhattan in all its big-city glory is worth the trip; so is the Hudson River, and the old-new mix of the Jersey City waterfront has its own appeal.

A newly cleaned and restored sign above a broad set of stairs leading up and away from the train shed reads "To upper decks of ferryboats." It's a tempting fantasy to walk up those steps and through the doors to see what lies beyond. The sign, however, is purely decorative. Although ferry service has returned to Hoboken, thanks to Arthur Imperatore's NY Waterway, the decks of the ferryboats aren't high enough to require those stairs; the ferry terminal, not as glamorous as the train station but clean, well-maintained, and boasting a café, is immediately adjacent to the terminal. Ferries make the short trip across the Hudson River to Lower Manhattan throughout the day.

NY Waterway (800-533-3779; www.nywaterway.com) does more than provide a scenic, efficient commute from Hoboken. The company also offers a number of cruises, most leaving from Manhattan. Among the highlights are the full-day cruise to Sandy Hook, with connections from Weehawken and Hoboken; harbor cruises; cruises around Manhattan, and, in season, baseball cruises to and from Shea and Yankee Stadiums. In addition to the Manhattan departures, the baseball cruises depart from Port Imperial in Weehawken for all games and from Hoboken Terminal on weekends and holidays. In addition to round-trip transportation, packages that include tickets to the games are available; these require advance reservations.

There is a lot more to Hoboken than its transportation hub. From Hoboken Terminal, follow the signs to the street and follow the street grid and your instincts. The old copper exterior of the station is beautifully green, a combination of patina and peeling that adds another dimension to the immaculate restoration of the interior. When you leave the station and turn north, you will be facing a new park along the South Waterfront. A plaque points out that this was an important port of embarkation during both World War I and World War II; the park allows biking and skating, and there is also fishing access. Benches and a good view of Manhattan make it a good place for a few minutes' relaxation. Stevens Institute, at Castle Point, rises rather majestically in the distance, and way beyond, you can see the George Washington Bridge. It is a good place for pushing baby carriages, stopping to chat, sitting to rest, or allowing restless, small children to let off steam before you corral them back into their strollers so you can admire the buildings and window shop.

After a few blocks in the park you will probably be ready to head west toward Hoboken's lively streets, with their low-rise buildings and varied commercial life. If you cut over to the intersection of Washington Street and First Street, you will find a good view of the handsome City Hall, which recently has been refurbished. Before you reach Washington Street, a barbershop on First Street just west of Hudson Street, complete with an old-fashioned awning and a green door, helps set the mood for the walk. If you need a break from admiring urban landscape, you can go west a few more blocks to get to the park south of Fifth Street at Park Street, also a place children will probably like. It's also worth a short detour because it's across from an impressive public library with a tall, massive tower; the building was completed in 1897 and looks like an idealized, healthily nostalgic version of New York's Washington Square Park.

Basically, a good walk will take you to and from Washington to the residential streets, following your mood. When you've seen enough, simply head back, exploring a different street or different side of the street. Hoboken isn't very large, and there are buses on Washington Street if you are too tired to enjoy the walk back. You can also break up the journey by stopping for refreshment of one kind or another—there are a lot of places to stop for food, drinks, and shopping, either real or wishful. Clothes, antiques, and housewares are offered at many of the retail stores.

Joseph G. Broda

Brownstones on Hudson Street, Hoboken

Food choices abound. Two among the many well-regarded Hoboken delis are **Vito's** (806 Washington Street, 201-792-4944) and **Lisa's** (901 Park Avenue, 201-795-3212). If you're after some crusty Hoboken bread, you will want to head for **Marie's Bakery** (261

Second Street, 201-963-4281) or **Antique Bakery** (122 Willow Street, 201-714-9323). **Lepore's** (537 Garden Street, 201-659-4783) occupies a delightfully traditional-looking corner shop, and sells homemade butter creams, among other tempting sweets. **Hobos Creamy Creations** (636 Washington Street, 201-963-3222) has a tiled entryway and old-fashioned interior; it sells homemade ice cream and candy, including seasonal treats such as pumpkin ice cream in October.

Hoboken isn't just a place to buy food to enjoy at home, of course. It is full of restaurants that cover a wide range of ethnic groups and price ranges. You can walk along Washington Street and smell good food as you pass a restaurant doorway (or smoke vent). A number of Hoboken's restaurants are open for dinner only, so you can top off an afternoon in Hoboken by having dinner at one of them before heading home. **Frankie & Johnnie's** (163 Fourteenth Street, 201-659-6202) serves American food in a turn-of-the-century setting. **Helmer's Café** (1036 Washington Street, 201-963-3333) is a reminder that Hoboken once had a substantial German population; it serves open-faced sandwiches, salads, meat platters, and other German fare daily (except Sunday) for lunch and dinner. The **Brass Rail** (135 Washington Street, 201-659-7074) has been around for nearly a century and has something of a dual identity: bar and burgers downstairs, Continental food upstairs. **Onieal's** (343 Park Avenue, 201-653-1492) is an American bistro that was one of the pioneers of the new Hoboken. **Amanda's** (908 Washington Street, 201-798-0101) is known for its lovely setting and for its contemporary American food. What about the Italian restaurants that tradition might lead you to expect? There are many. **Benny Tudino's** (622 Washington Street, 201-792-4132) is popular for pizza—and known for its large slices. **Tutta Pasta** (201 Washington Street, 201-792-9102) and **La Scala** (159 14th Street, 201-963-0884) serve other variations on the delicious theme of Italian food. There is even an outpost of Burritoville, known for its Manhattan locations. Hoboken's **Burritoville** (520 Washington Street, 201-418-0035), like its counterparts elsewhere, features very good, very large burritos with cute names—like Holy Molé—along with wraps, quesadillas, enchiladas, nachos, and other compatible items.

Chapter Three

On the Rocks: Above, Below, and Beyond the Palisades

Just as there's more to New Jersey than Turnpike exits and smoke-stack-dotted meadowlands, there's more to Bergen County than its admittedly terrific opportunities for retail adventures in dazzling malls and carefully maintained downtowns. As for the infamous traffic on Routes 4 and 17, most Bergen County stores are closed on Sunday, leaving more room for travelers pursuing activities other than shopping and work, so Sundays are especially good days to appreciate history and nature in Bergen County.

As unlikely as it may seem to the uninitiated, you can find more than enough of both to make a fine day trip, though they are often well disguised, hidden by the roads and densely packed residential and commercial development. Seen from upper Manhattan or somewhere on the Hudson, however, Bergen County's scenic potential becomes more obvious. The Palisades are truly spectacular. Those of us who have become accustomed to seeing them as we travel west on the George Washington Bridge or have gazed admiringly at them from an apartment somewhere on Riverside Drive tend to forget, as we drive along the Parkway and Turnpike or through local streets, that somewhere just east of us those same cliffs are waiting to be admired and explored. Cliff climbing is definitely not an option at

Walter Choroszewski

Palisades Interstate Park

Palisades Interstate Park (New Jersey section headquarters, Alpine Approach Road, Alpine, 201-768-1360). Boating, cycling, fishing, hiking, picnicking, and cross-country skiing—as long as there's snow, of course—definitely are. And it turns out that the park is full of historic sites and buildings, too, making the scenic New Jersey section of this sprawling 80,000-acre bi-state park a multipurpose destination.

Palisades Interstate Park, unevocatively abbreviated as PIP, has several distinct sections, each offering a mix of activities and attractions. Parking fees and road openings vary by season, so be sure to call before you go. Allison Park (off Hudson Terrace, between the George Washington Bridge and Palisade Avenue, Englewood Cliffs) is a landscaped park at the top of the cliffs. The grounds are open year-round, and parking is free. It is on the site of the estate of William O. Allison, a major landowner in the area in the late nineteenth century. The Alpine Area (at the base of the Alpine Approach Road, Alpine, 201-768-1360 for general information and slip rental; 201-768-9798 for the marina) includes both the Alpine Boat Basin and the preserved Blackledge-Kearney House. This riverfront picnic area—the open-air stone picnic pavilion dates from the 1930s—was the site of an Interstate Park beach in the early twentieth century. Before that, it was known as Closter Landing, part of a fishing settlement named Undercliff; appropriately, it is now a marina. The Blackledge-Kearney House is the only Closter Landing house that has survived; its oldest section dates to about 1750. The house is open from April to October on weekends and holidays from noon to 5 PM. For decades, the house was said to have been General Charles Cornwallis's headquarters, although it's unlikely that the British general in fact used it for that purpose. In any event, it was the supposed Cornwallis connection that saved the house from being torn down in the 1930s. The Alpine Area marina has a beach for car-top canoe and kayak launches, and the area has access to a number of hiking trails. There is a parking fee from April through October. The Englewood Area, which includes the Englewood Boat Basin and Bloomers Beach—named for a family, not the garment—is at the base of Dyckman Hill in Englewood Cliffs (marina, 201-894-9510). This riverfront picnic area and marina has a beach for canoe and kayak car-top boat launches, as well as access to the Palisades Interstate Park trail system. There is an April-to-October parking fee, and a refreshment stand is open from spring through fall. Until the late 1930s, a ferry from Dyckman Street in Manhattan landed here, and there was swimming at Bloomers Beach. The Undercliff Area is half a mile north of the Englewood Area; it, too, is a riverfront picnic area.

Fort Lee Historic Park (Hudson Terrace, Fort Lee, 201 461-1776) combines history with spectacular views of the Hudson River, the George Washington Bridge, and Manhattan. Here you will find a visitor center and museum, a reconstructed eighteenth-century soldier hut and campsite, and reconstructed gun batteries. Nearby Fort Lee was named after American General Charles Lee, whose retreat from the fort in 1776 preceded Washington's retreat through New Jersey. One quarter mile from the site of the fort, a visitor center and museum offer audiovisual displays, detailed exhibits, and a short film about Washington's evacuation of the area, as well as a public phone and information services. The main floor is barrier free. There is a parking fee from April to October. Hazzard's Boat Ramp in Fort Lee is a launching ramp for jet-skis and for registered, trailered boats less than twenty-four feet long. The launching fee is $10. Ross Dock, also in Fort Lee, is a riverfront picnic area with access to Hazzard's Boat Ramp and the trail system. Perhaps the most spectacular section is the State Line Lookout (opposite Exit 3, Northbound Palisades Interstate Parkway, Alpine). At an elevation of 532 feet, the lookout is on the highest point of the Palisades Cliffs, with views as far away as Long Island Sound. It has extensive hiking and more than five miles of cross-county ski trails. Lookout Inn, constructed of stone and chestnut wood, is a snack bar and information center, built in 1937 by the Works Projects Administration. Hours vary.

The fact that Palisades Interstate Park runs along and below cliffs should tell you something about its trails. Just because they have views of New York City does not mean they are easy walks; they are steep in parts, and because of the proximity of steep drop-offs, they are not ideal for small children.

Two main trails, both designated National Historic and Recreational Trails, cover most of the length of the Park. The Shore Trail, starting

at the Edgewater–Fort Lee border, leads down to the river, follows
it, then goes back up to the top of the cliffs. The Long Path goes
along the top of the cliffs north of the George Washington Bridge.
Five other trails running east to west connect the Shore Trail and
the Long Path.

Coming Down from the Cliffs

Massive and seemingly wild as the Palisades are, it is easy to
forget that people live below the cliffs. Along the roads leading down
from the cliffs are compact riverside communities. Among them is
Edgewater, a thriving factory town throughout much of the twentieth century that subsequently became the site of empty and torn-
down factory buildings. It's now evolved into a bustling community,
the site of interesting restaurants, clustered on and near River Road,
and **Yaohan Plaza** (595 River Road, Edgewater, 201-941-9113), the
largest Japanese shopping center in the area. It is anchored by a huge
Yaohan supermarket, part of a chain with branches elsewhere in the
United States as well as abroad. Although there are other shops at
the plaza, the supermarket alone is well worth a trip. Alongside
American soup, detergent, peanut butter, and instant coffee are intriguing arrays of Japanese products. A bakery sells fresh Japanese
pastries and confections; a fish department sells a wide variety of
fish and other seafood; and a produce section carries both Japanese
specialties and American items.

Back in Time

Behind the Palisades are equally distinctive destinations that reflect events that took place more than two centuries ago. **New Bridge
Landing Historic Park** (1201-1209 Main Street, River Edge, 201-
487-1739) encompasses the sites of several of these events. A sliding

drawbridge was built here in 1744. A newer bridge, made of iron, opened in 1889 and was closed to car traffic in 1956; it's now listed on the state and national registers as the oldest highway swing bridge in New Jersey. The Landing's signature structure, however, is the Ackerman-Zabriskie House, a state-owned historic site that displays the furniture collection of the Bergen County Historical Society. This Dutch Colonial house really is Colonial, if not quite Dutch; it has the classic look—gambrel roof, extended curved eaves, wooden roof shingles, and a sandstone lower level nicely balanced by a brick upper level. The original five-room sandstone portion was built in 1712, well after the Dutch had ceased to be the official power in the region that became New Jersey. The Zabriskie family, subsequent owners of the site, built a gristmill and made money from the mill and from transshipping Long Pond and Ringwood iron from their river landing. They expanded the house to twelve rooms in 1752, and you may be pleasantly surprised when you walk into the house and see how high the ceilings are and how spacious the rooms feel.

In November 1776, the site became, however briefly, historically significant. It was at New Bridge that George Washington led the American soldiers who were garrisoned at Fort Lee in an escape from the British and Hessian troops who had landed at Lower Closter Dock and climbed the Palisades. Thomas Paine, one of the most eloquent revolutionaries, marched with the troops from Fort Lee and wrote the lines that became his most famous: "These are the times that try men's souls."

Colonel Jan Zabriskie, who owned the house during the Revolutionary War, was a Loyalist, and his property was confiscated by the state of New Jersey in 1780. That fall, George Washington used the house as his headquarters, and later the estate was awarded to Baron Steuben, the Prussian general who helped train Continental troops at Valley Forge. In 1939, when the house was dedicated as a public museum, Franklin Roosevelt's Works Projects Administration laid the random-width flooring in the big parlor. The historical society has an impressive collection of Dutch furnishings made or used in Bergen County between 1680 and 1860. The trick is to visit the house during its somewhat limited hours, usually Wednesday through Friday, 10 AM to noon and 1 PM to 5 PM, and Sunday, 2 PM to 5 PM. Even if you plan to be there during the official hours, it's a good idea to call ahead to confirm open hours.

Several other period houses have been moved to New Bridge Landing from nearby. The Demarest House, a two-room sandstone structure dating from the eighteenth century, was moved to the Landing from New Milford in the 1950s. It is open by appointment and for special events, and it displays Demarest family possessions and Bergen Dutch artifacts. The Campbell-Christie House, a gambrel-roofed sandstone structure originally built in New Milford in 1774, was moved to its present location in 1977 to save it from demolition. It is open for special events. The Westervelt-Thomas Barn, built in Washington Township in 1889, was moved to New Bridge Landing in 1958.

Recently, New Bridge Landing also held the dubious honor of being on Preservation New Jersey's annual list of the state's most endangered historic sites. For all its significance, it has the disadvantage of being across the street from some very basic twentieth-century brick garden apartments. If you look in the right direction at the river and narrow bridge and read the explanatory signs in the right spirit, you do manage to get some sense of what the place once was like.

Farther west is **The Hermitage** (335 North Franklin Turnpike, Ho-Ho-Kus, 201-445-8311; www.thehermitage.org), another site with Revolutionary significance, and a romantic history to match. Thanks to an 1847 remodeling by the noted architect William Ranlett, this state and national historic landmark looks very Gothic, but in fact it predates the Revolution. The Hermitage is owned by the state of New Jersey and operated by the Friends of the Hermitage, Inc., a private, nonprofit corporation founded in 1972 to restore, maintain, and interpret the site as it appeared in the late nineteenth century.

As early as 1740, there was a house at this location. In 1767, Ann Bartow DeVisme bought the house; one of her daughters, Theodosia Bartow, and Theodosia's first husband, James Marcus Prevost, occupied another house on the property. In July 1778, Theodosia heard that George Washington and his troops would be passing through Ho-Ho-Kus on their way from the Battle of Monmouth to White Plains, and she invited Washington and his men to stay at the Hermitage. From July 10 to July 14, Washington and his officers were entertained at this site, though it is not known whether they actually stayed in the house. Franklin Turnpike, which ran past the Hermitage, was a main thoroughfare—literally, a turnpike—in its day, connecting Hackensack and inland settlements in New York and New Jersey. All sorts of people stopped by; other visitors to the house during the Revolutionary period included James Monroe, William Paterson, the Marquis de Lafayette, Alexander Hamilton, Lord Stirling, Peggy Shippen Arnold, and Aaron Burr. In fact, after Theodosia Bartow Prevost's husband died, she and Aaron Burr were married at the Hermitage in July 1782.

In 1807, the house was sold to Elijah Rosegrant and his wife, Cornelia Suffern. The Rosencrantz family (the name was changed from Rosegrant) owned the house from 1807 until 1970; the family also owned cotton mills, which paid for the house and its transformation from solid farmhouse to Gothic confection. Elizabeth Rosencrantz was the last family member to live in the house. Pictures on display in the house show her as a champion golfer. Although she was raised in comfort, even luxury, she had no real means of support, and in the 1920s she operated the house as a tearoom. New people were moving to increasingly suburban Bergen County, and they were eager to see how the grand old families had lived, even if they had to pay for lunch or tea in order to do so. The Depression ended that; people no longer had the money or time to sit in the front parlor of an old farmhouse, sipping tea and nibbling cakes. Parcels of the land that had surrounded the house were sold off over the years. Elizabeth lived in two rooms of the old house, set on five remaining acres; she wanted to leave the house to the state to preserve its heritage, and her own. A woman who had been a maid for the family lived with her. They heated the house by burning wood in the fireplace, and one day Elizabeth was badly burned. After she recovered from her burns, the county authorities refused to let her return to the house unless electricity was installed. It was, but Elizabeth died soon afterward, and the house became the property of the state, as she had wished. It was a leaky, drafty, unpolished treasure. The house has undergone restoration since then, but a walk through its rooms still combines reminders of the women's loneliness and financial struggle with the chance to admire and enjoy fine furniture and spacious rooms.

The Hermitage and the neighboring John Rosencrantz House have one of the largest collections of textiles in the area, including men's, women's, and children's clothing from 1750 to 1943; accessories (hats, shoes, parasols, belts, jewelry, and neckwear); and table linens, bedding, and window coverings from 1790 to 1940. The Hermitage is furnished as it appeared in the 1890s, and reflects the fact that one family lived in the house from 1807 until the middle of the twentieth century. Much of the furniture is Victorian, but some items date back to the eighteenth century; twentieth-century items in the collection are not routinely on display but may be seen in a variety of exhibitions and are available for study by prior appointment. The collection also includes paintings, kitchenware, tableware, lamps and tools, Victorian-era toys and games, athletic trophies won by Rosencrantz family members, musical instruments, and craft items. Guided public tours of the museum are offered Wednesdays through Sundays at 1:15, 2:15, and 3:15 p.m. Special events, such as lectures and crafts shows, are scheduled throughout the year.

For very young children—those of nursery school age or in the early elementary grades—the Palisades may be too rugged, and the historic sites a little too far removed from reality. If you're looking for a child-pleasing side trip, though, you don't have far to go.

In good weather, a trip to **Van Saun Park** (Forest and Continental Avenues, Paramus, 201-646-2680; zoo, 201-262-3771) is an adventure. This county-run park is probably best known for its zoo, which is home to a variety of wild and domestic animals. Your children can see exotic birds, snakes, lizards, and mammals, as well as chicken, sheep, pigs, and other familiar farmyard friends. The zoo is open year-round; an entrance fee is charged from May to October. Van Saun Park also has one of those miniature train rides that are so much fun if you are four years old or spending the day with a four-year-old. This one, pulled by a replica of a nineteenth-century locomotive, travels in a loop around the zoo, and of course goes through a tunnel. The park also has the usual amenities—picnic area, playground, fishing in Walden Pond, and ice skating and sledding when the weather cooperates.

If the weather suggests indoor activity, head for the **New Jersey Children's Museum** (599 Industrial Avenue, Paramus, 201-262 5151; www.njcm.com). This interactive museum is designed for children aged one to eight. It has fifteen thousand square feet of exhibit space divided into thirty different rooms. Exhibits include a medieval castle with a talking knight, a kid-sized charger, and costumes. Children can use a real flight simulator, climb on a real fire engine, visit a real helicopter, and exercise skills and imagination in a dance room and a garage. This is also the place to spin New Jersey's largest kaleidoscope. The museum is open daily, and admission is $8 plus tax for adults and children. Both hours and fees can change, of course, so be sure to call before you go. Note, too, that like most attractions of this kind, the museum can be crowded, both during school hours and on weekends, so be prepared for lots of company.

Food

Wherever your Bergen County trip takes you, finding a place to eat will not be a problem. For quick, easy, child-friendly meals, the restaurants and fast-food places on the various highway strips offer virtually limitless choices. If you prefer a more leisurely setting, the possibilities are equally endless. Among those you might consider for a serious meal at midday are **Azúcar** (10 Dempsey Avenue/River Road, Edgewater, 201-886-0747), a popular Cuban restaurant; **River Palm Terrace** (1416 River Road, Edgewater, 201-224-2013), a highly regarded steakhouse; and **Jamie's** (574 Sylvan Avenue, Englewood Cliffs, 201-201-568-4244), which features creative American dishes. More casual settings include **Baumgart's Café** (45 East Palisade Avenue, Englewood, 201-569-6267), known for American diner-style treats during the day and Chinese food at night, and the mini-chain **It's Greek to Me** (1636 Palisade Avenue, Fort Lee, 201-947-2050, and other locations in Bergen County). For the makings of a picnic with international flavor, shop at **Yaohan Plaza**.

Chapter Four

Newark? Yes, Newark

Like the rest of New Jersey, only more so, Newark has struggled for years with national perceptions and misperceptions. And just as most of us who live in the state know that most of New Jersey is interesting and some of it is beautiful, many have discovered that Newark is a city with a lot to offer visitors. It has a museum worth a trip from almost anywhere, a park whose design rivals that of Central Park, an intensely ethnic neighborhood known for fine restaurants, and a long and complex history. Two recent additions have sparked renewed attention from Newark's suburban neighbors. These are the highly publicized New Jersey Performing Arts Center (NJPAC) and the almost as highly publicized Riverfront Stadium, home of the new Newark Bears.

Since its gala opening in October 1997, the **New Jersey Performing Arts Center**, 1 Center Street (888-466-5722; www.njpac.org), has been a magnet for performers and audiences. Ample parking both aboveground and in the amazingly well-lit and secure-feeling Military Park Garage, help make NJPAC's culturally varied schedule even more appealing. It's probably fair to say that NJPAC has been the key ingredient in the perception of a Newark renaissance. The red-brick complex rising near the Passaic River waterfront is very visible and attractive, whether you see it from McCarter Highway or in the distance from the train near Broad Street Station on its way to or from the western suburbs. An appealing array of events, matinees as well as evening performances, makes this an obvious focal point for a day or day-into-evening trip.

The twelve-acre complex includes a 500-seat outdoor amphitheater, a 1,500-seat symphony lawn, and the star attractions, two theaters. Prudential Hall, with 2,750 seats and strikingly rich-looking wood walls, designed for both acoustics and beauty, hosts orchestras, operas, ballet and contemporary dance, jazz, popular music, Broadway shows—events suited to a large venue and expected to attract audiences of sufficient size to fill the space. The Victoria Theater, with 500 seats, hosts dramatic productions, acoustical concerts, lectures, films, and children's and family-oriented productions—events designed for a more intimate setting.

What can you see at NJPAC? More than 100 different performances each year. Obviously, the schedule varies by season and year, but typical offerings in a given season include New Jersey Symphony Orchestra concerts with guest appearances by notables such as flutist James Galway and cellist Yo-Yo Ma; appearances by other orchestras, including the Boston Symphony Orchestra; the (December) Holiday Klezmerfest; the Alvin Ailey Dance Company; *The King and I*; Audra McDonald of Broadway's *Carousel, Ragtime, Master Class,* and (TV movie version) *Annie* fame; several performances by Sweet Honey in the Rock; and the year-long Festival of Pan-African America. And NJPAC keeps even busier, thanks to summer youth workshops in singing, dancing, and acting, as well as rental of its spectacular spaces for social and community events.

Ticket prices are pretty much what you would expect to pay for major entertainment, although parking is somewhat less expensive than in New York. Getting to NJPAC is remarkably easy from the highways leading into and around Newark. If you choose public transportation, the purple Loop Shuttle bus connects the Newark cultural attractions with each other, and, most important, with both Penn Station and Broad Street Station, which in turn connect travelers to New York City and many New Jersey towns; it provides frequent service for a nominal fare. Note that although the views and acoustics are good throughout the house, some people find the balconies at Prudential Hall somewhat awkwardly designed. Last time I attended a performance there, I was impressed by how convenient my balcony seat was to a very elegant mosaic-brightened ladies' room, but the balcony rows also seemed very long. There are no center aisles breaking up the rows of seats, which can give you a feeling of being surrounded by more people than you are quite comfortable with; this also makes exiting after the show more difficult.

To see more of NJPAC, consider a tour. Guided tours are scheduled on Monday and Wednesday mornings, and on alternate Saturday mornings; the cost is $3 for adults and $2 for children ages 3 to 12. The tours last about an hour and are wheelchair-accessible. Reservations are required; call 973-287-5805 for information.

If you'd like to eat at NJPAC before a matinee or enjoy a pre-performance dinner, the well-regarded and very welcome **Theater Square Grill** (973-642-1226) is open for lunch on Monday through Friday and for dinner Tuesday through Sunday. It offers pre-performance prix-fixe dinners and "After Curtain" light meals; reservations, a good idea at any time, are required for pre-performance dining. From April to October, you can also punctuate your cultural tour of Newark with a meal at **Calçada**, a casual outdoor café on the patio between the main lobby and the waterfront. With offerings such as stone-oven pizza, fish, and steaks, it serves lunch on weekdays and dinner Tuesday through Saturday. Keep in mind that you don't have to attend a performance at NJPAC to enjoy its restaurants. There are other things to see and do in Newark, and many of them are only blocks from NJPAC.

One recently added attraction is **Riverfront Stadium** (973-483-6900 for information about game times, ticket prices, and promotions; www.newarkbears.com), home of the Newark Bears. The handsome new minor-league ballpark, which opened in the summer of 1999, has added another dimension to the neighborhood. The warm brick façade of the park is especially welcoming to drivers coming off Route 280 eastbound at exit 14. But whichever direction you are coming from, you will probably see an abundance of signs directing you to Downtown/Arts, and this includes the stadium. The city and the people in charge of signs on the highways have done their best to make it easy to find, and you certainly won't overlook it once you get there.

The ballpark has more than 6,000 seats, and 20 luxury boxes. It boasts two radio booths, two television booths, a state-of-the-art scoreboard, a removable fence in right field, and a concert stage. In addition to the April-through-September baseball schedule, which includes many evening games as well as weekend day games, the stadium is the site of soccer and football matches, concerts, and other events of community interest. (Tickets are available by calling 201-507-8900, and through Ticketmaster.) The star attractions, the new Newark Bears, established in 1998, are an Atlantic League team. The Atlantic League (www.atlanticleague.com) has two other teams in New Jersey—the Atlantic City Surf and Somerset Patriots, and despite the new league's short history, the team names evoke a sense of place and tradition: the Lehigh Valley Black Diamonds and the Nashua Pride are my favorites.

Newark itself has a place in baseball history. The old Newark Bears, who played in Ruppert Stadium until 1949, were a top Yankees farm team in the Triple A International League; Yogi Berra played for those Bears in 1946. The opponents of those Bears included teams with half-familiar names, like the Jersey City Giants. Another Newark team, the Eagles, were part of a now-vanished baseball world; they were a Negro League team. Many great athletes played on Negro League teams, because what we now call Major League Baseball was closed to minority players. New Jersey's own Larry Doby played for the Eagles before becoming the American League's first black player.

In keeping with Atlantic League policy, Riverfront Stadium is geared to family entertainment, with food concessions and on-site parking. Essex and Morris County suburbanites who have already made their way to the games for family excursions and birthday parties give it enthusiastic reviews.

Off-season note: If baseball isn't in season yet, you can travel a few miles out of Newark to visit the **Yogi Berra Museum** at Montclair State University. Open Wednesday through Sunday, noon to 5 PM, it is located at 8 Quarry Road, Little Falls, 973-655-2377.

Long before the Arts Center or the ballpark existed, there was the **Newark Museum** (49 Washington Street, Newark, 800-768-738; Newark Skyline, for planetarium information, 973-596-6529; www.newarkmuseum.org). The Newark Museum is a major museum, overshadowed only because it is so close to the wonders of New York City. This not-for-profit institution, funded by the city, state, the state council on the arts, and private donations, has such a colorful, detailed Web site that a quick on-line visit will leave you wondering why you haven't made the museum a more significant part of your weekend activities. At any rate, that's the effect it had on me. What a dazzling place on screen—and in reality.

I first visited the museum in the early 1970s, when a coworker and I were given tickets to the opening of a quilt show. We were junior employees of a large educational publishing company, and we didn't often get free tickets to even remotely glamorous events. The invitations must have filtered down to us through several layers of senior and associate editors. We somehow figured out how to take public transportation from Manhattan to Newark and, ultimately, to the museum. I remember liking the quilts and being impressed by the rotunda. After that evening, I forgot about the museum until I moved to New Jersey years later and became a resident of suburban Essex County. The museum then became a dependable place for our family to go on a chilly, cloudy weekend afternoon.

With 80 galleries of art and science exhibits, the Newark Museum can occupy you for hours. Founded in 1909 and still sparkling after a $23 million renovation by New Jersey's own world-class architect Michael Graves that was completed in 1989, the museum looks like—and is—a major cultural institution. Consider the mini-zoo, the sculpture garden, and the Alice and Leonard Dreyfuss Planetarium, which was established in 1953 and is the only one in the state that has a Zeiss Skymaster ZKP3 Star Projector. But most of all, consider the art.

The museum proudly claims the largest collection of Tibetan art in the Western Hemisphere. The Tibetan Collection includes paintings, sculpture, ritual objects, dance masks, tents, saddles, headdresses, and weapons. It has its origins in the collection donated by Dr. Albert L. Shelton, a medical missionary, and in three additional collections from other missionaries. The Tibetan Collection, highlighted by a Buddhist altar consecrated by the Dalai Lama in 1990, is just a part of the Asian Collection, which includes paintings, sculpture, and netsuke from Japan, pottery and porcelains from Korea, stone and wood sculpture from India, and Chinese art, including metalwork, ceramics, lacquer ware, wood and stone carvings, and ceramics.

The museum's Ancient Mediterranean Cultures Collection features the Coptic art of Christian Egypt and is highlighted by the Eugene Schaefer Collection of Ancient Glass and Classical Antiquities. If looking at really old glass—from 1500 BC to 1000 AD—intrigues you, visit the Decorative Arts Collection, another of the museum's star attractions. Among its highlights are American art pottery (including such *Antiques Roadshow* stalwarts as Fulper and Rookwood) and New Jersey ceramics. The collection also includes nineteenth-century furniture, Lenox porcelain, Orrefors glass, and Tiffany jewelry. The collection is housed primarily in the Ballantine Mansion.

The Ballantine Mansion is one of the treasures of the museum. This brick-and-limestone mansion, built in 1885 for the Ballantine brewing family, became part of the museum in 1937 and has been a National Historic Landmark since 1985. During the Christmas season it is a good place to take children, because the holiday decorations are particularly lovely. But it is truly a year-round attraction. Two floors of the house are open to the public. These include period rooms—Billiard Room, Parlor, Reception Room, Library, Dining Room, Music Room, Master Bedroom, Mrs. Ballantine's Bedroom, and Alice Ballantine Bedroom—restored to the height of 1891 fashion. Two hallways and six new galleries house the decorative arts collection, displaying items that might have been found in homes from the 1650s to the present.

The Newark Museum also has a substantial collection of American art, including works by Edward Hopper, John Sloan, Georgia O'Keeffe, Mary Cassatt, and Childe Hassam, and a sampling of the Hudson River School including works by Frederick Church and Thomas Cole. Romare Bearden is among the African American artists represented. You will also find folk art, Works Projects Adminstration prints, and Joseph Stella panels titled "The Voice of the City of New York, Interpreted." You may feel as though you have stepped into the pages of a luxurious art history book.

And that's just the adult part. The Junior Museum presents varied programs in both arts and sciences for ages three though sixteen. Eight-week Saturday programs are extremely reasonably priced; at this writing, $30 per child for Newark residents, $55 per child for nonresidents. There are also one-day science intensives and family-oriented workshops. The museum's mini-zoo has about 100 animals, and the interactive "Making Sense of the Natural World" exhibit is scheduled to open in 2001.

Directly behind the museum there is a parking lot, entered from either Washington Street or Central Avenue. The Museum is also served by the Loop Shuttle, connecting it to both train stations. When you walk from the parking lot to the museum itself, you will pass through a sculpture garden, which is an attraction in itself. In the garden, and especially appealing to children, are the Fire Museum, originally an 1860s carriage house, and the 1794 Schoolhouse.

A few blocks from the museum, and just down the street from NJPAC facing Military Park, is a new and old cultural attraction, the **New Jersey Historical Society** (52 Park Place, 973-483-3939). Relocated in the 1990s from its former home on Broadway, it now occupies the building that once housed the Essex Club. In addition to hosting special exhibits (recent subjects have included Teenage New Jersey and New Jersey Diners), it has a library and several permanent exhibits of particular interest to children. It may not be quite large enough to merit a special trip on its own unless the current exhibit is of real interest to you, but it is an appealing place, with a very elegant interior highlighted by a sweeping, curved staircase. The Historical Society is open Tuesday through Saturday from 10 AM to 5 PM, and admission is free.

There's a point on Route 280 West, just before you reach the Stickel Drawbridge, when you see a towered cathedral rising from a low hill behind the Colonnade Apartments. On a misty day it looks like a mirage, nothing like the square-topped buildings that make up most of the Newark skyline. The building that appears so tantalizingly in the distance is the **Cathedral Basilica of the Sacred Heart**, 89 Ridge Street, Newark (for information, call 973-484-4600). Built in the soaring French Gothic style and modeled to some extent after the thirteenth-century cathedral at Reims, Sacred Heart measures 365 feet long and 165 feet wide and is the fifth largest in the country. Started in 1899 and completed in 1954, the cathedral abounds in stained-glass windows, marble altars, pointed arches, limestone carvings, and woodwork. Its copper spire rises to 260 feet, and its 200 windows are made of antique glass and follow the color scheme used for the windows of Chartres. The south rose window, with a diameter of 35 feet, is the second largest in the United States.

The building has a complex design history; it doesn't trace its heritage back to any one famous architect. The original design contract went to Jeremiah O'Rourke and Sons of Newark. The O'Rourke firm was soon joined by E. M. Waldron and Company, also of Newark. The exterior walls of Vermont Rockport granite were erected under O'Rourke's supervision, but the two firms did not work harmoniously together, and in 1908 work on the cathedral halted. Isaac E. Ditmars assumed control of the project in 1910 and modified the design to favor the French Gothic style. The final interior work was done by the New York architectural firm of Paul C. Reilly, with construction handled by the George A. Fuller Company and interior ornamentation by Professor Gonippo Raggi and Sons of Orange. The rose windows were designed by Karl Jung of Munich, and all the cathedral's windows were executed by the studios of Franz Zettler, a stained-glass craftsman from

Walter Choroszewski

Cathedral Basilica of the Sacred Heart

Munich. In 1976, the building was designated a National Historic Site. On October 4, 1995, Pope John Paul II conducted evening prayers here; President Clinton attended the service.

Tours are given the second Sunday of every month after noon Mass and after Sunday afternoon concerts, which are scheduled most months from September through May. The building, open at other times as well, is impressive even when you walk through it on your own.

Quick Tips

Given the variety of Newark's attractions, a day trip might well include an evening out, a dinner at NJPAC or one of the restaurants nearby or in the Ironbound section of the city. Or you might see a matinee at NJPAC, after lunch on NJPAC's patio. Or just munch a hot dog at Riverfront Stadium. Think *The Nutcracker* with your children on a cold winter afternoon, baseball on a warm, breezy afternoon. Then on to dinner at one of the Ironbound restaurants. Try **Casa Vasca** (114 Elm Street, 973-465-1350), whose white sangria tastes good even to people who don't drink. **Tony de Caneca** (72 Elm Road—not the same as Elm Street, and at the other end of the neighborhood, so get directions when you call for reservations—973-589-6882) is also deservedly popular. Another favorite is **Don Pepe** (844 McCarter Highway, 973-622-4662), which is especially convenient to NJPAC and provides free attended parking as well as super-generous servings. Children will love the sliced fried potatoes, and so will you. In fact, if you want a free-form walk on city streets with something of a time-warp quality, you might just go to the Ironbound and stroll down Ferry Street. If you don't buy anything, it won't cost anything (other than parking or a train ticket to Newark's Penn Station, which is right at the edge of the Ironbound). In downtown Newark, a popular weekday food spot is **Hobby's Delicatessen** (32 Branford Place, 973-0410), regarded by knowledgeable regulars as among the best Garden State purveyors of pastrami sandwiches and related indulgences.

A Newark trip is great for grownups, too; a matinee doesn't automatically mean "bring a child," museums are often a peaceful refuge for adults, and there's nothing wrong with grownups going to ballgames on their own.

Something Special in the Spring

Seeing the cherry blossoms at **Branch Brook Park** (Park Avenue and Lake Street, Newark, 973-268-3500) is one of those rare activities that it is more fun to do on a crowded weekend than on a peaceful weekday. Observing and sharing other people's pleasure in the landscape is part of the experience. The cherry trees are indeed beautiful during that all-too-brief period in early spring when they are in bloom, and the trees arch over the paths or bob gently toward you in all their flowery glory. Branch Brook Park was the first county park in the United States, and the cherry trees that are its signature were originally planted in the late 1920s. The park, which is not as famous as Manhattan's Central Park or Brooklyn's Prospect Park, was designed by the firm of Frederick Law Olmsted, who had designed the two New York parks with Calvin Vaux several decades earlier. It's north of downtown Newark, stretching to the Belleville line.

One problem, or so it seemed when I last visited the park in early April 2000, is that Branch Brook, like other Essex County parks, suffers from a shortage of loving, skilled, and expensive maintenance. This is not to say that parks crews do not spend hundreds of hours caring for the trees and planting new ones, but that Branch Brook, like South Mountain Reservation, Verona Park, and other Essex County parks, tends toward bare spots and occasional litter. Another factor, of course, is that April isn't always sunny and mild, and the day you have decided will be your Branch Brook day may be gray, windy, and reminiscent of November. But the park does have a cherry tree–rimmed lake and a majestic view of the Basilica of the Sacred Heart across the lake. On a weekday afternoon you can pull over on the shoulder of the park's main drive and look and take pictures to your heart's content. Although it isn't desolate enough to feel dangerous, it does feel lonely and a little exposed. If you go in the afternoon on the peak weekend, which sometimes coincides with the Cherry Blossom Festival, it may be too crowded for you to pause and enjoy the pink-and-white vistas peacefully. But what you lose in solitude you gain in the pleasure of seeing dozens or hundreds of other people being dazzled by an extraordinary display of carefully cultivated "natural" beauty.

Food

If you make a late Saturday afternoon trip to Branch Brook Park, you may want to add another dimension to the experience: dinner at **Nanina's in the Park** (540 Mill Street, Belleville, 973-751-1230). Since 1953, this elegant restaurant has been serving Italian food to appreciative diners. It is also known for its extensive wine list. The restaurant serves dinner Wednesday through Saturday, starting at 5 PM, and reservations are required. Jackets are preferred on Saturdays, so you may want to take the dress code into account before you start your cherry-tree trip.

Lights, Camera, Action, History

At some point, usually around fourth grade, many New Jersey elementary school students visit the **Edison National Historic Site** in West Orange (Main Street and Lakeside Avenue, West Orange, 973-736-0550). In case you didn't grow up in New Jersey or don't have any children who are now growing up in New Jersey, here's a reminder that the site is a spot of real significance and interest— even worth a second trip as an adult or with your family. The site is just off Route 280 (280 westbound to exit 10, 280 eastbound to exit 9) and, although it is worth a trip on its own, it also fits easily into the beginning or end of a Newark or Paterson day trip.

The site, which reopened in September 2000 after having been closed for renovation, consists of Thomas Alva Edison's research and development laboratory on Main Street and his home, Glenmont, in Llewellyn Park. Edison worked at the Laboratory Complex for more than four decades; among the items he invented or developed there are the motion-picture camera, phonographs, sound recordings, and silent and sound movies. There are fourteen structures, including six that were built for Edison as laboratory space in 1887, the year he settled in West Orange. The Black Maria is a replica of the world's first specifically designed motion picture studio.

Nearby Llewellyn Park, site of Glenmont, was one of the first private residential communities in the United States. Glenmont was built in 1880; a brick-and-timber mansion, it contains furnishings and family items used by the Edison family. The grounds include about fifteen acres, a greenhouse and barn, and a poured cement garage. Thomas Edison and his wife, Mina Edison, are buried on the grounds.

The Edison National Historic Site also includes a Museum Collection and Archives, primarily consisting of the original contents of the laboratory and Glenmont; they represent the world's largest single body of Edison-related material. The Edison family donated the materials to the National Park Service during the late 1950s and early 1960s. According to the National Park Service, the collection "includes laboratory notebooks, sketches and working drawings made by Edison and his colleagues, specialized testing equipment and materials, master and unreleased sound recordings, and the prototypes and working models for important inventions, including the first phonograph, improved telegraph equipment and early motion picture apparatus."

The site is open for guided tours Wednesday through Sunday; weekend hours are 9 AM to 5 PM; on weekdays the site opens at noon. You can visit both the laboratory and Glenmont. Glenmont tickets are sold on a first-come, first-served basis and do sell out on busy days.

Food

A block or two away from the site, at the corner of Main Street and Babcock Place, just across the street from the Tory Corner branch of the West Orange Public Library, is the **Greek-American Deli** (239 Main Street, West Orange, 973-236-0836). It sells sandwiches and other takeout food but is especially interesting for its full line of Greek products, such as cheeses and olive oils, as well as packaged prepared foods such as moussaka and pastitsio. It also carries goods from a bakery in Astoria, Queens; the kourembiedes, covered with powdered sugar, rich, slightly crunchy, and gently flavored, possibly with anise, are delicious. For a simple eat-in setting, there's the nearby **Wagon Wheel** (255 Main Street, West Orange, 973-731-4191), a luncheonette and ice-cream parlor.

Chapter Five

Iron and Silk: Paterson

As tourist attractions go, Paterson is still a work in progress. As a place with real significance in the history of American labor and industry, however, its role is assured. You just have to be prepared to make the leap between past and present and allow for a certain inconsistency in the urban landscape. Yes, there are great old mill buildings; there are also some empty lots. Yes, some of the buildings are nicely restored; others are somewhat desolate. Yes, the seventy-seven-foot Great Falls of the Passaic are impressive; you may not, however, find the footpath leading to the best view of the falls terribly appealing. In short, Paterson, conceived by Alexander Hamilton as a great American industrial center, is worth a visit. But if you choose to visit, go knowing that Paterson isn't—or at least wasn't yet in late summer 2000—a place to meander through a carefully manicured, well-funded historic park.

Alexander Hamilton, later to be fatally injured by New Jersey's own Aaron Burr in a duel fought elsewhere in New Jersey, thought the Great Falls of the Passaic River would be an ideal site for industry. Under Hamilton's guidance, the Society of Usefull Manfactures (S.U.M.) was established in 1791, and the Great Falls was chosen as its development site. The area was essentially planned and laid out by Alexander Hamilton and Pierre Charles L'Enfant in 1792, making it the nation's first planned industrial city. It was named for William Paterson, then governor of New Jersey. Cotton mills were among the first industries. The first lock-out of workers in American industrial history occurred at a Paterson mill in 1794. The first factory strike in America took place in a Paterson cotton mill in 1828; it was accompanied by a sympathy strike on the part of masons, carpenters, and other skilled workers in the city.

The opening of the Morris Canal in 1831 and the arrival of the railroad a year later encouraged other types of industry, notably the Colt revolver mill established by Samuel Colt in 1837. That year a locomotive was built in Paterson; over the next four decades thousands of locomotives were manufactured in the city. The silk industry came to Paterson in 1840, and by 1850, it was known as Silk City, a nickname that lasted well into the twentieth century. The industry attracted immigrants, many of whom had been politically active in Europe. In 1886 there was a brief strike, and in 1902 a three-week strike made a lasting impression. There were twenty-five thousand silk workers in Paterson in 1910, and they made nearly one-third of the silk manufactured in the United States.

In 1900, Paterson was much more than just another large New Jersey town with factories: at the turn of the last century, it was among the twenty largest cities in the United States. The Great Paterson Silk Strike of 1913 is legendary; it's the strike whose picketers, calling for an end to child labor, an eight-hour workday, and improved working conditions, were led by well-known activists such as "Big Bill" Haywood and Elizabeth Gurley Flynn and journalist John Reed. For all the glamour and widespread support in the outside world, the strike did not achieve the workers' goals. By the mid-1920s, the silk industry in Paterson was beginning to decline, a process hastened by the increasing production of synthetics after World War II.

The **Great Falls of the Passaic/(S.U.M.) Historic District** was listed on the National Register in 1970 and designated a national historic landmark in 1976. The historic district encompasses the streets and factories near the river. The visitor center (corner of McBride Avenue and Spruce Street, 973-279-9587) is open year-round on weekdays and seasonally on weekends. It is across the street from Haines Overlook Park, which provides a view of the falls and a place

Walter Choroszewski

Great Falls of the Passaic

to park your car. You can get a walking tour map there, as well as a great deal of supplementary information about the S.U.M. hydro-electric project, specific mill buildings, the Paterson Museum, the city's important churches, and more. At the very least, you should pick up a copy of the walking tour guide booklet in order to get a sense of where you are and what you are seeing; at least when I visited, there were very few signs. The old painted-on names of the mills are still visible in some cases, but except for the Rogers Build-ing, which now houses the Paterson Museum, and the neatly labeled Thompson house on Mill Street, there isn't much in the way of spe-cific information on-site. Nor are there many signs pointing the way from Paterson's commercial downtown to the historic district.

For the best view of the falls, cross the Passaic River and take the path behind the hydroelectric plant. Completed in 1914, it was one of the first hydroelectric plants in the country. The nearby footbridge gives you a fine vantage point, and there is a park at the top of the falls. It is named for Mary Ellen Kramer, who worked to gain land-mark status for the area when her husband was mayor of Paterson in the 1970s. The walking tour map will also take you to Raceway Park; this is the starting point for the district's canal system, which brought water from the river to the waterwheels and turbines of the mills. It was the first major water-power development in the country. The

Society of Usefull Manufactures developed most of the raceway system during the early decades of the nineteenth century. In about 1900, the emphasis shifted from individual waterwheels to central generating stations, which increased the power potential.

Near Raceway Park and the 1840s Gatehouse built to regulate the amount of water drawn from the Passaic River into the raceway, you can see the Ivanhoe Wheelhouse, a sole remnant of the Ivanhoe Manufacturing Company's vast, ten-building paper-production facility. The wheelhouse was restored in 1981.

Walking down Spruce Street to Market Street will provide you with a nice vista of brick mill buildings. It will also take you to the **Paterson Museum**, housed in the very handsome brick Thomas Rogers Building (2 Market Street, 973-881-3874). This is one of the district's fully restored buildings, and the museum's interior still evokes the space and layout of a factory floor. Even if you choose not to walk to the falls or stroll around the neighborhood, you may want to stop in at the museum. At the entrance are two locomotives, a reminder that the Rogers complex once housed the post–Civil War Rogers Locomotive Erecting Shop and the Rogers Administration Building. The Rogers Locomotive Works was the largest of five steam locomotive manufacturers in Paterson in the middle of the nineteenth century. The museum, with collections reflecting local archaeology, history, and mineralogy, has a display devoted to Paterson's industry, including Colt guns, the only two surviving Holland submarines, a weaving industry exhibit, and more; there are also rotating art and historical exhibitions. The museum is open Tuesday through Friday, 10 AM to 4 PM, and Saturday and Sunday, 12:30 PM to 4:30 PM.

John P. Holland built a fourteen-foot submarine in 1878; it sank on its first trial run. He persevered with varying degrees of success, eventually building six submarines. In 1900, his Holland VI submarine became the first vessel in the American submarine fleet.

A walk along Market Street to Mill Street will lead you to a number of other architecturally and historically interesting buildings, including the Franklin Mill, the Essex Mill, the Nag's Head Tavern (where John Reed, Helen Gurley Flynn, and John Sloan, among others, gathered during the 1913 Silk Strike), and Old School No. 2, a beautifully rehabilitated Victorian Gothic building. The 1836 Colt Gun Mill Historic Site was in the process of being preserved when I last visited. The front section of the Phoenix Mill on Van Houten Street, built about 1816, is the oldest surviving mill in the historic district.

The massive mills are only part of Paterson's architectural presence. There are also several interesting churches. The cornerstone of the **Cathedral of St. John the Baptist** (Main and Grand Streets) was laid in 1865. The building, in the style of European Gothic cathedrals, was dedicated in 1870. It is a national historic landmark and serves as the principal church of the diocese of Paterson. Closer to the mill district, **St. Michael's Roman Catholic Church** is a distinctive structure of yellow brick and topped by campaniles. It contains a "Cherub Head" relief by the sculptor Gaetano Federici. Dedicated in 1929, it, like St. John's, is a national historic landmark.

Paterson was also the birthplace and home of a variety of famous people. Near the corner of Cianci and Ellison Streets, there is a memorial statue of comic Louis Costello of the Abbott and Costello duo. Across the street is Federici Park, named for Gaetano Federici, with a Federici bust of Christopher Columbus. The poet Allan Ginsberg grew up in Paterson, too, of course, but his monuments are in words rather than stone.

The American Labor Museum/Botto House National Landmark

Given the importance of the labor movement in Paterson's history, it's not surprising that the **American Labor Museum** is nearby. The museum is located at the **Botto House** (83 Norwood Street, Haledon, 973-595-7953), only a few minutes' drive from the Great Falls Historic District. Once again, there are no signs leading directly from one place to the other. When you get to Haledon, there are signs, but they are small, so be alert. The museum is on a quiet residential street, and the open hillside that once lay in front of the Pietro and Maria Botto home (there are other houses on the hillside now) was a meeting place for the 1913 strikers. As the Bottos' granddaughter Bunny Kuiken, who also acts as a tour guide, explains vividly in the video that introduces you to the museum, the police in Paterson were sympathetic to the mill owners and hostile to the strikers, while the mayor of Haledon was sympathetic to the workers. Pietro Botto, a skilled weaver from northern Italy who worked in the silk mills, invited the strikers to gather at his home, and its second-floor balcony served as a podium for speakers such as writer Upton Sinclair, "Big Bill" Haywood, and many others.

The Botto House is both a theme museum and a house museum. There are exhibits about present-day labor, as well as the history of the 1913 strike, and there is a small, specialized research library. Better still, several rooms are still furnished and decorated as they were when the Botto family lived there, and the house and its neatly maintained grounds are very welcoming. Each room is filled with items that highlight an aspect of the family's life and add a dimension to a visitor's understanding of the strikers' era and the years that followed. Matrimonial certificates and Mr. Botto's American citizenship papers hang on the walls; the dining table is nicely set for dinner; Mason jars in the kitchen contain fruits and vegetables canned decades ago by family members. When I was there, Mrs. Kuiken, a wonderfully gracious and informative guide, mentioned that the tomatoes in one jar had been put up by her mother-in-law seventy-five years ago. Pointing out the copper polenta pot on the stove, she noted that in her family, polenta or rice rather than pasta served as the customary starch at a meal. Even if this house had no significance in the greater historical scheme, it would be a fascinating place to visit, because it provides so many insights into a particular lifestyle of early-twentieth-century New Jersey. The American Labor Museum/Botto House National Landmark is open Wednesday through Saturday from 1 PM to 4 PM.

The Other Half

Pateron's privileged residents, the mill owners and other prosperous families, lived close to the workers' neighborhoods. The recently renovated **Lambert Castle** (Valley Road, on the Clifton/Paterson border, 973-881-2761), also known as Bella Vista, was built in 1891 by Catholina Lambert, a wealthy immigrant silk manufacturer. A formal, elaborate stone building with towers, balconies, and terraces, it's definitely worth seeing. There is a museum, run by the Passaic County Historical Society, featuring a gallery of local history, sculpture, and period rooms reflecting the styles of 1900 through 1913, when life at the Castle was at its peak of activity. The main entrance atrium is especially impressive. Lambert Castle is set in Passaic County's **Garrett Mountain Reservation** (Valley Road, Paterson, 973-881-4832). Trails and picnic areas are to be found throughout the park, and fishing is permitted in the stocked pond.

Food

Paterson is a densely populated city in a densely populated county, so there is a lot of food, representing many ethnic groups. Pizza, a sandwich, or fast food can be found on almost any block. You may want to try **Shish-Kebob** (970 Main Street, 973-977-4888) or **Albasha** (1076 Main Street, 973-345-3700), which are among the several Middle Eastern restaurants on Main Street and elsewhere in the city that reflect Paterson's substantial Middle Eastern population. **La Tia Delia** (28 Market Street, 973-523-4550) is one of a number of Peruvian restaurants on Market Street, reflecting another of the city's immigrant communities. Residents and visitors enjoy **Meson Galicia** (58 Ellison Street, 973-684-4250), which serves Italian and Spanish food. **E & V Ristorante** (322 Chamberlain Avenue, 973-942-8080) is a long-established and popular family-friendly Italian restaurant. For a local classic, try a Texas wiener—a deep-fried hot dog served with spicy mustard, chopped onions, and chili sauce. Texas wieners are supposed to have originated in Paterson, and **Libby's** (98 McBride Avenue, 973-278-8718), near the Great Falls Visitor Center, has been serving them since 1936.

Chapter Six

Ringwood State Park: Something for Everyone

Tucked away off Route 511 in the northern reaches of Passaic County, **Ringwood State Park** (1304 Sloatsburg Road, Ringwood, 973-962-7031) is a place with diverse attractions, rich in both nature and history. It isn't very close to major population centers, and the side roads that lead to it aren't especially clearly marked, but it is one of those places that has something for everyone in a setting of considerable natural beauty.

In almost every case, if you are visiting Ringwood from within New Jersey you will be coming from the south, very likely from Interstate 287. That means you will be introduced to this still-remote part of the state by driving along the stretch of Route 511 that goes through the town of Wanaque. The Wanaque Reservoir, a major source of water for northern New Jersey, provides the area's underlying identity. Driving past its entranceway you get a glimpse of the imposing dam and dramatic stonework in the dam itself and the structures in front of the dam. The commercial strips have a largely pre–World War II look; they are interesting because they reflect a certain part of the past that much of suburban New Jersey has left behind.

As you drive north on Route 511, the glimpses and broad views of the reservoir are beautiful, at least during seasons when there is lots of water in the reservoir system. It looks like a lake surrounded by low, wooded hills. On sunny days, the water is very blue. During droughts, the view is less reassuring, with dried mudflats visible well away from shore. There is a sign for Ringwood State Park where Sloatsburg Road angles off from Route 511, and from Sloatsburg Road you can get to the various attractions at the park. Call before you go, and select your specific destination with an eye to your particular interests.

Ringwood Manor

The standard-issue brown wood signs for the various attractions within Ringwood State Park are not very legible from a distance. As you drive along Sloatsburg Road, you may overshoot Ringwood Manor's driveway before you can decipher its sign. Then you will have to drive all the way to New York State to turn around conveniently—at least, that's what happened to me the first time I visited. Once you reach the manor, however, you will find that it was worth the trouble.

For two centuries, starting in the 1740s, Ringwood and its environs were part of an active iron-mining area. **Ringwood Manor**, which has been designated as a National Historical Landmark, is an elegant country house that served as the home of several ironmasters of the Ringwood Company and their descendants. The first house was built in the 1760s; the British burned part of it during the Revolution, and the existing mansion was built and added on to for decades during the nineteenth century. As it now appears, the house particularly reflects the tastes and style of the Cooper-Hewitt family from 1854 through 1936. Its owners included Robert Erskine during the American Revolution, Martin Ryerson in the early 1800s, Peter Cooper (of Cooper Union fame) in the mid-1800s, and Peter Cooper's son-in-law, Abram Hewitt, in the later 1800s. Abram Hewitt was elected

Photograph courtesy of Friends of Ringwood Manor

Parlor at Ringwood Manor

mayor of New York City in 1887. The family donated it to the state in 1937.

According to the brochure prepared by the Friends of Ringwood Manor (973-962-6118), a nonprofit organization of enthusiastic and knowledgeable volunteers dedicated to restoring and preserving the mansion, the 3-story, 51-room house has 28 bedrooms, 13 bathrooms, 24 fireplaces, and 250 windows. Officially, the house, which contains an interesting collection of nineteenth-century American painting and furniture, is open Wednesday through Sunday year-round. If you are intent upon seeing the interior of the house, be sure to call to confirm that tours will be available when you make your trip. Beautiful as the grounds are, seeing the interior of the house and hearing about its owners makes the trip more meaningful.

The cherry woodwork in the dining room and the elaborate carving in the gun room are especially eye-catching; the airy French drawing room and somewhat more intimate Ryerson parlor provide vivid hints of the rhythm and quality of life at Ringwood Manor. The delightfully furnished family bedrooms and period bathrooms upstairs offer lovely views of the carefully landscaped grounds and glimpses of how luxurious life could be a little over a century ago.

If the house is not open, you still can get a good view of the spacious, newly renovated sunroom, or piazza, a recently completed project of the Friends of Ringwood Manor. Thanks to the room's floor-to-ceiling windows, you can see inside quite well from the stone terrace outside. Decorated with statues and ferns, the room has a beautifully refinished wood floor and white wicker furniture softened with green and flowered cushions.

The grounds are lovely, with ample parking and benches everywhere so that you can sit and enjoy the views of lawns and meadows and ponds and hills. Not surprisingly, I saw about a dozen people sketching from various vantage points when I was there. There are French and Italian statues, garden ornaments, and various examples of ironwork strategically placed throughout the grounds, as well as gates from the Astor home on Thirty-third Street in Manhattan, gate posts from the old Columbia College campus, and columns from the old New York Life Insurance Building on Madison Square in Manhattan. The formal gardens were inspired by the European travels of Mrs. Hewitt and her daughter.

A picnic grove just down the driveway from the first parking lot has plenty of shade, a small playground, and the usual state-issue grills. Seasonally, the Friends operate the Victorian Coffee Shop in the old laundry building across the way from the mansion. Inside the Coffee Shop, there is a small gift shop which sells a variety of tempting, historically appropriate mementos.

Iron from Ringwood was used for parts of the chain that American forces used in an attempt to block the British from sailing up the Hudson River during the Revolutionary War; Ringwood was also a major supplier of iron to the Union armies during the Civil War. The last Ringwood mines closed in the 1950s. One place to explore this now ghostly aspect of the area's history is at the **Long Pond Ironworks Historic District** (1334 Greenwood Lake Turnpike,

Hewitt, 973-657-1688). Long Pond Ironworks is several miles past Ringwood State Park on Route 511, which at this point is called Greenwood Lake Turnpike. The ironworks began operation in the mid-1700s and continued until the 1880s. The remains of the village—a very small church, a couple of houses, and the visitor center housed in the old company store—are along the road. Industrial structures from the eighteenth and nineteenth centuries, including furnaces, ice houses, and waterwheels, also remain. The Friends of Long Pond Ironworks lead tours of the furnace area and village on the second Saturday of the month, from April to November. The visitor center is open seasonally on Saturday and Sunday afternoons. The recreational section of **Long Pond Ironworks State Park**, on Monksville Reservoir near the historic district, is open to the public twenty-four hours a day year-round. The reservoir has two boat ramps and is heavily used by anglers, sporting clubs, and the United States Sailing Association.

Outdoor Activities

Like any good state park, Ringwood provides ample opportunity for outdoor activities, particularly at **Shepherd Lake Recreation Area**, and you can combine an afternoon at the lake with a quick visit to Ringwood Manor or Skylands. From Memorial Day weekend through Labor Day, when lifeguards are on duty, swimming is permitted at spring-fed Shepherd Lake. There are bathhouses and a concession stand. Rowboats, canoes, and small sailboats are allowed on the lake and can be rented at the recreation area (boathouse, 973-962-6999). Fishing is allowed in season at the lake, home to trout, largemouth bass, sunfish, pickerel, and catfish, and at Ringwood Brook, which is stocked with trout. Hunting is permitted in designated areas in season.

There are more than forty miles of trails throughout the park. The trails are designated either hiking-only or multi-use, and depending upon the season and conditions, the latter are used for horseback riding, mountain biking, cross-country skiing, and snow-mobiling. Trail markers specify the designated use.

A Garden Walk

Not far down the road from Shepherd Lake, with an entrance drive flanked by two impressive stone eagles standing guard in front of rhododendrons, is another of New Jersey's not-quite-discovered treasures: **Skylands, the New Jersey Botanical Garden** (973-962-7527; www.njbg.org). This thousand-acre-plus combination of formal plantings and beautiful vistas has its origins in the private luxury enjoyed by two wealthy men and now is supported in part by the NJBG/Skylands Association, a nonprofit volunteer group that works in partnership with the New Jersey Department of Parks and Forestry.

Skylands Farm was the name of a country estate assembled by Francis Lynde Stetson (1846–1920), a prominent New York businessman. He had a granite mansion built and hired Samuel Parsons Jr., a protégé of Frederick Law Olmsted, to design the grounds, roads, and drainage systems. Parsons, a founder of the American Society of Landscape Architects, used photographs of his work at Skylands to illustrate a landscape architecture text that he published in 1915. In 1922, not long after Stetson's death, Skylands was sold to Clarence McKenzie Lewis (1877–1959), an investment banker. Lewis had the Stetson house torn down and replaced it with a Tudor mansion. A plant collector himself, Lewis hired a prominent landscape architecture firm, Vitale and Geiffert, to design the gardens around the house. The state purchased Skylands in 1966, and in 1984, the ninety-six acres immediately surrounding the mansion were designated by Governor Thomas Kean as the state's official botanical garden.

Skylands is open daily from 8 AM to 8 PM. The setting is so beautiful that even if there are not many flowers in bloom, you will have a lot to look at in this sheltered valley surrounded by rolling hills and views of the Ramapo Mountains. If you visit in the fall, you will get to see brilliant foliage, but no rhododendrons. (You may also miss many of the insects that often join you on a summertime walk in any garden.) If you go in late May, you may get to sniff the lilacs, but the annuals won't be in yet. There is no parking fee on week-days; a nominal fee is charged on weekends between Memorial Day weekend and Labor Day.

You can pick up a self-guiding tour brochure at the Visitor Center at the Carriage House. Here you will also find a small gift shop, rest rooms, pay phone, and vending machines. The brochure is a key part of appreciating your surroundings, since there is very little explanatory material in the gardens themselves.

After you pass through the Annual Garden, which is just beyond the Carriage House, you will come to a field-path framed by young crab-apple trees. This is known as Crab Apple Vista; at the end of the vista stand the graceful Four Continents statues and a grove of horse chestnut trees. The Perennial Garden is next to the Annual Garden; depending upon the time of year, it can be either very colorful or barely noticeable.

One of the sights that intrigued me as I walked toward the statues were the dark-leaved column-shaped maple trees that accent the skyline to the right. They are not shaped like traditional maple trees—they look more like a variation on Lombardy poplars—so it was a bit of a surprise to read the label when I reached the road along which they are planted. If you are in the mood for a short walk or have small children with you, this is a good place to cross Maple Avenue and start exploring the formal gardens on the other side of the road. If you want to explore beyond the main attractions, the brochure map will guide you to paths and informal gardens beyond Crab Apple Vista, including a wildflower garden, a heather garden, and a bog garden.

After crossing Maple Avenue, you will be near the Lilac Garden; in late May, this is a very fragrant and restful place; even without the flowers, it is delightful. In summer, there is a good display of day lilies in the next garden, going toward the house. A reflecting pool and a fountain with a boy riding a dolphin make the nearby Azalea Garden a special treat even when the azaleas are not in bloom.

Food

Most of Ringwood State Park is a good place to picnic. Picnics are not permitted at Skylands, but there are plenty of picnic facilities at Ringwood Manor and Shepherd Lake. Like other state parks, Ringwood is part of the carry-in/carry-out program: Bags are distributed throughout the park, and you are asked to take your trash out with you and dispose of it at home. It's probably best to bring food from home, but you could stop and pick up food in Wanaque or on the way to Long Pond. You might be lucky enough to be at Ringwood Manor when the Victorian Coffee Shop is open. Refreshments are available seasonally at Shepherd Lake, and the vending machines just outside the rest rooms at the Skylands Carriage House can tide you over in a culinary emergency.

If you leave Ringwood in the late afternoon or early evening, you might want to stop for dinner at **Berta's Chateau** (7 Grove Street, Wanaque, 973-835-0092) on the way home. This long-established local favorite serves northern Italian food. It is open daily from 5 PM, Sunday from 1 PM. It offers a children's menu and is noted for its wine list.

Chapter Seven

Our Own North Woods: Sussex/Passaic Wilderness

People who drive the New Jersey Turnpike on their way to someplace else—the Green Mountains, Cape Cod, Williamsburg—would probably be surprised to know that the Appalachian Trail runs through the same state that this traffic-clogged highway does. The Appalachian Trail, after all, is a byword for serious hiking, a two-thousand-mile challenge, anchored by Maine's Mount Katahdin at one end and by Springer Mountain in Georgia at the other. Of course, it is also a trail whose segments are easily broken down into hikes of varying length, manageable by hikers of more modest ambitions.

New Jersey claims seventy-four miles of the Appalachian Trail, which runs through the state's northwestern highlands and includes parts of the trail network in several state parks and forests along and around the Kittatinny Ridge. While hiking may be the prime motivation for a visit to this corner of the state, it is by no means the only reason to come.

The thirteen thousand-plus acres of **Wawayanda State Park** (85 Warwick Turnpike, Hewitt, 973-853-4462) are surprisingly close to populated resort areas such as Highland Lakes, but civilization will seem far away once you are in the park. Its twenty miles of the Appalachian Trail are just a fraction of all the trail miles inside its boundaries, and the view from the top of Mount Wawayanda is one of those spectacular rewards that hardworking hikers get for reaching a rugged elevation. Lake Wawayanda, once the site of nineteenth-century ironworks, provides a scenic setting for swimming, boating, and fishing (there is also fishing in Wawayanda Creek); canoe and boat rentals are available seasonally. It is a beautiful lake at any time of year; fall foliage in the park can be spectacular, and the trails also lend themselves to cross-country skiing. Horseback riding and mountain biking are also permitted in the park. Wawayanda sometimes has snow cover when the suburban areas to its south and east do not, so cross-country skiing, as well as snowshoeing and snowmobiling, may be possible even on winter days when your lawn and driveway are clear. There are several special natural areas in the park. Bearfort Mountain Natural Area (1,325 acres) has several types of forest: swamp hardwood, hemlock-mixed hardwood, and chestnut oak. It has 360-degree views of the surrounding highlands and is a good location for observing hawks. Wawayanda Hemlock Ravine Natural Area (399 acres), a hemlock-mixed hardwood area, rises three hundred feet from Doublekill Creek to surrounding hills. The Appalachian Trail runs along the area's western boundary. Wawayanda Swamp Natural Area (2,167 acres) includes an Atlantic white cedar swamp, mixed oak-hardwood forest, and a glacially formed spring-fed lake. Among its wildlife inhabitants are red-shouldered hawks, barred owls, and great blue herons. There are several trails in this area.

The nearly fifteen thousand acres of **High Point State Park** (Route 23, Sussex, 973-875-4800) are at the northwestern tip of New Jersey. High Point Monument, 1,803 feet above sea level, is built on the highest point in the state. Its attractions include swimming in spring-fed twenty-acre Lake Marcia, boating on Sawmill Lake and Steenykill Lake, fishing, winter sports, and hiking on a number of blazed trails. The **High Point Cross-Country Ski Center** is a special feature. The park has fifteen kilometers of groomed trails, half of them covered by artificial snow. Cross-country skis and other winter sports equipment are available for rent. The center, on Lake Marcia, serves food. For information about cross-country skiing at High Point, call 973-702-1222. The Dryden Kuser Natural Area (1,500 acres), 1,500 feet above sea level, includes the highest-elevation Atlantic white cedar swamp in the world. There is a self-guided trail booklet for the swamp trail. The Appalachian Trail, which for a time follows a rocky ridge, provides vantage points from which to view the surrounding area. Going north, the trail descends from the ridge and passes through areas that once were farm fields. Park maps are available at the visitor center.

In 1923, the land for High Point State Park was donated by Colonel Anthony R. and Susie Dryden Kuser and dedicated as a park. The landscaping was designed by Boston's Olmsted Brothers firm; the Olmsted brothers' father was Frederick Law Olmsted, who designed Central Park. The Kusers also paid for 220-foot-tall High Point Monument, which was completed in 1930 in memory of the state's wartime heroes. There is a parking lot at the monument for those who would like to limit their hiking to the monument's stairs; a restoration program projected to last fourteen months was underway as this book went to press, and the monument was closed to the public.

Stokes State Forest (1 Coursen Road, Branchville, 973-948-3820) encompasses more than 15,735 rugged and beautiful acres and is popular with hikers, campers, fishermen, and photographers. Its trails offer opportunities for the usual pleasures of the state parks, including winter sports and horseback riding. Big Flat Brook is stocked with trout yearly and is a popular fishing site; the forest's other ponds and other streams are also popular. Perhaps the two best-known areas of the park are Tillman Ravine and Sunrise Mountain. The steep sides of Tillman Ravine Natural Area (525 acres) are covered with a hemlock forest, and there are several trails in the ravine. Several bridges cross Tillman Brook, which runs along the bottom of the ravine, and as you follow the trail you will see waterfalls, rock outcrops, and a smooth-sided sandstone hollow called the Teacup below the Lower Falls. Sunrise Mountain (elevation 1,653 feet) provides a spectacular view of the surrounding countryside. You can hike or drive to a summit pavilion built by the Civilian Conservation Corps in the late 1930s. The Appalachian Trail runs along the ridge. Sunrise Mountain is a difficult environment for plants. Mountain laurel, wild blueberry, pitch pine, and scrub oak are among the natural vegetation found throughout the area.

Swartswood State Park (off Route 619, Swartswood, 973-383-5230), with about thirteen hundred acres, is the smallest of the northwestern rustic retreats. Its glacial lake sets the scene for sailing, fishing, and swimming in summer, and ice boating and ice skating in winter. There is a trailer launch and a cartop launch, and boat and canoe rentals are available seasonally. Trails, including a handicapped-accessible trail, provide ample opportunity for hiking, biking, horseback riding, and, in season, cross-country skiing and snowshoeing.

The land for **Kittatinny Valley State Park** (Andover, 973-786-6445) was acquired by the state in 1994. Fishing and boating are permitted on Lake Aeroflex and Gardner's Pond, both of which are part of the Pequest River's headwaters. Two hiking trails in the park, the twenty-seven-mile Paulinskill Valley Trail and the twenty-mile Sussex Branch Trail, lie along unused rail lines and are used for hiking, horseback riding, biking, cross-country skiing and dog sledding.

Food

Picnics are the obvious meals for outdoorsy day trips in the Great Northwest, though food concessions operate seasonally at some locations. If you plan a full day on the trails, you should plan food and drink accordingly, but if you have a shorter session in mind, you can always head south or east a bit to nearby towns such as Newton for a meal on the way to or from your trip destination. In fact, Newton is worth at least a side trip even if you don't want to eat there. The Sussex County seat is built around a hilly courthouse square, and many of its buildings project a delightfully nineteenth-century mood.

Sun and Snow

Not far from the natural attractions of the state-owned lands is a place for a different kind of outdoor adventure. **Mountain Creek** (Route 94, Vernon, 973-827-2000) is a great destination for organized play in both summer and winter. During snow season, it is a remarkably close downhill ski and snowboard area. It has more than forty trails, eleven lifts and tows, and a vertical drop of more than 1,000 feet. Lessons and rentals are available. The season usually runs from mid-December to mid-March. In summer, the focus of the trip is Water World, a trip in itself or a nice way to cool off after a warm half-day hike on a rugged trail. Water World, which is closed after Labor Day, includes children's attractions such as the Lost Island fun area, a wading pool, bumper boats, and a multilevel interactive water play fort with water slides, spray cannons, and water hoses. Water World's Adventure Ridge is geared toward adults and older children, with heavier-duty attractions such as Cannonball Falls, a speed slide, and water speed coasters. The Wild River Canyons provide a taste of white-water excitement in the form of a raft ride, tube rides, and a cliff leap. There is also a powerful wavepool, with a body slide nearby for younger children. Although the water park itself is closed in the fall, Mountain Creek's Amazing Maize Maze™ remains open on weekends through the end of October. This professionally sculpted corn maze covers more than four acres and has two miles of paths.

Mountain Creek serves a variety of food in a variety of settings. Possibilities include burgers, sandwiches, salads, pizza, soft drinks, even ribs and corn, along with soft drinks, beer, and cocktails.

Chapter Eight

Child's Play and More: The
Sussex/Passaic County Circuit

If you grew up backpacking and hardly felt the weight of your trail supplies the last time you climbed a mountain, you may be the kind of day hiker who can strap your toddler on your back and spend the afternoon climbing Sussex County's peaks. If, however, you are less rugged and your children less portable, there are many other things to do in the northwestern corner of New Jersey. An array of long-established attractions, including Space Farms, Fairy Tale Forest, and Wild West City, are traditional family fare. A new attraction that fits right in is Skylands Stadium, where the Cardinals (of the St. Louis Cardinals farm system) play. Two mining museums are the educational icing on this family-oriented cake.

Perhaps the most intriguing, because it's so varied and quirky, is the **Space Farms Zoo and Museum** (Route 519, Sussex, 973-875-5800; www.spacefarms.com). Open daily May through October, it is set on more than one hundred acres in the crossroads settlement of Beemerville. The zoo's collection of hundreds of animals includes bobcats, tigers, lions, leopards, monkeys, buffalo, hyena, llamas, yaks, wild ponies, timber wolves, foxes, bears, snakes, and deer. Even more interesting, at least for me, are the displays of historic and collectible items. There is a huge old barn filled with carriages, wagons, and antique cars and motorcycles. You can also see rifles and other weapons from the Revolutionary and Civil Wars, a barn with a fascinating display of old tools, a doll museum and toy museum, a hand-built train set, a miniature circus, and American Indian artifacts. The site also has a family restaurant, gift shop, picnic and barbecue area, country store, and playground with miniature golf. Space Farms dates back to 1927, when Ralph and Elizabeth Space started with a quarter-acre of land and a general store, repair shop, and animal shelter. The enterprise expanded over the years and continues to be a surprise worth discovering.

Reflecting its abundant mineral resources—zinc ore so rich that much of it is fluorescent—northwestern New Jersey has not one but two mineral and mining museums. Some of the minerals found here are not found anywhere else in the world. The **Sterling Hill Mining Museum** (30 Plant Street, Ogdensburg, 973-209-7212; www.sterlinghill.org) is the site of a world-famous underground zinc mine that is open for tours. The last operating underground mine in the state, Sterling Hill Mine closed in 1986, and the nonprofit museum opened in 1990. It hosts visitors daily April through November and weekends in March. The air in the mine is cool enough to make wearing a sweater or light jacket a good idea; the museum also recommends proper footwear (that means no high heels, flip-flops, or mules). The **Franklin Mineral Museum and Mine Replica** (Evans Street, Franklin, 973-827-3481) is also on the site of an old zinc mine; it is open daily from April through November. The museum displays fluorescent minerals, and the mine replica is housed in an adjacent building. You can gather your own rocks and minerals at the mine's old waste pile, known as the Buckwheat Dump, and buy a variety of souvenirs at the museum shop.

In a less glittery but more fanciful vein, and possibly more appealing for younger children, **Fairy Tale Forest** (Oak Ridge Road, West Milford, 973-697-5656) brings children's favorite storybook characters to life. On twenty acres of woodland, children can ride the Candy Rock Line train past the Three Pigs' Cottage, Rapunzel's tower, and Humpty Dumpty's wall. Fairy Tale Forest is open daily in summer and on weekends in late spring and early fall.

Although the Wild West may seem like a fairy tale to many young (and not-so-young) minds, it's also a historic reality. **Wild West City** (off Route 206, Netcong, 973-347-8900) is an authentic reproduction of Dodge City. Its live-action Western dramatizations are augmented by a petting zoo, spacious picnic grove, the Golden Nugget Saloon, and shops. Regular events include an opening ceremony, acts called "Gunslinger," "Pony Express," "Art of Bullwhips and Dancing Ropes," and mock stagecoach and bank holdups. There are also special events throughout the season; some from the summer of 2000 include demonstrations of domestic life on the frontier; Native American dancers; Civil War interpretations and weapons demonstrations; and a tribute to the American Cowboy, with the "Wild West City Cowboy Roll Call" and live western music at the Opera House. Wild West City is open from late April through October.

There aren't too many images more American than an old Western town. A baseball diamond with uniformed players in all the right places may be one of the few. And you can see that image and watch a ballgame, right in Sussex County. The **New Jersey Cardinals** of the Class A-NY-Penn League are part of the St. Louis Cardinals farm system and play from late June through early September. Rising from the fields just off Route 15, the Cardinals' stadium, **Skylands Park** (94 Championship Place, Augusta, 973-579-7500; toll-free, 888-NJ CARDS/652-2737), may remind you of the film *Field of Dreams*. The league includes more than a dozen teams from places such as Auburn and Batavia, New York; Pittsfield, Massachusetts; Winooski, Vermont; and Niles, Ohio.

Northwest New Jersey also offers unstructured fun. Lake Hopatcong, the state's largest lake within New Jersey, straddles Morris and Sussex Counties and is a giant version of a classic swimming hole. **Hopatcong State Park** (Landing Boulevard, Landing, 973-398-7010) has a lawn that slopes down to the lake, a bathhouse, and a concession stand. Call before you go to confirm that lifeguards are on duty. There is boating, fishing, and picnicking; in winter, weather permitting, Lake Hopatcong's ice fishing is considered to be among the best in the state.

A Detour for the Grownups

When you head north on Route 15, instead of taking the road that leads to Skylands Stadium or Space Farms, you can head for Lafayette, instead, and the pleasures of one of New Jersey's most appealing antique centers. The **Lafayette Mill Antiques Center** (Morris Farm Road, 973-383-0065) is open Thursday through Monday and closed Tuesday and Wednesday. Looking much like the 1840s gristmill it used to be, the Antiques Center is full of delightful shops, representing more than forty dealers. One of the more unusual is the Boathouse, which sells model boats and ships, as well as old books on sailing-related subjects and other items that fit a nautical theme. Ruth Fassel's Victoriana shop, just inside the main entrance to the mill, is also appealing. One of my favorites is the 1880 House, with shelves full of wonderfully evocative old food and home-product containers, as well as other kitchen items. Tom Mitchell has an array of old sporting equipment, including racks of old baseball bats, some with Hall of Fame credentials. The upper level of the mill is also well worth exploring; perhaps its star attraction is Sign of the Tymes, which sells nostalgic old toys and advertising materials. Several other shops on the upper level offer nice selections of wood furniture, especially dressers.

Several buildings face the Mill directly across the parking lot/courtyard. The **Night Watch**, 973-383-1611, purveyors of "good eats and antiques," serves a dual purpose, and is made more intriguing by its bilingual—Dutch and English—menu, posted in the doorway. For those with a sweet tooth, there's the **Chocolate Goat** (103 Route 15, 973-383-5560), a lovely gift shop that also sells Neuhaus chocolates.

Just south of old Lafayette is **Olde Lafayette Village** (Routes 15 and 94, 973-383-8323). This small outlet-style shopping village also includes specialty shops, so you can browse at Bass, Bugle Boy, Izod, and Van Heusen and then take a look at jewelry, art, and collectibles.

Food

Certainly you can bring a picnic along on a day trip to Sussex and Passaic counties; picnic areas abound. Or you can eat at any one of the many family/fast-food restaurants nearby or add another dimension to your trip by stopping for a leisurely meal. **Lafayette House** (Olde Lafayette Village, 973-579-3100) has a colonial-style dining room and a downstairs pub. Open for lunch and dinner Monday through Saturday, and for brunch on Sunday, it has a children's menu (in the pub) and a liquor license. The **Black Forest Inn** (249 Route 206, Stanhope, 973-347-3344)—also convenient to Waterloo Village, featured in chapter 10—is a well-regarded German-Continental restaurant that has been thriving for more than two decades. It is open for lunch several days during the week and for dinner every day except Tuesday. The **Front Porch Grille** (75 Sparta Avenue, Newton, 973-300-9801), a casual but sophisticated place, is open for lunch Tuesday through Friday and dinner Tuesday through Saturday.

Chapter Nine

Bridging the Gap:
Delaware Water Gap
National Recreation Area

Delaware Water Gap National Recreation Area is huge, at least by mid-Atlantic standards. Since it spans the Delaware River, it has lots to offer in both New Jersey and Pennsylvania. (Even though this is a book about New Jersey day trips, I've considered anything in the Delaware Water Gap an honorary part of New Jersey; some things are too good to miss just because you have to cross a bridge to get to them.) It is probably fair to say that the park has something for everyone except for visitors who absolutely must have paved sidewalks to pound. There are boardwalks and hard-packed dirt or gravel roads for those whose mobility is limited, but as far as I know, no sidewalks.

Delaware Water Gap National Recreation Area preserves 40 miles of the middle Delaware River, and almost 70,000 acres of land along the river's New Jersey and Pennsylvania shores. The Gap is the point at which the river curves through the Kittatinny Ridge, in a steep-sided opening that is visible for miles and looks especially dramatic when you drive through it on Route 80 going from New Jersey toward Pennsylvania. It's much tamer driving east, though you get a better view of the river itself from that direction. The park's Kittatinny

Walter Choroszewski

Delaware Water Gap

Point Visitor Center (908-496-4458), just off Route 80 on the New Jersey side of the river, is open daily from 9 AM to 5 PM spring through late October, and on most weekends in winter. (Note that the park is officially headquartered in Bushkill, Pennsylvania; phone, 570-588-2435; other visitor centers are open seasonally.) At Kittatinny Point, you will find information, an audiovisual program, displays, a sales outlet for park-related items, restrooms, and telephones. There is no admission fee to the park, though recreational fees are collected at Smithfield Beach, Milford Beach, Bushkill Access, Dingmans Access, and Watergate.

At various times of year and in various spots, visitors to the park can canoe, camp, fish, swim, hike; view wildlife and geological features; discover historical sites; and drive or bicycle to look at the scenery. The road that parallels the river on the New Jersey side is romantically and traditionally known as the **Old Mine Road.** The road is believed to have been built by the Dutch in 1650 to connect early mining areas near the Water Gap and Kingston, New York. The precise chronology of the first century or so and the precise route of the original road may be a bit hazy, but in 1777, Robert Erskine, George Washington's surveyor general, mapped the area. The Old Mine Road follows his route. The park includes historic Millbrook Village and several environmental education centers. The surrounding area was once destined to be flooded as part of the proposed and highly controversial Tocks Island Reservoir. In 1978, Congress designated the section of the Delaware River within Delaware Water Gap National Recreation Area as part of the National Wild and Scenic Rivers System, and in 1992 the Tocks Island Dam project was deauthorized.

Gap Basics

Delaware Water Gap National Recreation Area is a four-season destination. A day trip can focus on anything from the river itself to rock climbing to history to simple admiration of the scenery. There is swimming at Milford Beach and Smithfield Beach; both are on the Pennsylvania side. Although the Delaware River rarely looks threatening, it is unpredictable, with drop-offs and currents; there have been a number of drownings in recent years. Park and local authorities emphasize that visitors should swim only at officially designated and guarded beaches, and use caution and wear life jackets while boating or engaging in any other river activity. There are access points every eight to ten miles for canoeing, tubing, and rafting, which are all popular activities. Boating maps are available at the visitor centers, and you can rent tubes, canoes, and rafts from private concessions at several locations. The park office has a list of licensed liveries who rent equipment and transport you between access points. For example, **Kittatinny Canoes** (800 FLOAT-KC/356-2852) has a base just on the Pennsylvania side of the Dingmans Ferry Bridge. Hunting is permitted throughout the area in season; check at the visitor center or ranger stations for details. River fishing requires a license from either New Jersey or Pennsylvania. Required state hunting and fishing licenses are sold at local sporting goods stores. The park is also a good place for watching birds, especially raptors during their autumn migrating season. According to the park's informational brochure, the Delaware Water Gap is one of the few places in the East where bald eagles spend the winter, and the best time to view them is in mid-morning or late afternoon in January or February.

A snowmobile trail runs from Smithfield Beach through the fields, and a longer loop leads up to a ridge. Unplowed roads as well as hiking trails provide ample cross-country skiing opportunities, and if the winter is cold enough, you can ice skate and ice fish on lakes and ponds.

The park has more than sixty miles of hiking trails, and more than twenty-five miles of the Appalachian Trail run through the park. The narrow roads of the park are generally scenic. The Old Mine Road is a popular drive; hardier travelers can bicycle along park roads, and the Blue Mountain Lake Mountain Bike Trail opened recently. Bicycling is not permitted along the hiking trails.

Being There

The Water Gap makes its presence known miles before you reach it, especially if you are traveling west on Route 80 in Allamuchy Township, where a scenic pullover will provide you with a great view of the Gap. The scene always reminds me of the prehistoric land-scapes in *Land Before Time,* a movie about sweet but hungry dinosaurs.

You don't necessarily approach the Gap from Route 80, of course. You can avoid the highway by driving the state and county roads of Sussex and Warren Counties. Route 15 to Route 206 through Lafayette will get you to the northern reaches of the park, and if you pay careful attention to the signs once you pass Culver Lake, you will be able to turn onto Route 560, the road that, depending upon which forks you take, leads to Layton, Peters Valley, Dingmans Ferry, and Dingmans Falls. Layton's red-painted corner store still has a Mail Pouch Tobacco sign on one side. Dingmans Ferry isn't a ferry anymore; it's the name of a narrow metal toll bridge that crosses a placid-looking stretch of the Delaware. The toll is 75 cents each way and there is a fifteen-mile-an-hour speed limit. The bridge was originally built in 1834, and tolls are taken by hand by people standing in the middle of the roadway.

Once you cross the bridge, which is the only one between the Route 80 and Route 206 toll bridges, you are in Pennsylvania. Suddenly, you are on Route 739; take it a short distance to Route 209 and turn south, following the signs for Dingmans Falls (the turn-off is very close to the intersection; this isn't a major trek). There's a parking lot and a May-through-October **Visitor Center at Dingmans Falls.** The key thing is the boardwalk that leads through the woods to the real point of this detour—the waterfalls. The board-walk is very solid and wide enough for several people to walk next to each other. The stream that runs through the woods is wide and shallow and, if the season is right, bubbling just enough to provide good sound effects. One side of the valley rises steeply from boardwalk level, high and almost clifflike, though heavily forested. You will smell pine needles and see lots of wild rhododendrons. If you visit at the right time, late June or early July, you will have the added treat of seeing an abundance of very pale pink blossoms on the rhododendron bushes. Cross the stream along a wide pedestrian bridge and you will be at Silver Thread Falls. Tall (eighty feet, in fact), slender, and true to their name, the falls come straight down in a narrow, glistening rush all the way from the top of the cliff to just in front of the boardwalk viewing point. Admire it, then keep going. Your first glimpse of Dingmans Falls may be disappointing, since the bottom part of the falls are at a more gentle angle than the perpendicular Silver Thread Falls. But when you get closer, you will not be disappointed. The gentler, though wide and rushing, bottom part is just the beginning of the experience. The top is far away, high above you, and the water rushes straight down. This is a real waterfall, with a 130-foot drop. The boardwalk has a good, wide viewing area, as well as reassuringly solid railings. The more adventurous or agile can take an excellent wooden stairway that zigzags up the hill all the way to the top of the falls for a view from above.

Back on the New Jersey side, **Peters Valley Craft Education Center** (19 Kuhn Road, Layton, 973-948-5200; www.pvcrafts.org) is quiet and tucked-away, and can have the air of a tiny, undiscovered village even on a summer weekend afternoon. The center has resident and visiting artists who teach both beginning and advanced courses. Peters Valley also offers workshops on "Epoxy Resin: Create with Color," "Advanced Chainmaking," "Northeastern Woodland Style Indian Wigwam Construction," and "Copperplate Calligraphy," to name just a few among dozens of intriguing summer 2000 classes. Workshops are scheduled during the spring, summer, and fall, with educational programs throughout the year. The Studio Interpretive Program gives the public a chance to see Peters Valley's facilities, with the studios open during the workshop season every Saturday and Sunday from 2 PM to 5 PM. Twice a year, in spring and in fall, Peters Valley holds an open house; studios are open, with ongoing demonstrations.

Throughout the year, the Peters Valley Store and its upstairs Sally D. Francisco Gallery show and sell the work of more than 250 craftspeople.

The quiet of Peters Valley disappears temporarily on the weekend in late September when the annual outdoor craft fair is held. During the fair, the place is bustling with visitors eager to browse and buy. In 2000, about 170 juried contemporary and traditional craftspeople participated in the thirtieth annual fair.

Peters Valley also has an educational outreach program called Craftsmen at Work. It brings contemporary and traditional crafts to schools, with studio department heads or local artists presenting craft demonstrations. If you would like to get a preview of what goes on at Peters Valley, the Gallery Without Walls may appeal to you. It consists of nineteen pedestals and one wall case distributed among nineteen public indoor sites in Morristown (including Epstein's and the Morris Museum). Each pedestal houses a work of contemporary craft as well as a brochure featuring statements from the artists and a map linking the pedestals together.

The landscape and roads become curvier and steeper as you travel through the Walpack Wildlife Management Area. The road loop near Flatbrookville is very scenic. The part closer to the river is the Old Mine Road; the road slightly inland is Route 615. If you feel as though you are driving in circles, you may very well be, but checking the map in the park's brochure should help you find your way. *Fishing note:* Trout are regularly stocked in Big Flat Brook and Little Flat Brook, and they are popular fishing spots.

About ten miles from Peters Valley is a bridge over Flat Brook and a sign for Millbrook Village and Blairstown. Follow the signs to Millbrook; along the road there are several spectacular vistas of mountains framed by forest. **Millbrook Village** (908-841-9531), about two miles down this road, is a restored nineteenth-century rural community operated seasonally by the National Park Service. Selected buildings in the village are staffed Friday through Sunday, 9 AM to 5 PM, from spring through late fall; crafts are demonstrated on Saturdays and Sundays. You can walk through the village at any time of year to appreciate its architecture and historic setting. When you are ready to leave Millbrook, you can either retrace the route you took to get there and resume your drive along the stream valley, or continue past the village to the fork in the road, where signs will direct you either to Blairstown or the Delaware Water Gap.

Food

Delaware Water Gap National Recreation Area has nearly everything you might want in a day out—except, possibly, a wide choice of restaurants. With all those picnic areas, however, and if you come equipped with a well-filled picnic basket and cooler, that's not a major weakness.

The **Walpack Inn** (Route 615, Walpack Center, 908-948-9849), just south of the abandoned village of Walpack Center, remains in business. It is open for dinner from 5 PM to 10 PM on Fridays and Saturdays and from noon to 8 PM on Sundays. The combination of its beautiful, remote setting, limited hours, and good food makes it something of a local legend.

Over the River and Down the Hills

The Poconos lie just beyond the western edge of the officially designated Delaware Water Gap Recreation Area on the Pennsylvania side of the river. It's true that neither the ambience nor the skiing itself is much like New England, but it's equally true that you can reach the slopes, notably those at Shawnee and Camelback, and enjoy a few hours' skiing without a long drive. And for people like me who do not downhill ski but have children who do, the trip is well worth it. As long as you go equipped with plenty of reading material, needlework, or some other relaxing project, it's rather pleasant to have your family zipping down a snowy hill while you gaze out at the lifts from the warmth of the lodge.

Shawnee Mountain Ski Area (Exit 52 off Route 80 West, Shawnee-on-Delaware, Pennsylvania, 570-421-7231) is the closest of the Pocono ski areas. It has rentals, lessons, tubing, snowboarding, night skiing, and makes its own snow. In the summer, Shawnee is also a popular destination because right at the bottom of the mountain is Shawnee Place, with more than fifteen outdoor play activities especially for children aged two to twelve, two waterslides, and an activity pool. There is also a "river" ride featuring miniature canoes in a slowly moving flume.

Just a few miles farther west is **Camelback Ski Resort** (Exit 45, Route 80 West, Tannersville, 570-629-1661; ski conditions, 800-233-8100). It, too, has rentals, lessons, night skiing, snowboarding, tubing, and snowmaking capabilities; its vertical drop is slightly greater than Shawnee's. One very cold weekday in January 2000, I drove my teenage daughter and a friend to Camelback (they had no school), then settled myself to read at a table in the large and not yet overcrowded lodge. A number of other adults were doing the same thing, and no one seemed to mind. The girls and I had arranged to meet for lunch. After that, they went back out for a few more runs downhill and I made a quick trip to another spot that makes a trip to the Tannersville area inviting—the **Crossings Factory Stores** (Exit 45 off Route 80 West, Tannersville, Pennsylvania, 570-629-4650). Although I had not intended to do any serious shopping, I was pleasantly surprised by how large and varied the Crossings is; in fact, it has more than ninety outlets, as well as restaurants and a food court. I stopped in at the Coach outlet and a few other stores, then quickly returned to Camelback to resume my chaperone/chauffeur duties. It seemed to me that the Crossings would make a nice shopping excursion in its own right at any time of year.

Camelback does of course provide food and drink at the lodge. There's an appealing alternative just down the road, as well. The **Barley Creek Brew Pub and Restaurant** (Sullivan Trail and Camelback Road, Tannersville, 570-629-9399), housed in a renovated nineteenth-century farmhouse, serves lunch and dinner. Ales and lagers are brewed and served on-site, and in addition to its own products, Barley Creek serves "guest" brews, cocktails, and specialty drinks. The ten-barrel brewhouse features a copper-topped, brick-encased brew kettle, a grist mill, beer and lager conditioning tanks, open fermentation tanks, and more. There are free brewery tours on week-days at 12:30 PM; the bar and the Fermentation Lounge have views of the brewhouse, so even if you don't take the tour you can see what's going on.

Chapter Ten

Spanning the Centuries at Waterloo

A trip to the Village of Waterloo is a good, old-fashioned family trip in every sense of the word. In a rural setting not far off a major highway (Route 80), the village is a living example of a nineteenth-century New Jersey canal town, ideal for families whose children are just approaching the middle-elementary grades, since most New Jersey schools cover the state's history in fourth grade.* You—and they—will learn a little about the canal, about iron mining in northern New Jersey, about life in the old days in general. You will see a remnant of the Morris Canal, enjoy the sight of surviving residential and commercial structures, and, for a bit of historical variety, visit the recreation of a Lenape village.

---

*You might want to check with your child's school to make sure that your family trip won't duplicate a planned school trip; Waterloo is a popular destination for school trips and although it's well worth more than one visit, seeing it twice in one school year might be a bit too much. And don't feel that you need to have a child along to enjoy Waterloo; last time I was there, on an overcast Sunday afternoon in August, I was surprised to see a substantial minority of visitors were adults in couples or groups, who seemed to enjoy visiting as much as the family groups did.

Restored and peaceful, the **Village of Waterloo** (525 Waterloo Road, Stanhope, 973-347-0900, www.waterloovillage.org) is highly evocative of another century, but it is hardly a figment of someone's romantic imagination; not only was it really a village on the Morris Canal, it has a history older than the canal's by many decades. In the 1760s, it was the site of the Andover Iron Works. Loyal to England during the Revolution, the owners supplied England with iron ore at the beginning of the Revolutionary War. In 1778, the American Board of War confiscated the ironworks and used its production to supply the Continental Army. After the war, Andover Iron Works was sold, and the area, then known as Old Andover, was settled by a man named John Smith, who invested in land, agriculture, and the iron industry. Smith become a general in the War of 1812; his son Peter served as a state senator and banker. When the Morris Canal opened and the village became a port, Peter Smith opened a general store and sold dry goods to the boatmen. At about this time, the village was renamed Waterloo. It thrived throughout the nineteenth century but with the decline of the Morris Canal became somewhat forgotten in the twentieth.

The Morris Canal opened in 1831; its primary purpose was to provide transportation for industrial and agricultural goods, including iron ore, coal, grain, and wood; it brought anthracite coal from Pennsylvania's Lehigh Valley to New York, and by the 1840s it also carried high-grade iron ore from New Jersey to the furnaces of northern Bucks County and the Lehigh Valley. The canal extended from Phillipsburg in the west to Jersey City in the east and was a tremendous engineering feat; most of the canal is gone now. The canal was about one hundred miles long and reached a higher elevation than any other canal—from sea level at Jersey City to 914 feet at Lake Hopatcong, which was its primary water source. From Lake Hopatcong to Phillipsburg it dropped 760 feet. A complex lock system was devised to handle these major elevation changes: it included 34 ordinary lift locks and 23 inclined planes. Lift locks are standard canal features; you can see them in operation at canals throughout the world, and though they are impressive, they are not unique. It was the inclined planes that made the Morris Canal famous. They were set up like short railroads that operated on waterpower and carried boats across changes in elevation that ranged from 35 to 100 feet. The canal and the ports that had grown up along it prospered for much of the nineteenth century, but the railroads that crossed New Jersey on routes pretty much parallel to the canal put it out of business; they provided faster and cheaper transportation for both goods and people. The Morris Canal was closed in the 1920s and most of it was drained. There are only a few places where you can still see any water at all along the canal's route. Waterloo is one of those places.

Like many other nineteenth-century towns in the region, Waterloo at its peak had a grist mill, a sawmill, a forge, a tavern, and more than a dozen homes. When the railroad bypassed it in 1901, the canal trade died, and the village lost its vitality. After several decades of obscurity, Waterloo Village returned to, if not the spotlight, more widespread public awareness. Percival H. E. Leach and Louis D. Gualandi restored the village and opened it to the public in 1964; they founded the Waterloo Foundation for the Arts in 1967. Now it's a place to observe life as it was lived along the canal nearly 150 years ago.

There are more than twenty restored buildings, many but not all of which are open to the public. The village is populated with costumed guides and craftspeople working at historic crafts; not all the crafts were practiced in the village, but they are appropriate to the era. There are demonstrations in the Blacksmith Shop, Grist Mill, and Weaving Barn, among other buildings. The Canal Museum, with its exhibits about the construction of the canal and life along it, is fascinating, and will almost certainly tell you things you didn't know about New Jersey history. Because it isn't interactive or three-dimensional, it may be of less interest to children, though. Other highlights include the Homestead, where Peter Smith lived, and the Pottery Shed, once used to store wood and ice.

Winakung is a re-created Minisink Indian village whose design is based on archaeological and scholarly research; it was added to

View of Smith Store, taken from the canal side, with Waterloo Methodist Church in background.

Winter view of the Blacksmith Shop, showing remaining lock area (on right), part of the mule bridge, and inclined plane.

Photographs courtesy of the Waterloo Foundation for the Arts, Inc.

Waterloo after the initial restoration. The Minisink lived in northeastern New Jersey and were part of the Lenape "nation," which also included the Raritan, Hackensack, and other groups indigenous to New Jersey, eastern Pennsylvania, southeastern New York, and northern Delaware. The village includes huts, longhouses (not teepees, which are part of Great Plains Indian culture, not Northeast Woodland culture), and dugout canoes representing regional American Indian life in 1625.

To reach the village from the rest of Waterloo, you walk along an unpaved trail; there are bark wigwams, a garden, and a grove along the way. You then cross a bridge to the island where the village is located. There are a number of structures, including an Indian museum and gift shop, but the two most noticeable are the longhouses. A sixty-foot-long bark longhouse is furnished to resemble a trading scene. At the time reflected in the re-creation, European traders had already made contact with the Indians and begun to trade metal tools and utensils, cloth, glass beads, and other items for furs and skins. A forty-foot-long longhouse is furnished with deerskin-covered bunks and shelves holding baskets, pots, and pelts. Firewood is stored beneath the bunks, and braided ears of corn hang from the roof.

Logistics

When you purchase admission ($9 for adults, $8 for senior citizens, $7 for children) to Waterloo you get a brochure that contains a clear, simple map; sites are numbered, and brief explanations of each site help point you to what interests you most. Most people explore Waterloo on foot, but on weekends and holidays, weather permitting, you can take a twenty-minute ride ($4 for adults, $3 for senior citizens and children) on a hay wagon pulled by two Belgian horses. The tour leaves from the picnic pavilion and goes past the Wellington House and out along the Morris Canal, passing Peter Smith's General Store, the Grist Mill, and the Canal Museum.

Waterloo is certainly appealing enough to keep you busy for several hours—long enough to get hungry while you are there. In addition to picnicking along the canal there are several other options for food. The Pavilion Café is open daily for snacks, beverages, and light lunches. The Towpath Tavern, located below Smith's General Store on the banks of the canal, is open daily in summer and on weekends in spring and fall. It serves daily specials and familiar favorites such as chili; wine and beer are available. During concerts and festivals, there is a food court near the concert tent.

If you are at Waterloo on a good picnicking day, keep in mind that you can also picnic along the Musconetcong River at **Allamuchy Mountain State Park—Stephens Section** (Waterloo Road, 908-852-3790). (The Village of Waterloo is actually located in the park and leased and operated by the Waterloo Foundation for the Arts.) The Musconetcong is a popular trout-fishing stream, so if you prefer fishing to history, you may want to head straight for the riverbank.

The Village of Waterloo is a seasonal destination. It is closed from December to March, open Wednesday through Friday in April and November, and open Wednesday through Sunday in May through October.

The Other Waterloo

People who don't know Waterloo for its earlier history may know it for its special events. The popular summer festival features well-known performers and caters to a variety of tastes and ages. Musicians who played there during the summer of 2000 included Bob Dylan and his band; Willie Nelson; Lyle Lovett; Peter Frampton; and the traveling Metropolitan Opera. The Dylan concert took place on the same day as a Village-sponsored nineteenth-century embroidery demonstration and the New Jersey Storytelling Festival. The seasonal antiques shows and crafts shows at Waterloo are great, too; they are well publicized in local and regional media and can get crowded, but they're worth the trip.

New Jersey's mining industry is all but defunct now, but its mining history predates the Revolution. During the period that iron mining flourished in New Jersey, most of the iron mined in the state came from a strip of territory that runs northeast to southwest, with sprawling Rockaway Township at its heart. Rockaway mines, such as those at Hibernia and Mount Hope, supplied American troops during the Revolution and continued to produce iron until well into the twentieth century. In 1997, the Morris County Park Commission (973-326-7600; www.parks.morris.nj.us) opened **Mount Hope Historical Park** off Teabo Road in Rockaway. The park occupies what was once the Mount Hope mining tract, containing the remains of the Teabo, Allen, and Richard Mines; walkers get a chance to see one of the places where the iron shipped along the Morris Canal was mined. For example, mule-drawn trams carried ore from the Richard Mine to the Morris Canal in the 1830s; the Mount Hope Mineral Railway replaced the trams in 1867 and carried ore to the canal docks at Wharton. This once-bustling mining and processing site is now a wooded hillside with many traces of the area's iron mining history visible along several marked trails. What's left of the industry consists mostly of depressions known as subsidence pits created by the collapsed tunnels and shafts. Two main trails, the Red Trail (1.5 miles) and the Orange Trail (1.2 miles at the far end of the Red Trail), loop along the hillside, providing glimpses of the past.

As soon as you turn onto Mount Hope Road off Route 80, the road becomes narrow, winding, and hilly, strikingly different from the stretch of development across the interstate where Rockaway Townsquare Mall is located. It suddenly seems surprisingly remote from the metropolitan area, and easier to imagine as the site of thriving iron mines. Brown signs point to Mount Hope Historical Park. There is a parking lot at the entrance to the park, and a loosely graveled path leads up the hill to the point where the marked trails branch off. It's not exactly a hike, but it's not ideal for pushing strollers or wearing open shoes.

Chapter Eleven

Morristown:
History, Horses, Houses

If Morristown were in Massachusetts, it surely would be famous for its Revolutionary War connections. As soon as anyone said 1776, the Ford Mansion would come to mind almost as quickly as Boston's Old South Church. There might even be a poem about the Morristown Green, as a companion to the one about Concord's Bridge. If Morristown were in Pennsylvania, it would be famous for the suffering of the Continental army in the snowy fields just outside town. But Morristown is in New Jersey, and its fame, like the fame of most Revolutionary War sites in the state, is overshadowed by the glamour of Concord, Lexington, and Valley Forge.

To be fair to Morristown, there is a lot more to it than the Revolution—wraparound interstate and unrelenting traffic patterns notwithstanding. The late eighteenth century and **Morristown National Historical Park** (973-539-2085; www.nps.gov/morr) are as good places as any to start discovering Morristown, though.

What happened in Morristown to justify the creation of a national historic park? During the Revolutionary War, troops spent a lot of time in New Jersey; in the 1770s, they spent two winters in Morristown. Early victories at Trenton and Princeton took a toll on the Continental army, and in January of 1777 the army settled into Morristown for the winter. Morristown was sheltered from the British army by the Watchung Mountains to the east, and lookouts were posted on high ground to watch out for British troops approaching from New York, which the British controlled. The Morristown Green was an open field in those days, and the town itself was not large; farmers in the countryside around town raised a variety of fruits, vegetables, and grains, and a great deal of forest was still standing.

The 5,000 or so soldiers in Morristown were quartered in tents and in public and private buildings, including stables and barns. Some troops from Delaware lived in the Colonel Jacob Ford mansion. It was a harsh winter. Some men deserted, some left when their enlistments were up; smallpox spread, and George Washington ordered soldiers and townspeople to be inoculated against the disease. Supplies didn't always make their way past the British. The winter passed, and the Continental army forced the British, who had advanced into New Jersey, to retreat back to New York. The Continental army left Morristown, and the British were defeated at Saratoga. The Americans spent a bitter winter in what became legendary suffering at Valley Forge (in Pennsylvania, remember), and the Battle of Monmouth, which took place in June 1778, became the last major battle fought in a northern colony.

In late 1779, Morristown became a center of attention again, largely because of its strategic location behind the mountains and not too far from New York. Washington's army came south from West Point, New York and joined troops coming from the middle and southern colonies. George Washington reached Morristown in a storm on December 1. He used the Ford mansion as his headquarters, and senior officers lived in other private homes in the area. The soldiers and junior officers—ten thousand soldiers—spent the winter several miles outside town at Jockey Hollow. The winter that followed turned out to be the worst winter of the eighteenth century. The soldiers built more than one thousand huts; there were two hundred huts on the hill where five reconstructed huts now stand. There were twenty snowstorms, not enough food, and insufficient clothing. Donations of supplies helped, but morale remained low. In the spring of 1789, American forces left Morristown to turn back British and German troops. Six brigades were sent to nearby Springfield, where a battle was fought on June 23, and the British were turned back. Soon after, all American troops had left Morristown, although there were small encampments during the next two winters.

What It's Like Now

When you approach Morristown by highway, you see those familiar brown historic site signs. The Ford Mansion, Washington's winter headquarters, seems like a relatively luxurious place. It's a gracious home with nice furniture and woodwork, and it is certainly interesting, especially for elementary school children, to see some of Washington's belongings. The museum is worth a visit too; the medical tools are a dramatic reminder of how life has changed in two hundred years. The mansion and the adjacent museum are open daily from 9 AM to 5 PM; so is the visitor center at Jockey Hollow. It's only when you follow the signs out of town to Fort Nonsense and Jockey Hollow that you begin to get a sense of the separation, both social and geographic, between the fairly comfortable few and the thousands of freezing soldiers in their drafty wooden huts. Driving out of downtown Morristown along Western Avenue, you will see nineteenth-century houses, tightly packed for several blocks; gradually the neighborhood opens up. About two and a half miles outside of town the landscape turns to country, with old and beautiful houses at considerable distances from each other. Soon you are at Jockey Hollow, about three miles out of town. The elegant white Guerin House at the entrance to the park provides an introduction; Washington's soldiers occupied some of the land owned by blacksmith Joshua Guerin, and part of the house was here at that time.

There is an admission fee for the museum and other buildings, but the park at Jockey Hollow is a popular place for joggers, walkers, and bikers who use the beautiful rolling countryside as a recreation area. There are twenty-seven miles of trails and enough explanatory signs (the Old Camp Road and the First Maryland Brigade, for instance) so that you get a sense of who lived where during the winter of 1779–80, and how difficult things were. There are parking areas along the road so you can stop and explore the trails.

The road through the park is mostly one way and will lead you to the Visitor Center, where you are asked to pay the entrance fee. If you prefer to walk and hike through the park, pick up a map at the Visitor Center; both local trails and Patriots' Path offer plenty of options for exploring on foot.

The key building at Jockey Hollow, other than the Visitor Center, is the Wick House. American General Arthur St. Clair used this farmhouse as his headquarters. It is usually open from 9:30 AM to 4:30 PM. The smell of wood smoke indoors and out, the small, dark rooms—keep in mind that this was a prosperous, comfortable house for its day—and the small red barn, well house, and well-kept garden help bring history to life, especially for young visitors who know the story of Tempe Wick, who supposedly hid her horse in the house so it wouldn't be taken by the army. The tale is the basis of two popular children's books: *This Time, Tempe Wick*, by Patricia Lee Gauch, for young children, and *A Ride into Morning*, by Ann Rinaldi, for intermediate grades. If your child already knows these books, then seeing the Wick house will be an extra treat, and if the books are new to you, visiting the house will probably spark an interest in one of them. On a warm spring afternoon, the house and its surroundings look like the perfect New Jersey country cottage; on a cold, damp, day, the house is chilly. Either way, this is a good way to make history part of a family excursion.

A Present-Day Park

Lewis Morris County Park/Cultural Center (270 Mendham Road; swimming information, 973-267-4351 or 973-326-7600; information about picnic reservations, 973-326-7631) is immediately adjacent to Jockey Hollow. It opened in March 1958 as the first park in the Morris County Park System. In addition to pretty surroundings and the usual camping, picnicking, and hiking opportunities, it has an attractive playground with slides, rings, and climbing structures. In summer when lifeguards are on duty, the park allows swimming at Sunrise Lake, which has a sand beach. Boating and fishing are also allowed at Sunrise Lake. Lewis Morris Park also has five miles of equestrian trails. In addition to parking for horse trailers, the park offers stream water for the horses to drink.

Tempe Wick Road will take you to the **New Jersey Brigade Area** of Morristown National Historical Park, where about 900 soldiers camped in 1779–80. The members of the brigade were the last troops to arrive in Morristown that winter, and presumably there was not enough room at the main encampment two miles away. Follow the signs from Tempe Wick Road, along a winding, hilly road that leads across the Morris Township line into Bernardsville. Along the way are fields and woods punctuated by lovely houses, some old, some new. There is a small parking area for the path to the New Jersey Brigade Area.

After you have explored this section, follow the signs for the **Cross Estate Gardens** (973-539-2016). The gardens were a totally unexpected treat for me, and probably will be for most other visitors who enjoy privacy and quiet outdoor places. Although the gardens are part of Morristown National Historical Park, they derive from a more recent era. The Cross Mansion, a relatively modest stone-and-stucco house, was built as a country vacation residence in the early 1900s, one of a number of estates in the "Mountain Colony," which was then a wealthy resort area on the mountain in Bernardsville. The original Cross Gardens are a series of secluded areas, almost like outdoor living rooms, connected by walkways and separated by various types of old-fashioned gates. The formal brick walkways and the stone-pillared arbor are especially delightful. Volunteers from the New Jersey Historical Garden Foundation work with the National Park Service to preserve the Cross Estate Gardens; if you would like to volunteer, call 973-267-4283.

Once you leave Morristown National Historical Park you may be tempted to drive along the back roads enjoying the scenery and houses. Hardscrabble Road is especially pretty; barns with stone foundations and small old houses preserve the feeling of the past even though you are no longer in a historical park. You may feel you are in a peaceful landscape painting as you cross from Bernardsville into Mendham.

Eventually, most of the side roads lead to Route 24, and if you go east on Route 24 you will get back to Morristown. If you want to stray off Route 24, follow the sign for Brookside Historic District, a tiny community with its own post office and miniature general store. The quietly charming Brookside Community Church, a stone building with a white steeple, looks as though it was built on a slightly smaller scale than most other buildings. East Main Street, the little road that parallels Route 24 and goes through Brookside past small, sweet, and now expensive houses, is exceptionally peaceful and quaint. The road will take you back to Route 24.

More than twenty years ago, my husband and I, who had just moved to New Jersey, were enchanted by this stretch of Route 24 and its environs, and although there has been tremendous development in Morris County, these few miles are as peaceful and elegant as ever. Farther east off the main road is Washington Valley, another beautiful, secluded stretch of old houses and open fields.

After the Revolution

Several sites from other periods are also worth a visit. Although not all of them revolve around history in the formal sense, each is a historic property. If you have lots of time and energy, you can work at least one of them into a trip to Morristown National Historical Park. Depending upon your interests and proximity to Morristown, any one of them could also be a worth a trip of its own.

Photograph courtesy of Craftsman Farms

Craftsman Farms, Parsippany

Craftsman Farms

Gustav Stickley was the leader and and spokesman for the American Arts and Crafts Movement of the early twentieth century. When you walk up to the **Stickley Museum at Craftsman Farms** (just off Route 10 West at Manor Lane, Parsippany, 973-540-1165; call for hours, which vary by season), you may feel as though you've stumbled upon the original New Jersey lake cottage, with a big stone chimney, log walls, and smallish diamond-paned casement windows. With its log walls made from chestnut trees that grew on the property and great chimneys cut from local fieldstone, the house is true to the Arts and Crafts (or Craftsman) philosophy of giving function precedence over form and show, of using natural materials and building in harmony with the environment, as stated in the brochure distributed by the Craftsman Farms Foundation. Stickley intended Craftsman Farms to be a school for boys to learn farming and a trade, and the main house, set on 600 then-rural acres, was designed as a clubhouse. Stickley lived here from 1910 to 1917, commuting to Manhattan, designing homes and furniture, publishing *The Craftsman* magazine, and struggling economically. He filed for bankruptcy in 1915, and Craftsman Farms was sold in 1917 to a family who maintained it as Stickley had. In 1989 the property was threatened by townhouse development, and the Township of Parsippany-Troy Hills acquired the site through eminent domain. The gardens and farm animals that were an integral part of the experience are gone, but the house remains. It has large rooms that manage to seem cozy and dignified at the same time. The house is furnished with the massive, simple yet somehow spectacular pieces that typify Craftsman style at its best. The grounds are open year-round, and the house is open several afternoons a week, April through October. While it isn't grand, it's certainly significant, and its very familiarity is a sign of Stickley's success. Elements of this house and Stickley's vision can be found in lake communities and railroad suburbs throughout the state.

Incidentally, the museum shop at Craftsman Farms is excellent. Located in the home's original kitchen, it sells reproduction Arts and Crafts items, books about the movement, and original works by artists and craftspeople who use the Arts and Crafts movement as a basis for their own creations. Stationery, pottery, tiles, lamps, clothing, metalwork, and furniture are just some of the items you will find here.

Frelinghuysen Arboretum

Driving up the curving entrance road to **Frelinghuysen Arboretum** (53 East Hanover Avenue, Morris Township, 973-326-7600) feels a little like driving up to a very elegant country house, especially after you glimpse the spacious white Colonial Revival mansion that now serves as headquarters for the Morris County Park Commission. Although the first floor of the house is open to the public, it's the grounds that make the arboretum special. Walking trails and lawns that visitors are welcome to sit on make Frelinghuysen an especially welcoming place. Even on a weekday afternoon it is likely to be well attended, because it's a convenient lunch and relaxation spot for people who work in nearby corporate offices.

The specialized garden areas are especially appealing. These include flowering cherry trees; a rose garden near the house; the Mary Lindner Perennial Garden near the arboretum's Haggerty Education Center; and the Beth Fisher Winter Garden, which features holly trees and hawthorne brightened by colorful berries, and various winter-blooming hellebores, such as the Christmas Rose, which usually blooms in February. The Pikaart Garden at the Braille Nature Trail is another special place, with a trompe l'oeil "pond" made up of ajuga, or bugleweed, bordered by plants that would ordinarily grow at the edge of a pond. The Braille Trail, dedicated in 1973, leads through a "see, touch, and feel" garden. Braille markers identify plants, and a rope rail outlines the edge of the path.

The Frelinghuysen Arboretum is also a regional center for horticultural activities, including educational programs, and the Joseph F. Haggerty Education Center and Home Demonstration Gardens have been designed to be barrier-free environments, adding to the arboretum's accessibility.

Fosterfields

The Morris County Park Commission keeps its parklands clean and pretty. It posts maps and explanatory brochures on signboards at the entrance to the parks, makes brochures available to the public at many of the locations, and even has an informative Web site that

leads you to park information (www.parks.morris.nj.us). One especially appealing county property is **Fosterfields Living Historical
Farm,** just west of Morristown off Route 24 (73 Kahdena Road, Morris
Township, 973-326-7645). This beautiful farmstead, open from April
through October, Wednesday through Sunday, gives visitors a sense
of what life was like on a farm around the turn of the twentieth
century; in fact, its activities reflect the 1900 farm journal of one of
its former owners. It's a lovely place to explore at any time, and scheduled events add a great deal to the experience. Additionally, tours of
the Willows, the Gothic Revival home of the Foster family at
Fosterfields, provide insights into life on a prosperous farm of the
period; the Willows is open Thursday through Sunday.

In addition to the daily farm chores, such as cleaning stalls and
milking cows, performed by the staff, programs, usually involving
observation and participation, are scheduled on most weekends April
through October. They are usually planned for family enjoyment
and many are especially geared to children's involvement. Events in
2000 included spring plowing, planting potatoes, Butter Day, a
pressed-flower workshop, harvesting oats, and helping interpreters
in period costume with the tasks of washing and ironing clothes at
the Willows. Another event is the celebration of Miss Foster's twenty-
third birthday as it would have been celebrated in 1900. There is
usually a Civil War weekend in late October.

Speedwell Village

Historic Speedwell (333 Speedwell Avenue, 973-540-0211;
www.speedwell.org) is Morristown's own reconstructed village. The
Vail Homestead at Historic Speedwell is across the road from the site
of the Speedwell Iron Works, which thrived in the early nineteenth
century and became a cotton factory in the 1820s. The forge,
workmen's cottages and the workshops are now gone, although there
are a few stone walls remaining near Speedwell Lake. Near the house
is the building, now known as the Telegraph Factory, where Alfred
Vail (son of the Stephen Vail who established the ironworks) and
Samuel F. B. Morse worked on the telegraph. The Telegraph Factory

is a National Historic Landmark and has been restored to its 1838 appearance; it was at Speedwell, in 1838, that the telegraph was demonstrated to the public for the first time.

Incorporated in 1966 as a nonprofit historic restoration, Historic Speedwell, which is on the National Register of Historic Places, covers more than seven acres. It includes three farm buildings dating back at least to Stephen Vail's ownership and three late-eighteenth- and early-nineteenth-century houses that were moved to the site—the Gabriel Ford Cottage, Moses Estey House, and L'Hommedieu-Gwinnup House—to save them from demolition.

Historic Speedwell is open from May through October, Thursday through Sunday afternoons; call before you go.

Macculloch Hall

Macculloch Hall Historical Museum (45 Macculloch Avenue, Morristown, 973-538-2404; www.machall.org) is tucked away on a street that runs parallel to South Street in the Morristown Historic District. This Federal-style brick mansion was completed in 1819 for George Perrot Macculloch, who was a guiding force behind the Morris Canal, which connected coal mines in Pennsylvania with iron foundries in Morris County. The house is furnished with period pieces and has permanent exhibits focusing on American and English decorative arts of the eighteenth and nineteenth centuries, local history, and the work of Morristown's own political cartoonist, Thomas Nast, who lived across the street at 50 Macculloch Avenue. The museum is open Wednesday, Thursday, and Sunday afternoons, although group tours can be arranged for other times by appointment; the historic gardens are open daily. Macculloch Hall makes a nice footnote to a day in Morristown.

As you might expect in a place with such a rich and diverse history, Morristown has an active information center. **The Historic Morris Visitors Center** (6 Court Street, Morristown, 973-631-5151; www.morristourism.org) is worth a stop for maps and advice.

Food

For a change of pace after a day immersed in the Revolution, there are two especially appealing possibilities for dining in Morristown.

Moghul (35 Morris Street, Morristown, 973-631-1100) is a gracious, comfortably elegant Indian restaurant that is open for both lunch and dinner. Whether you and your family already love Indian food or are trying it for the first time, this is likely to be a place you want to return to. **Pamir** (55 Washington Street, Morristown, 973-605-1095) is a well-regarded Afghan restaurant open daily for dinner and weekdays for lunch.

If more familiar cuisine beckons, there's the **Office Beer Bar & Grill** (3 South Street, Morristown, 973-285-0220), one of several throughout the Morris/Union/Somerset County area, for burgers, fajitas, and other staples. Despite the official name, the Office is a family-friendly chain. The **Famished Frog** (18 Washington Street, Morristown, 973-540-9601), cousin of the Thirsty Turtle in Bernardsville, is a relative newcomer and a popular destination for burgers, sandwiches, and the like. It's open for lunch and dinner Monday through Saturday and closed on Sunday.

C'est Cheese (64 South Street, Morristown, 973-267-2941)) is a good spot for ready-made and made-to-order sandwiches, salads, and other picnic food. The **South Street Creamery** (146 South Street, Morristown, 973-267-8887) offers a tempting variety of ice cream and gelato, as well as coffees and other light refreshments. It's a great place to stop for dessert or a treat.

Chapter Twelve

Natural Beauties:
The Great Swamp and Beyond

The Great Swamp is awfully close to Morristown geographically; in fact, part of it is in Morris Township. But its past goes far beyond the colonial history that sets Morristown and its environs apart. What's more, the preservation of the Great Swamp in its present form is a result of twentieth-century efforts to keep development at bay.

The heart, though by no means the total acreage of the Great Swamp, is the **Great Swamp National Wildlife Refuge** (headquarters, Pleasant Plains Road, Basking Ridge, 973-425-1222), a place of flat wetlands, wooded hillocks, gravel trails, and raised boardwalks where my family used to go for walks on weekend afternoons or the occasional weekday holiday. I associate those excursions with side trips to Wightman's Farm Market for cider and doughnuts, and casual spins through the countryside looking for glimpses of secluded houses.

A trip to the Great Swamp can be as serious or as low-key a wildlife-watching trip as you want it to be. You can spend time in the bird blinds, waiting to spot one of the hundreds of species of birds— they're not all there at once of course, since habitats vary seasonally—listed in the refuge's bird brochure. (This brochure, and several others on subjects such as wildflowers and reptiles, amphibians, and fish, is available at the refuge headquarters.) Mammals include

the white-tailed deer, beaver, muskrat, raccoon, skunk, red and gray
fox, woodchuck, and cottontail rabbit. You certainly don't have to go
to a wildlife refuge to see deer, but it's a pleasure to see them in a
protected environment where they are neither a nuisance nor endangered.

Surprisingly, given the "swamp" in its name, the Great Swamp
has large oak and beech trees, as well as stands of mountain laurel.
The swamp is typically mid-Atlantic, like New Jersey itself, with plants
of northern and southern botanical zones to be seen. On a golden
fall day after the mosquitoes have fled or died, you can simply walk
the trails, enjoying the mix of trees and marsh grass. Looking across
the flat scenery, you may get a sense of what the land was like just
after the lake drained away; it can be very peaceful. On weekdays,
you are likely to be alone; on weekends it can be crowded.

Ten thousand years ago, the Great Swamp and much more of north-
central New Jersey was covered by water—a lake created by the
melting of the Wisconsin Ice Sheet. The lake, referred to as Lake
Passaic, eventually drained out through the gap at what is now
Little Falls in Passaic County. Many marshy areas remained; in
addition to the Great Swamp, these include Black Meadows, Great
and Little Piece Meadows, Troy Meadows, and Hatfield Swamp.
The flat area that is now the Great Swamp remained marshy and
never became thickly populated when the surrounding area was
being settled.

In the late 1950s, the Port Authority of New York and New Jersey
seriously considered building a jetport in the Great Swamp. Local
opponents of the plan formed the Great Swamp Committee and
raised enough money to buy three thousand acres; this land was
given to the Department of the Interior and dedicated as a wildlife
refuge in 1964. Since that time, thousands more acres have been
added to the refuge.

For casual visitors and dedicated wildlife observers, one key spot in the Great Swamp National Wildlife Refuge is the Wildlife Observation Center, with its gravel parking lot off Long Hill Road. There are information boards at the entrance to two trails that lead to bird-observation shelters; one shelter is two-tenths of a mile away, the other four-tenths of a mile away. Both walks are easy and pretty, though less appealing in warm, humid, buggy weather. Their length makes them ideal for family walks with small children. One highlight of a trip my family made about ten years ago was the spotting of a medium-size snake underneath the boards of a loose section of boardwalk. My son loved it, from the safe distance of an intact section of boardwalk. We also have enjoyed seeing turtles resting, very still, in the water off to the side of one of the boardwalks.

Bike Rides

The roads that wind through the wildlife refuge not only make for lovely car rides, they are also very good for biking because the immediate area is level. The roads are narrow, however, and visibility is sometimes limited, so they are not ideal for biking with small children.

Not too many miles east of the Great Swamp, however, there are two Morris County bicycle trails that are deservedly popular and, when they aren't too crowded, fine for children accompanied by adults. The bike path at **Loantaka Brook Reservation** (Kitchell Road and South Street, Morris, Chatham, and Harding Townships) has two sections that run through woods and occasional open areas. The main parking area for the bike path is on Loantaka Way, off Shunpike right on the border between Morris and Chatham Townships. The drawback to this path is its popularity with everyone from children on training wheels to people riding their bikes as fast as possible to people walking dogs on long leashes to people walking slowly. It isn't a wide path, and for everyone to enjoy it safely requires a certain amount of courtesy and common sense, which is usually to be found, but occasionally not. (Loantaka Brook Reservation also has three miles of equestrian trails. There is parking for horse trailers but no water. Like the bike trail, the bridle trail terrain is flat.)

The **Traction Line Recreation Trail**, most easily entered from the parking lot at the Convent Station railroad station near the gates of the College of St. Elizabeth, is a popular multipurpose trail with about three miles of bikeway. It is ideal for jogging and, snow permitting, cross-country skiing, as well as biking, and it has a nine-station parcourse fitness circuit. The trail, along the route of the abandoned trolley line of the Morris County Traction Company, parallels New Jersey Transit tracks between Morristown and Madison. Much of the property for this trail was donated by the Jersey City Power and Light Company, now GPU Energy. This trail isn't as winding and pretty as the one at Loantaka, but it does provide a pleasant and easy bike ride away from motorized vehicles.

The Great Swamp is well served by several education centers on county lands adjacent or very close to the national wildlife refuge. The Morris County Park Commission maintains about forty acres on the east edge of the Great Swamp. There are several loop trails, and a short trail leading from the parking lot to an observation blind; there is also an observation deck just off the boardwalk section of one of the loop trails. Morris County's **Great Swamp Outdoor Education Center** (247 Southern Boulevard, Chatham, 973-635-6629) is open seven days a week, although it is closed on holidays. The building has classrooms, an auditorium, a reference library, and an exhibit hall. Special programs and nature walks are scheduled on weekends.

Another beautiful setting, this one at the western edge of the Great Swamp, is **Lord Stirling Park** (Lord Stirling Road, one mile off South Maple Avenue, Basking Ridge, 908-766-2489). The park and its Environmental Education Center are operated by the Somerset County Park Commission Department of Environmental Services.

Lord Stirling Park has miles of dirt paths, mown grass paths, and boardwalks. Even a short walk that never strays far from Branta Pond, just out of sight of the education center, gives you a chance to feel pleasantly lost in a lush, level, civilized wilderness. The trail map, available at the education center, is very clear, and the trails are blazed with bright-colored plastic markers. The plank bridges that punctuate the paths are named for aphids, back swimmers, and other creatures of the swamp. The trails, although level, can be fairly rough-textured, so they don't lend themselves to baby carriages. There is, however, a special-use boardwalk near the education center. Built in 1981 by the Telephone Pioneers, it offers wheelchair users, carriage and stroller riders, and walkers unsure of their footing a good opportunity to enjoy the beauty of the Great Swamp. The trails are open from dawn to dusk, weather conditions permitting, and the Education Center, which has restrooms and a book shop/gift shop, as well as exhibits, is open from 9 AM to 5 PM daily, except holidays.

An added attraction at Lord Stirling Park is **Lord Stirling Stable** (256 South Maple Avenue, Basking Ridge, 908-766-5955; TDD 908-766-4620 for individuals with hearing impairments). At Lord Stirling Stable, the Somerset County Park Commission conducts a full program of equestrian instruction in English horsemanship for youth and adults from beginner through jumper. There are ten miles of trails on 450 acres of woods and fields, as well as one indoor ring, two outdoor rings, and an outdoor jumping course. Boots and hard hats are required and may be rented at the stables. All riders must be at least nine years old and weigh not more than 240 pounds. For an annual fee, people who have their own horses may enjoy the trails or outdoor rings.

About a mile from Lord Stirling Park is the **Raptor Trust** (1390 White Bridge Road, Millington, 908-647-2353). This rehabilitation center for wounded wild birds is run by a nonprofit organization. The birds are brought in by people who have found and rescued them. The Raptor Trust, located on sixteen acres bordering the Great Swamp, is one of the foremost privately funded facilities of its kind in the United States. It has a fully equipped infirmary, as well as aviaries and flight chambers containing approximately 130,000 cubic feet of space. The Trust has returned more than twenty-five thousand birds to the wild since 1982; birds that have not recovered sufficiently to be released live at the Trust permanently. Although recuperating birds are not available for viewing, resident, nonreleased raptors, such as hawks, eagles, owls, and vultures, can be viewed. The resident raptors are also available for breeding and for behavioral studies. The Raptor Trust also presents slide programs about raptors and the organization itself. The programs are presented to school and other groups throughout New Jersey; there is also an on-site education building. The Raptor Trust is open seven days a week during daylight hours.

If spending time at the Great Swamp has made you want to find even more outdoor destinations in the area, you are in luck, because there is an abundance of them. One of the most peaceful and beautiful is the **Scherman-Hoffman Wildlife Sanctuaries** (Hardscrabble Road, Basking Ridge, 908-766-5787). The sanctuaries, operated by the New Jersey Audubon Society, are very close to Morristown National Historic Park geographically, and very close to the Great Swamp in ambience. They cover more than two hundred acres of lovely countryside. You can get a trail guide at the Hoffman House, which also has a gift shop/book shop. There is a short self-guided nature trail, and other trails, some of which connect to Patriots' Path.

Leonard J. Buck Gardens (Layton Road, Far Hills, 908-234-2677) is a bit farther afield. This thirty-three-acre garden is in a quiet setting of woods, streams, and unusual rock outcroppings. Its deep gorge was once the outlet of Lake Passaic. The land was donated to the Somerset County Park Commission in 1974 and opened to the public in 1984. The garden's visitor center was once the carriage house of the Buck estate, and you can get a map and other information there. The garden is especially colorful in the spring, when its azaleas, rhododendrons, and dogwoods are in bloom.

Food

A day trip in and around the Great Swamp can send you to a number of different communities, and the eating options are wide-ranging, too. At the Chatham/Madison end of the trip, there is **Bean Curd** (275 Main Street, Chatham, 973-635-5333). This long-established Chinese restaurant is open daily for lunch, dinner, and takeout. You can expect friendly service, cheerful surroundings ideal for a family meal, and good food.

At the other side of the Great Swamp, you might consider **The Store** (555 Finley Avenue, Basking Ridge, 908-766-9853). As its name suggests, it serves American food in an old-fashioned country store setting and is a relaxed spot for lunch and dinner. For American food in a gracious setting right near the Scherman-Hoffman sanctuaries, there's the **Grain House** at the Olde Mill Inn (225 Route 202, Bernardsville, 908-221-1150). It has a children's menu and is open Monday through Saturday for lunch and dinner, and on Sunday for brunch. Down Route 202 a mile or two is the main branch of **Monterey Gourmet** (167 Morristown Road/Route 202, Bernardsville, 908-766-2000), an excellent source for sandwiches on chewy long rolls and other above-average take-out foods.

Although you can't eat a meal at **Wightman's Farm Market** (Mt. Kemble Avenue/Route 202, Morristown, 973-425-9819), you can certainly buy very good food and beverages there, including apple cider, sold year-round, and an interesting variation—cherry-apple cider. Depending upon the season, you will find local strawberries, fresh corn, figs, many varieties of apples, and a selection of other produce. Wightman's also sells freshly made doughnuts and good pies, as well as preserves, some frozen foods, and various other food items. Outside the building you can select pumpkins in the fall and flourishing plants in spring and summer. In the autumn Wightman's also offers hayrides and the chance to pick-your-own pumpkins. Although it can be crowded on those perfect fall days when the sun is shining and the air is cool enough to make you think of jack-o'-lanterns, it's always a pleasure to go there.

If you are in the heart of the Great Swamp at the wildlife observation area, you aren't too far from **Hillview Farms** (223 Meyersville Road,

Meyersville, 908-647-0957). You can pick raspberries, apples, pumpkins, and other produce here, depending upon season, and Hillview Farms also sells fruits and vegetables, cider, pies, and jams and jellies. There was a great deal of residential development on Meyersville Road east of the farm in the late 1990s, but at this writing, the farm was still there and still a popular destination for families and school trips.

Chapter Thirteen

Chester: More Than Shopping

One beautiful September afternoon several years ago, I picked my daughter up at school and headed for the Alstede pick-your-own farm a few miles out of Chester to gather fall raspberries. The berries were just the right shade of soft, dark red; the buzzing insects never got too close, and the hillside and the view were, as always, beautiful. It was one of the nicest afternoons imaginable. The hour or so that we spent picking berries in the golden sunshine, balanced right on the border between late summer and the new school year, is still one of our favorite shared experiences. And we came home with enough berries to top the breakfast cereal for several days, bake a pie, and crush the leftover berries for syrup.

We've enjoyed many other items purchased at the Alstede farmstand across the road from the pick-your-own fields: peaches, corn, and tomatoes head the list. An additional attraction at Alstede is the collection of farm animals housed behind the parking lot. The pigs are particularly popular with my family. The **pick-your-own Alstede Farm** is on Pleasant Hill Road, which runs out of town from Hillside Avenue; there is also an **Alstede farmstand** and garden shop on Route 24, just west of town (www.alstedefarms.com; 908-879-7189).

When I think of a trip to Chester, it is as much for the hillside at Alstede Farms as for the myriad shops along Main Street. Fortunately, since the distances once you get to Chester are quite short, there's likely to be time to do a bit of everything in the course of a day trip to this bustling town.

Chester is an old town; it was settled by Europeans well before the Revolutionary War, and before that, the Lenni-Lenape traveled along the Black River. The European settlers established farms, mills, and blacksmith and cabinet shops. By 1740, the place where two of the main Lenni-Lenape trails crossed was known as Black River, and by 1771 a weekly stage wagon route connected Jersey City to the crossroads community. In the early 1800s, the Washington Turnpike (now Route 24) was chartered to run through what had become known as Chester. Chester became an overnight stop for travelers on the Turnpike. The Brick Hotel on Main Street was the main lodging. By the 1830s, roads were better and fewer travelers had to stay overnight; to make matters worse, from the Chester hotel business point of view, the Morris Canal was handling much of the freight that had once traveled by road.

In the mid-nineteenth century, iron mining resulted in a new wave of prosperity. Morris County was one of the nation's leading producers of iron ore by 1880. The iron ore only lasted a couple of decades, however, and by about 1900 Chester's prosperity and activity had subsided. The buildings that characterized the thriving nineteenth century give the town much of its present charm, although they now house very different businesses. For example, 71 Main Street was once the home of James Topping, a master cabinetmaker. He lived in the house early in the nineteenth century, then bought the farm that became Larison's. In the early twentieth century, the building housed a store that sold newspapers, candy, and hot roasted peanuts.

By the 1950s, the area around Chester was becoming increasingly suburban; the main crossroads of Route 24 and Route 206 were by then a little west of the main commercial activity on Main Street, and Larison's Turkey Farm Inn was advertising widely, bringing people from outside the immediate area to its restaurant in one of Chester's older buildings. The Brick Hotel, then known as the Chester House, was attracting Sunday diners from the city. In 1969, the Chester Lions Club opened a flea market in town; in the early 1970s the first tourist-oriented shops opened. Most of the old wood buildings that line Chester's Main Street were once workers' housing and factories.

In the past two or three decades, Chester has come to epitomize the weekend excursion town; now it is bustling even on weekdays. It is in many ways both trite and charming. Some might say that Chester has been almost too successful in its turnaround. In addition to the shops that front on Main Street, there is newer, mini-mall–style construction behind the older buildings, convenient for strolling and browsing but less distinctive in architecture and ambience. Crafts, gifts, and home accessories seem to make up the bulk of the offerings. There are still a few antique shops, though; if you are in the mood for antiquing rather than general recreational shopping, you might prefer to go to Chester during the week, although of course weekends are the best time to find all the shops open.

Chester is full of appealing gift, accessory, home décor, and antique shops. **The Whistling Elk** (44 Main Street, 908-879-2425; www.thewhistlingelk.com), **Chester Timepiece** (58 Main Street, 908-879-5421), and **The Quest** (50 Main Street, 908-879-8144) are among the ones I enjoyed last time I visited Chester, but just about every store in town is worth at least a peek.

One long-time favorite is the **Chester Carousel** (125 Main Street, 908-879-7141), which carries an appealing mix of country antique furniture and new decorative accessories, such as lamps, place mats, and wooden fruit. The old wood items at the Chester Carousel are always in good condition, carefully maintained (or perhaps refinished) in a style that's compatible with the newer merchandise. The shop is in a restored late-nineteenth-century store, which gives a trip there a little added historical flavor, and it is right across Hillside Avenue from the Publick House.

One of the most unusual stores in town is **World of Birds** (15 Perry Street, 908-879-2291; www.worldofbirds.com). It is a colorful and musical specialty bird store; when you walk in, you will probably be greeted by a flying bird. As well as all sorts of birds, the shop also sells cages, seeds, and other things that birds like or need, but the birds themselves are fascinating even if you don't think you are in the market for a new pet.

Before you leave town, take a look at the Chester behind Chester. The street that parallels Route 24 is narrow, with old houses that look like original miners' homes and give a clearer sense of Chester's past.

The Parks

Even if the thought of picking berries on a sun-warmed hillside doesn't make you smile in anticipation or happy memory, and you have no interest in shopping, Chester may still be worth a visit, because it is the site of two terrific parks.

Cooper Mill County Park (66 Route 24, 908-879-5463) is just west of town. The parking lot has a picnic table and rest rooms and is connected by a short path to historic Cooper Mill. The beautiful stone mill was built on the Black River in the 1820s to grind wheat, corn, and other grains for the inhabitants of the Chester area. The Morris County Park Commission bought the mill in 1963 after it had been vacant for some time, and it was opened to the public in 1978. You can see the six-and-a-half-ton water wheel in action when the mill is open; while supplies last, you may also get a free bag of corn meal or whole-wheat flour after you tour the mill. The mill is open for tours weekends May through October, Friday through Tuesday in July and August. On many weekends, there are family-oriented programs focusing on the social, agricultural, and technical history of the neighborhood once known as Milltown that surrounded the mill. A yearly calendar of special events at Cooper Mill, Fosterfields, and Mount Hope Historical Park is available at the mill and from the Park Commission (973-326-7645; www.parks.morris.nj.us). During daylight hours when the mill building is closed, the grounds are open, and the walkway that leads behind the mill gives you a good look at the millwheel at rest.

If you'd like a longer walk than the trip from the parking lot will provide, you will be pleased to know that Morris County's linear **Patriots' Path**, a network of multipurpose trails, crosses underneath Route 24 through a giant culvert right at the mill's front door. It continues from behind the mill to the Kay Environmental Center about a mile away. If fishing rather than walking appeals to you, you probably already know that the Black River is a popular fishing river in season; note that the section at Cooper Mill is closed to fishing on Thursdays.

Just west of Cooper Mill on Route 24/513 is the turn for the road that leads to **Hacklebarney State Park** (119 Hacklebarney Road, Long Valley, 908-879-5677). It takes a while before you get to the park, but trust the signs; you will get there after you have driven for about two miles through some lovely New Jersey countryside. Just before the entrance to the park you will pass Hacklebarney Cider Mill, a popular stop in the autumn to watch cider being made, and to buy apples, cider, and pies. There is a lovely nineteenth-century white house with green shutters adjacent to the mill, and across the road there is a lovely old brick house, whose sign identifies it as Stone Meadow, 1775.

There is a stone courtyard at the entrance to the park, with a monument explaining that woodlands were donated to the state in 1924 by Adolphe Edward Borie in memory of his mother, Susan Parker Borie (1835–1913), and her granddaughter, Susan Ryerson Patterson (1892–1921), "to be preserved for the benefit of youth." The park is beautiful, and the donation would seem to have benefited everyone, young or old, who takes the opportunity to visit the park.

The park itself is a walking/hiking destination with about five miles of trails, several picnic areas (with charcoal grills), and nice rest rooms near the parking area. At the parking lot, there's a signboard and trail map to point you to attractions such as Rock Grove and two Black River tributaries, Trout Brook and Rinehart Brook. It is definitely worth the time to take the trail all the way to the boulder-strewn gorge of the Black River. The river doesn't always have a lot of water in it, and it sometimes looks like a brook rather than a source of water power for Cooper Mill, but it is beautiful at all times of year. It is the kind of river that dogs love to splash in and children love to skip stones on; remember that all pets must be leashed in state parks, and the rangers do enforce this rule, very politely, at Hacklebarney.

Food

As Chester has become an increasingly popular shopping destination, it has also become a place to eat. **Sally Lunn's Tea Rooms and Restaurant** (15 Perry Street, 908-879-7731) is perhaps the most ladylike of its dining establishments, with lace tablecloths gracefully draped over flowered tablecloths. One recent indication of Chester's tremendous popularity was the line of people waiting to get in early on a Wednesday afternoon in midspring. Sally Lunn's serves homemade baked goods, soups, and similar items. It opens in mid-morning and closes at 5:30 or 6 PM, depending on day of the week, so plan on it for lunch or tea or snack rather than dinner. It also sells antiques, and china, tea, and other food items.

The **Publick House** (111 Main Street, 908-879-6878) used to be the Brick Hotel, and it still provides overnight accommodations. Year-round in its dining room or May through October on its great street-view veranda, you can enjoy lunch, dinner, or Sunday brunch.

For light refreshment, **K.C.'s Coffee Place** (56 Main Street, 908-879-9932) is a gourmet coffee bar as well as gift shop. **Roma Italian Deli** (30 Main Street, 908-879-6606) is another place to go for cappuccino, espresso, and pastries. As its name suggests, it specializes in Italian delicacies and also sells subs and cold cuts. Chester also has a **Dairy Queen** (30 Main Street, 908-879-5546), a pizza parlor, a sub shop, and several other restaurants. It is not a town where you are likely to go hungry.

If you prefer to picnic in one of the parks, you might want to stop at the Chester branch of Bernardsville's **Monterey Gourmet** (350 Route 24 East, 908-879-0300), just east of downtown. It offers an appealing variety of sandwiches (the grilled vegetable and mozzarella sandwich is one favorite), salads, and prepared foods. It also sells wine, but remember that alcoholic beverages are not permitted in state and county parks.

Chapter Fourteen

Princeton Proper and Beyond: Perfection and Variety

Princeton and privilege have more in common than their first three letters. From the architectural dazzle of the Princeton University campus to the tree-lined streets of big houses—call them mansions, it's fair in many cases—the town and the university look like seats of power, whether it's based on wealth, luck, SAT scores, or some other combination of factors. You don't have to be a high school senior to be impressed by the place. Princeton is the site of a world-famous university; it's a supremely desirable business and residential address, a town with an abundance of old and attractive buildings and thriving, varied businesses geared to both students and affluent adults. There is even a Revolutionary War battlefield, not to mention easy access to a scenic state park and lovely countryside nearby. A trip to Princeton will work for almost any age group and set of interests.

The University

Who can say whether Princeton would be glamorous without the university? It has lots of natural advantages and a historic location. However, the university, the sixth-oldest college in the United

States, shares much of the town's history and helps makes it special. Founded in Elizabeth in 1746 as the College of New Jersey, the school moved to Newark in 1747 and to Princeton in 1756, the year Nassau Hall was completed. The school's second president, Aaron Burr Sr., was the father of the Aaron Burr who became Thomas Jefferson's vice president and killed Alexander Hamilton in a duel. In 1776, the university's president, John Witherspoon, signed the Declaration of Independence, and for several months in 1783, Nassau Hall was the meeting place of the Continental Congress.

Now, Princeton University covers more than 600 acres and includes more than 100 buildings. It's a monumental institution, with architectural and historic as well as educational significance. You can walk around by yourself or join an organized tour, which you will probably share with eager prospective students and their parents. The University's Orange Key guide service organization (609-258-3603) leads several tours daily, including two on Sunday. Perhaps the most memorable building on the tour is Nassau Hall. It originally housed the whole college, and now is the site of administrative offices. There is still the mark of a cannonball on the west wing of the building from the 1776 bombardment by the British. Most of the original 1756 building was destroyed by fire in 1802, and the replacement was rebuilt based on a design by Benjamin Latrobe, one of the leading architects of the era. In 1855, a second fire led to other exterior changes. The entrance hall is especially moving. Known as the Memorial Atrium, it was designed in 1920 as a memorial to Princeton University's war dead from the Revolution and later wars. The names and class years of each are listed. Of the seventy Princetonians who died in the Civil War, half fought for the North and half for the South. On Cannon Green, behind Nassau Hall, is a cannon that was used in both the Revolution and the War of 1812. A smaller cannon that stands between two striking Greek temple–style buildings known as Whig Hall and Clio Hall, was also used in the Revolution. As you walk around the campus you will see the chapel, the Firestone Library, imposing stone, brownstone, and brick buildings, modern sculptures, and, at most times of year, lots of people.

Walter Choroszewski

Princeton University

The Battlefield

On a sunny June afternoon, **Princeton Battlefield State Park** (Mercer Street, a little more than a mile west of downtown Princeton, 609-921-0074) looks like a very pretty, peaceful stretch of parkland.

It isn't a park with heavy-duty outdoor recreational facilities, nor is it battle-scarred. In late spring, the lawns are green, with people stretched out on the grass reading, talking, and relaxing. There are paths for walking, and in winter, it is a pleasant site for cross-country skiing if there is enough snow. On a hillside across the road from the main park entrance, there is an elegant colonnade masquerading as a classical ruin, like something you might see in an English garden, or at the battlefield at Gettysburg. The Battle of Princeton is one of those pivotal New Jersey Revolutionary War battles that seem to be much better known among New Jersey elementary school children than among the general American population.

Because this was a cold-weather battle, a midwinter visit gives a better sense of what it was like when the encounter took place on January 3, 1777, a few days after Washington's famous crossing of the Delaware to Trenton. American troops made their way from Trenton to Princeton along icy roads to surprise the British early on January 3. In what was then the orchard of a Quaker farmer, Thomas Clarke, 350 American soldiers, led by General Hugh Mercer, fought and defeated two British regiments. Mercer was mortally wounded and supposedly took shelter under an oak tree. The last remnants of that tree, which became a historic icon known as the Mercer oak, were felled by winds in March 2000; the Mercer oak has since been replaced by a young oak tree grown from one of its acorns.

The Clarke House, where General Mercer was brought after the battle, and where he died several days later, serves as a museum. It is open a few hours a day Wednesday through Sunday; in addition to rooms furnished in the style of the late eighteenth century, there is a display of Revolutionary War maps and weapons. Battle Monument, showing George Washington leading his troops and General Mercer dying, was dedicated in 1922 to commemorate the battle. The colonnade across the road is, in fact, a relic of a house that was demolished in the twentieth century; it is there for decoration. It lends an elegant Princetonian touch to the park.

The Town

One of the intriguing things about Princeton is the way several worlds meet across Nassau Street. On one side is the university; on the other side, both on Nassau Street itself and along the side streets around Palmer Square, is a bustling town with dozens of stores. These range from the usual upscale mall chains such as Ann Taylor and Talbots, to specialty shops such as Simon Pearce Glass and the Graves Design Studio Store.

There are also one-of-a-kind-Princeton classics that combine the expected with the unexpected. **Landau's** (102 Nassau Street, 609-924-4394) is a quintessentially Princeton clothing shop. It is also, according to Robert Landau, one of the store's owners, the site of the only museum in the world dedicated to Albert Einstein, whose name and brilliance are forever linked with Princeton (and its Institute of Advanced Study, where he worked); although he lived there from 1933 to 1955, nothing anywhere else in town commemorates his nearly quarter-century of Princeton life.

Landau's opened in Princeton 1955, the year that Einstein died. Over the years, the store became something of a fixture on Nassau Street, and people often came in search of directions, often asking how to get to the Einstein Memorial; there was no answer to that one. In 1995, when the movie *I.Q.*, with Meg Ryan, Tim Robbins, and Walter Matthau (as Einstein) was being shot in Princeton, it occurred to Robert Landau that the moment had come to do something about the absence of an Einstein site, and to be associated with the movie. First, people were asked to bring to the store clothing they had worn when Einstein was in Princeton, to be used in a window display. But people often give away their old clothes rather than storing them, and only two people brought items in. Next, Landau's asked for memorabilia, which turned out to be a much more abundant resource. Among the items lent and displayed were a crystal-and-silver desk set, valued at $15,000, purchased at the house sale that followed Einstein's death and assumed to be the one Einstein used; photographs of townspeople with Einstein in many everyday contexts (one resident brought in a photograph of her son with Einstein at a Princeton University Hillel meeting); even recently manufactured Einstein popcorn—"Eat it and it makes you brilliant." The display was a great success, attracting not only passersby but also tour buses and school groups. Landau's became so closely associated with Einstein in the public mind that one day Walter Matthau, who played Einstein in *I.Q.*, came in to ask where the day's shooting was, because he had lost his schedule and assumed Landau's would have the information.

The display was taken down later in 1995; the Princeton Historical Society used it as a basis for a hugely popular but temporary Einstein exhibition. There was clearly a great deal of interest in Einstein, and Princeton Borough resident and Temple University scientist Mel Benard asked for Landau's support in raising money for an Einstein "something." In four weeks, a couple of thousand dollars had been collected at the store. An offer to the Borough Council to fund a statue to Einstein was not accepted. Also during this time, Gillett Griffin of the Princeton University Art Museum, who had been a friend of Albert Einstein's daughter, Margot, noted that there should be a place where he could "show [his] stuff": things he had acquired after Einstein died, including Einstein's compass, a statue Margot Einstein had made for her father, family photographs, about 100 love letters (which Griffin gave to the University), handwritten work sheets, handheld games that Einstein liked to play with, even the paddles and cushions from Einstein's boat. Griffin had lent some of the items to Landau's for its first window display, and afterward most went back into storage.

At that point, Robert Landau decided to prepare another exhibit, which will remain in place at least until a more formal museum is established. With display cases lent by the university and with curatorial assistance from the Arts Council of Princeton, photographs from the Institute of Advanced Study, and other support from members of the community, Landau's now has the

Einstein Museum in a corner all its own. Opened in June 1999, the exhibit includes mainly photographs, the handheld games, the compass, and newspaper clippings.

Robert Landau and the many people who have contributed to the exhibit are eager to commemorate not just Einstein's brilliance but also his human qualities, both philanthropic and playful. There is a sign in the store window, and the "museum" is noted on a map of Princeton that is available at Palmer Square. It attracts both casual visitors and tour buses on a side trip from New York City. Some people come in just for the museum; others come in both to visit the museum and to shop. Landau's welcomes all.

Princeton is full of places in which to browse and buy and eat, and it has street after street of large, old, and often historically significant houses. It isn't overwhelmingly urban, though, and it makes for a pleasant shopping and strolling excursion of any length. There are plenty of things to see that are not officially part of the university, such as **Princeton Cemetery** (609-924-1639) on Wiggins Street, which contains the graves of Grover Cleveland, both Aaron Burr Sr. and Aaron Burr Jr., John Witherspoon, Jonathan Edwards, and other notables. Princeton has also been home to many luminaries. Their homes are not open to the public, but walking past them or stopping briefly in front of them is an unobtrusive way to get a sense of the lives and times of a diverse group of high achievers. Paul Robeson spent his early childhood in Princeton at 110 Witherspoon Street at the corner of Green Street. Albert Einstein lived at 112 Mercer Street from 1933 until his death in 1955. At his request, his house on Mercer Street did not become a public site but remained a private home. Woodrow Wilson, who served as president of Princeton University and governor of New Jersey before he became president of the United States, had several residences in town over the years—two houses on Library Place, 25 Cleveland Lane, and then when he became university president, on campus at Prospect House, which now serves as a faculty club. Grover Cleveland, who was born in West Caldwell, lived at 15 Hodge Road from 1896 until his death in 1908. Even if you aren't quite sure who lived where as you walk along Library Place and Hodge Road, you will be impressed by the houses, which are generally big and beautiful. Along Alexander Street there are somewhat more modest houses that also make a major impression; the white frame Greek Revival houses date from the 1830s and 1840s and have an air of elegant simplicity

---

The Historical Society of Princeton headquarters at the **Bainbridge House** (158 Nassau Street, 609-921-6748) is generally open Tuesday through Sunday afternoons and is a good place to turn for detailed historic-site information. The Society, founded in 1938, has a collection of more than 40,000 artifacts and manuscripts. In addition to exhibits and lectures, it sponsors weekly walking tours of historic Princeton on Sunday afternoons at 2.

Bainbridge House was built in 1766 by Job Stockton, a cousin of Richard Stockton, who was one of New Jersey's signers of the Declaration of Independence. It is one of the oldest buildings in Princeton; members of the Continental Congress stayed there during the Congress's 1783 sojourn in Princeton. Later it was a student boarding house, and still later it housed the public library. The Society restored the exterior in 1969 to its original eighteenth-century appearance, and in the early 1990s the interior was renovated. Most of the original structure is still there, however.

South of town going toward Lawrenceville on Route 206, known as Stockton Street, are two historic homes that are open to the public. They are driving rather than walking distance from Nassau Street. **Morven** (55 Stockton Street, 609-683-4495), which served as the governor's residence from 1953 to 1981, was built for Richard Stockton and later became the home of Robert Wood Johnson, founder of Johnson & Johnson. During most of the year, tours are available on Wednesdays from 11 AM to 2 PM. **Drumthwacket** (354 Stockton

Street, 609-683-0057) is now the official governor's residence. It was built in 1835 by Charles Olden, who served as governor during the Civil War, and was restored and furnished by the New Jersey Historical Society. Tours are offered on Wednesdays from noon to 2 PM, except in August.

Not everything about Princeton is serious, historic, or academic. The lifelike sculptures of Seward Johnson add a whimsical touch to several spots. Probably the most visible are the men who are always reading—the newspaper reader in front of Borough Hall, the book reader in Palmer Square. Sculpted year-round fishermen are a nice surprise at **Community Park North**, off Route 206 just north of town. This seventy-acre park has six picnic sites, an exercise course, walking trails, and an amphitheater for concerts and dramatic productions. Adjacent to it and sharing a parking lot is the ninety-acre **Mountain Lakes Nature Preserve** (Mountain Avenue). Four streams, three lakes made by damming brooks, wetlands, and trails turn this area into a restful retreat from the more built-up parts of Princeton. **Delaware and Raritan Canal State Park** (732-873-3050), an idyllic place to walk, bike, picnic, canoe, or just birdwatch, is accessible from Princeton's Basin Park on Alexander Street, as well as from Washington Road and Harrison Street. (For more about Delaware and Raritan Canal State Park see chapter 18 of this book, as well as the Millstone section of this chapter.)

For children too young to understand that they are supposed to be dazzled by Princeton—actually, for anyone in the mood for a terrific farm market or pick-your-own excursion—**Terhune Orchards** (330 Cold Soil Road, 609-924-2310; www.terhuneorchards.com) may be the high point of a Princeton trip. You can pick apples, pumpkins, and raspberries, buy a variety of produce as well as pies, muffins, and other baked goods, and say hello to farm animals. It is open daily, so even if your visit doesn't coincide with a picking season, there will be something to buy and see. If picking is your primary goal, however, be sure to call before you go to make sure the produce you want is being picked when you plan to be there.

To get to Terhune's if you are heading south from Princeton on Route 206, turn right on Carter Road, then left onto Van Kirk Road for the part of the farm with pick-your-own apples and raspberries. For the main farm, take Carter Road to the first traffic light and turn left onto Cold Soil Road.

Food

Any place that is full of college students is also going to be full of places to eat, and since Princeton is also home to many affluent adults, the options for food are even better. The ideal way to choose is to walk around until you see a menu or window-view that appeals to you. Several establishments have become favorites over the years, including **P.J.'s Pancakes** (154 Nassau Street, 609-924-1353). Back in its role as a Nassau Street classic after being closed by a fire several years ago, P.J.'s is open daily from early in the morning until late at night (or very early the next morning) for standbys such as pancakes, eggs, and burgers. The **Alchemist and Barrister** (28 Witherspoon Street, 609-924-1555) is a reliable, rather upscale source for hamburgers as well as more ambitious food. It is open Monday through Saturday for lunch and dinner and Sunday for brunch and has both a wine list and a children's menu. If you happen to be celebrating a special occasion, you may want to consider a pilgrimage to **Lahiere's** (11 Witherspoon Street, 609-921-2798), an icon of Princeton dining that has been around since 1919. It is open Monday through Friday for lunch, Monday through Saturday for dinner. **The Ferry House** (32 Witherspoon Street, 609-924-2488) has been in Princeton only since 1998, but it had established a following when it was in Lambertville. Like Lahiere's, the Ferry House is open Monday through Friday for lunch, Monday through Saturday for dinner, and it is primarily a place for adults to enjoy their food and their surroundings.

There are also many possibilities for quick and/or familiar refreshment. Two branches of **Chesapeake Bagel** (179 Nassau Street,

609-497-3275; 301 North Harrison Street, 609-921-8646) help meet the ongoing demand for bagels. Long-established **Conte's Pizza** (339 Witherspoon Street, 609-921-8041) is open Monday through Saturday from late afternoon through 11:30 PM. If a picnic appeals to you, **Chez Alice** (54 Nassau Street, 609-921-6707) offers takeout food. Among Princeton's many coffee places is **Bucks County Coffee Company** (Palmer Square, 44 Nassau Street, 609-497-6877), which is open daily and also sells sandwiches. For ice cream and homemade chocolates, you can join forces with other seekers of treats at **Thomas Sweet** (33 Palmer Square West, chocolate, 609-924-7222; ice cream, 609-683-1655; 179 Nassau Street, ice cream, 609-683-8720).

Somerville: Sidewalks and More

Somerville, thirteen miles north of Princeton on Route 206, is likely to surprise you the first time you visit. Its name appears so often on road signs, from Routes 202 to 287 to 22, yet none of those roads will quite take you there. But once you turn down Route 28—which at various stages is called West End Avenue, West Main Street, then East Main Street—toward downtown, you will soon find yourself in an established downtown, a place with brick sidewalks and varied storefronts punctuating well-maintained nineteenth-century buildings. You may get the feeling that 1965 wasn't so long ago after all; here is a living business district where you can buy useful items as well as appealing extras, and some parking meters still welcome nickels. Somerville is within sight and walking distance of Bridgewater Commons; in the past several years, probably not coincidentally, some but not all of Somerville's everyday business have given way to antique shops and centers, including **Somerville Center Antiques** (34 West Main Street and 9-17 Division Street, 908-595-1294) and **County Seat Antiques** (41 West Main Street at the corner of Division Street, 908-595-9556). They make for a fun afternoon of browsing. **Candyland Crafts** (201 West Main Street, 908-685-0410) is perhaps the most unusual store in town. Its shelves are filled with cake pans, decorating tools and ingredients, candy molds, candy boxes, gum-paste flowers, and just about anything else that has to do with baking, making candy, or decorating cakes. Stalwarts such as **Lloyd's Furniture**, at the corner of Main and Davenport· Streets (908-526-4344; www.lloydusa.com), still anchor the downtown shopping district to its past as the regional shopping town for what was once a thriving agricultural area. You don't have to look far for restaurants, either. Possibilities include **Bobby B's Best in BBQ** (42 West Main Street, 908-429-0707); **Martino's** (212 West Main Street, 908-722-8602) for Cuban food; **da Filippo** (132 East Main Street, 908-218-0110); and **Il Pomodoro** (1 West High Street, just off Main Street, 908-526-4466). Somerville is also the Somerset County seat; the beautiful marble courthouse built in 1908 toward the eastern end of Main Street is still in use, and a newer courthouse and county administration building are nearby. In short, if you like to walk on sidewalks, peek into shop and restaurant windows, and browse or go antiquing, you can have an enjoyable few hours in town even if that were all that Somerville offered. It is not all, however.

Somerville has history. Its earliest buildings date to well before the Revolutionary War. The thirteen miles of road leading to Princeton once wound through rolling countryside. While navigating the Somerville Circle, or zipping past the Somerville exit signs on Routes 22 and 287, it's easy to assume that you are simply bypassing another somewhat interchangeable central New Jersey town. Even a stroll or drive along Main Street will not fully reveal the more distant past, unless you notice the historic site signs pointing to the Old Dutch Parsonage and the Wallace House.

They are both a few blocks away from the main business section of downtown, separated by railroad tracks from the more bustling area. The **Old Dutch Parsonage** (65 Washington Place, 908-725-1015) was in the midst of restoration last time I visited it, but even without furniture the simple brick house was interesting both historically and architecturally. It was built in 1751 for the Reverend John Frelinghuysen, who established the first Dutch Reformed seminary in America at the house. The Reverend Jacob Hardenbergh lived there from 1756 to 1781; in 1766 he founded Queen's College, which in turn became Rutgers. This is not quite the original site of the house; it once stood on the banks of the Raritan River. The **Wallace House** (38 Washington Place, 908-725-1015) is diagonally across the street. Built in 1777, it was a relatively large and comfortable house for its time, having been the home of a prosperous merchant, John Wallace. George Washington chose it as his headquarters for the winter of 1778–79, while his troops camped nearby at Middlebush. It's not the Ford Mansion, but it's pleasant and evocative of its particular moment in history, with its airy Georgian floor plan, modestly elegant furniture, and much of its original woodwork still intact. Both the Wallace house and the Parsonage are officially open from Wednesday through Sunday from 10 AM to noon and 1 PM to 4 PM and on Sunday from 1 PM to 4 PM, but call before you plan to visit to be sure they will be accessible.

Duke Gardens

Despite its name, **Duke Gardens** (Route 206 south of Somerville, 908-722-3700) is not a summer destination. In fact, the gardens are closed from June 1 through September 30. Duke Gardens is at its best on a cold, blue-sky winter day, preferably when there is snow on the ground. That's because this lovely place, set back from the road on the stone-walled Duke Estate, consists of connected glasshouses housing eleven distinctively themed gardens. Doris Duke opened the first garden to visitors in 1964; her father, James Buchanan Duke, the first president of the American Tobacco Company, spent millions of dollars to develop the estate decades earlier, but it fell into disuse and disrepair for several decades before Doris Duke undertook her renewal efforts. She remained personally involved with the gardens until the mid 1980s.

This is not a spur-of-the-moment trip. You must call ahead to make a reservation for the day and time you wish to visit Duke Gardens, and there is an admission fee. At the appointed time you will be led through the gardens in a group by a guide; no strollers or cameras are allowed. Despite the rules and relative lack of flexibility, or perhaps because of them, a visit to Duke Gardens is always a treat, full of delightful things to see without being chaotic or noisy or pressured.

One highlight of the visit is the spacious Indo-Persian Garden, which is exceptionally restful as well as decorative. It was designed to reflect the landscaping of Mogul Emperor courtyards. It has fountains and geometric terraces and is patterned in a Moorish arch; among its plantings are orange trees, Mediterranean cypress, and a Persian rose garden.

All the gardens are wonderful, though, and each visitor is likely to have a favorite. The first garden on the tour is an Italian courtyard, followed by a Colonial garden designed to resemble a garden in the southern United States, with camellias, azaleas, magnolia, and crepe myrtle. The Edwardian garden treats you to masses of orchids, and the formal French parterre garden impresses with its latticework wrapped in ivy. The varied English gardens include topiary, a rock garden, herbaceous borders, and an Elizabethan knot garden. The succulent garden in the Great American Desert glasshouse boasts barrel cactus, giant aloe, and crown of thorns, among other unfriendly but interesting plants. The Chinese garden features a walkway over a stream, as well as plantings such as bamboo, camphor trees, and jasmine. A Moon Gate leads to a lattice courtyard. In the Japanese garden a narrow footpath leads from a bonsai display past a teahouse; the sandy soil near the path is raked into careful patterns. The tropical rain forest is a dramatic contrast to the gardens that precede it; next door, bird of paradise flowers are a highlight of the semitropical garden.

Millstone Miles: Bicycle, Drive, Walk, or Even Get a Horse

Anyone who doesn't believe that New Jersey is beautiful should take a drive in Somerset County along the Millstone River and the Delaware and Raritan Canal. For the brave of heart, a bike ride along all or part of the route will work, too. This is a trip you can make at just about any time of year as long as the road isn't covered with ice or snow or it isn't too hot to enjoy being out of doors. (If the roads are clear but the trails are snow covered, you can always snowshoe or cross-country ski.) The main road is Route 533, also known as Main Street or River Road depending on where you are. If you take it south from Millstone, which has a picturesque historic district of its own around the intersection of Main Street and Amwell Road, you will find yourself driving through the River Road Historic District, past fields and a scattering of old, very nice houses, with the Millstone River on your right. (Of course, this trip works just as well if you are coming from points south and drive north along Route 533.) This pleasant state of affairs continues for miles, into Montgomery Township. The road is level, which makes for nice bike riding, but it is quite winding, there is no shoulder, and there is a fair amount of traffic, so be careful. River Road is just across the Millstone River from a segment of **Delaware and Raritan Canal State Park** (634 Canal Road, Somerset, 732-873-3050). You will probably want to cross the river and get to the park for further exploration.

The Delaware and Raritan Canal is one of New Jersey's two great nineteenth-century canals (the Morris Canal is the other one; see chapters 9 and 10, about Delaware Water Gap and Waterloo Village, for more about it). Construction of the D & R Canal began in 1830 and was completed in 1834. Its purpose was to provide an efficient freight connection between Philadelphia and New York City. The main canal ran forty-four miles from the Delaware River just north of Bordentown to New Brunswick, where the Raritan River was navigable for large vessels. A feeder canal ran south along the Delaware River from its highest elevation at Raven Rock and joined the main canal twenty-two miles later at Trenton, fourteen feet closer to sea level. The canal thrived through the 1870s; 80 percent of its cargo consisted of coal traveling from Pennsylvania to industrial furnaces in New York City. In 1871, the canal carried nearly three million tons of cargo—more than New York State's famous (and longer) Erie Canal ever did.

If you are in a hurry to find a road that is narrower and even more picturesque, take the bridge at Blackwells Mills Road. There is parking at **Blackwells Mills,** as well as access to the canal, towpath, and river. The canal and towpath in the park are part of the National Recreational Trail System. You'll see the Blackwells Mills Canal House, a wooden bridge, and a mill site. There are picnic tables and grills in a field with views of the river. There is also horse-trailer parking near the park office just south of Blackwells Mills on Canal Road. This is where you will find the trail head for Six Mile Run Reservoir, a 3,000-acre natural, cultural, and historic site for hiking, biking, and horseback riding.

Or give yourself a few more miles on River Road, then take the one-lane bridge that will lead you directly to a parking area for a Delaware and Raritan Canal State Park day use area. A sign will tell you that River Road was the route Washington's army took after the Battle of Princeton and that the same route was used by American armies traveling from New York to Yorktown, Virginia, in 1781. Whether it's history or nature you're in the mood for, this is a good place to pause. You can picnic, walk, or take your bikes off the car and start exploring. You can ride, walk, or drive to Canal Road and **Griggstown,** where you will see a wooden canal bridge, the Mule Tender's Barracks Canal Museum (closed since the flood of September 1999), a bridge tender's house, and the site of the Griggstown Mill. You can walk along the towpath to Griggstown Lock, where there are picnic tables and grills. You can also rent a canoe at a private concession on the canal at Griggstown. Canal View Stables is on Canal Road south of Griggstown, so if you have a spontaneous urge to enjoy the equestrian trails at the park, here is your chance.

Blackwells Mills Canal House was built around 1835 to house the men and women who operated the swinging bridges. Although the canal closed in 1932, the house was occupied until 1970, when its last occupant, a ninety-year-old retired canal worker, died. Along with the canal, the house belonged to the state of New Jersey. In

1971, the Blackwells Mills Canal House Association was formed. The group leased the house from the state and began to restore it as a community center, museum, and library.

Plumbing, electricity, heat, telephone and other amenities were installed, along with a curator's apartment. The house serves the area with such programs as craft and antique shows, open-house tours, art exhibits, canoe instruction, children's events, market days, plant sales, exhibits, and weekend instruction in such fields as gardening, canoeing, bird-watching, and photography. It is now maintained by the nonprofit Meadows Foundation (732-828-7418), which oversees five other historic properties in the area, including the **Franklin Inn** (2371 Amwell Road, East Millstone), built in 1752 and also restored by the Blackwells Mills Canal House Association.

If you are bicycling, you won't go wrong heading either north or south on Canal Road. In either direction you will pass old houses of wood and stucco, get many glimpses of the canal and the towpath, and pass several places to stop and rest or picnic; signs point to the park, and there are little bridges across the canal. The only potential difficulty for bicycle riders is the narrowness of the road, which is also part of its charm. North of Griggstown, the road, although it doesn't go up and down hills, is higher in the middle than on the sides, which means you will be tempted to ride in the middle of the road to avoid feeling as though you are falling over. There isn't room for cars to pass middle-of-the-road riders comfortably, so someone will have to swerve.

Because there are so many parking areas for visitors to this seventy-mile linear park (the Millstone section is just one part of it; for more, see chapter 18, about Frenchtown, Lambertville, and Stockton), your trip here can be of any length and include whatever combination of activities you wish. You can do a short loop bike ride from the parking lot to Canal Road, north or south a bit, and back. Or you can ride from here to Canal Road, turn north and about three miles later cross the bridge at Blackwells Mills, ride south on River Road, and return to your car that way. You can go farther than that, of course, since both River Road and Canal Road extend south of the parking lot.

May/June Special

Not too far north and east of the Millstone section of Delaware and Raritan Canal State Park is the **Rudolf W. Van Der Groot Rose Garden at Colonial Park** (Mettler's Road, Franklin Township, 908-722-1200). In fact, the park includes frontage on both the canal and the Millstone River. Although Colonial Park is a great recreation facility at any time of year, there is an added benefit if you make the trip from late May to mid-June when the roses are in full bloom (or in early October for the second blooming). A stroll through the formal gardens in full flower is a delightful way to top off a day of biking, hiking, or scenic driving. The rose garden, adjacent to a five-and-a-half-acre arboretum, has brick walkways, an abundance of both climbing and shrub roses, and plenty of benches to sit on while you enjoy the view. It's a popular destination in a well-used county park, so you probably won't have it all to yourself on a sunny late-spring day, but there are enough roses for everyone to admire. It's also a popular place for wedding ceremonies and photographs (the fee is $50 an hour), so you may get to see part of someone's wedding festivities, which adds to the romantic appeal of a bower of roses. Behind the rose garden is the Braille and Sensory Garden, with Braille labels inviting visitors to feel the interesting texture or sniff the distinctive scent of a plant that is connected to the label by a guiding metal bar.

The horticultural displays may be among the more glamorous attractions, but Colonial Park really has something for everyone, and many things for many people. The county acquired land for this 568-acre park in 1965 and has developed it to maximize its recreational potential for every segment of the population. There are picnic tables and grills throughout the park. There is a fitness par-course laid out along a paved path used by walkers, joggers, and bicyclists. Three fishing ponds are stocked each year by the state. The Morgan Pellowski Playground features barrier-free equipment. The Lois Howe Nature Trail goes through a remnant of the oak, hickory, and beech forest. Ice-skating and cross-country skiing are offered when weather permits. Paddleboats can be rented at Powder Mill Pond, and a boat with hand pedals is available for people with limited mobility. There is even an eighteen-hole golf course—Spooky Brook—within the park. All in all, the park might even be worth a trip by itself, without the added attraction of the rest of the Millstone Valley.

Food

Obviously, this is a great picnic trip, whether you bring food from home or stop at a nearby supermarket to stock up. Keep in mind that the Amwell Road (Route 514)/Main Street (Route 533) area is completely noncommercial, so you will have to purchase food before you get there. Of course, there's no reason you can't end the day indoors at one of the many restaurants in New Brunswick, Princeton, and surrounding areas. Just figure out the best route home and then check your favorite restaurant guide.

Flemington

When I first went to Flemington, I was about six years old, and my parents were shopping at the Stangl Pottery, whose festive yellow-banded fruit-pattern dishes my mother used when we had guests. We drove from New York, in the days before Route 78, and all I remember from the visits is the kiln, and a roundish room with plates displayed along the walls.

Now, Flemington is New Jersey Outlet Central, or one of several New Jersey Outlet Centrals. The old houses lining the approaches to downtown are still beautiful, gingerbread-trimmed and close enough together to make the whole town seem like a neighborhood. Each time you visit Flemington, though, you are likely to find fewer local-service, everyday businesses. Even so, what sets outlet shopping in Flemington apart is that in addition to bargain hunting, you see a real town—a historic and very attractive town, in fact. Liberty Village is on the edge of (and walking distance to) downtown Flemington, site of the old Hunterdon County Courthouse, where the Lindbergh trial took place, and the red-brick Union Hotel, where the press stayed during the trial. Liberty Village has a huge parking lot, and even on weekends (except, perhaps, in Christmas season), you can usually find a spot there.

Shopping Specifics

Liberty Village Premium Outlets (908-782-8850; www.chelsea.gca.com) is relatively compact and easy to navigate on foot. Its well-known stores include Brooks Brothers, Polo Ralph Lauren, Villeroy and Boch, and Nine West.

Additional outlets on Main Street itself are even closer to the courthouse and the hotel: **Mikasa** (95 Main Street, 908-788-3620) and **Le Creuset** (156 Main Street, 908-782-1224, in the Flemington Cut Glass building) across the street are the notable examples. **Pfaltzgraff**, across the parking lot from the main Liberty Village complex, occupies the former Stangl pottery. Color-coded signs throughout the downtown point the way to centers and specific retailers. The additional Flemington centers, however, are not part of a single geographical unit; some are on the town's periphery, and you will need to drive to them. **Dansk Plaza** (Routes 202/31, 908-782-7077) houses a Lenox outlet, and, of course, Dansk.

The various Flemington outlets are open daily, with schedules that vary somewhat by season, so call before you go.

Visiting Flemington does not always mean going shopping. Its history and architecture are also worth the trip. Many of the buildings in town are listed in the state and/or national historic registers, and much of the downtown is a historic district. Even if you don't know much about the specifics of a given building, there's a lot to admire. For example, the building at the corner of Main Street and Bloomfield has a huge green-painted clock tower on it. At the corner of Main and Court Streets, the old Hunterdon County Courthouse, recently refurbished, is a fine example of Greek Revival grandeur. At this writing, applications were underway for funding to renovate the interior to match the fine work on the exterior. The Hunterdon County Sheriff's Department (908-766-1166) provides tours.

An even more imposing building across the street from the courthouse houses the **Hunterdon County Historical Society** (114 Main Street, 908-782-1091). Known as the Doric House, this beautiful structure, painted yellow and with the narrow horizontal top-floor windows characteristic of the Greek Revival style, was designed by Mahlon Fisher, who was responsible for many beautiful local buildings.

The **Union Hotel** (76 Main Street), with its mansard roof and double-deck porch, is an impressive sight even without the hordes of reporters who stayed there while covering the Lindbergh kidnapping case.

The **Black River and Western Railroad** (908-782-6622; www.brwrr.com) is another attraction that has nothing to do with shopping, though the station is at the edge of Liberty Village. The railroad, which started operating in 1965 on tracks formerly operated by the Pennsylvania Railroad (in 1970 it bought the entire line from what had become the Penn Central), describes itself as the only scheduled steam-powered passenger railroad in New Jersey. The trains carry passengers from April through December between Flemington and Ringoes, with connections to Lambertville from May to October. It's worthwhile not only for railroad buffs and children, but for all passengers who enjoy a taste of an earlier method of travel. The schedule varies depending upon when in the season you plan to ride the rails, so call for trip times. Incidentally, the BRWRR carries freight year-round—it isn't just a toy train set.

If you like toy trains, **Northlandz** (Route 202 South, 908-782-4022; www.northlandz.com) is the place for you. The outside of the exhibit building, perched right along the road and rather plain looking, doesn't give much idea of what awaits you inside. There, for an admission fee of less than fifteen dollars for adults and substantially less for children, you will discover a complex wonderland of model train sets, with a few added attractions, such as a doll museum and a 5,000-pipe organ. You walk a mile, admiring eight miles of track and well over one hundred trains; there are mountains and cities, hundreds of bridges, and scenery and vignettes of trackside life.

Food

If you get hungry while you are in Flemington, the **Market Roost** (65 Main Street, 908-788-4949) is definitely a good place to stop for lunch. Its roasted vegetable melt (including carrots, zucchini, onions, bell peppers, and cheese on a toasted English muffin) is filling and delicious. Other appealing possibilities include a French pâté platter with potato salad, cornichons, cheese, mustard, tomato, onion, and a croissant, fresh or roasted turkey breast with orange marmalade mayonnaise, and many more just-sophisticated-enough combinations. After you place your order, find a table at the front of the shop, then wait for your name to be called. While you are waiting, take a look at the elegant desserts on display near the takeout counter, and see if you can resist a slice of coconut cake or cherry pie or a large and luscious-looking lemon sour-cream muffin. You can always bring it home with you.

There's also a restaurant in the **Union Hotel** (908-788-7474) itself, which posts an easel-mounted menu on the hotel porch. The restaurant is open daily for lunch and dinner.

Just outside town is the popular **Jake's Restaurant and Bar** (253 Route 202/31, 908-806-3188). This casual American watering hole is open daily for lunch and dinner and has a children's menu.

Chapter Fifteen

Monmouth Battlefield and More: Churches, Cemeteries, and Orchards

New Jersey has a relatively moderate climate compared to lots of other places, but the history of its Revolutionary War battles might make it seem otherwise. There was snow and starvation at Morristown, icy roads at Princeton. The story was quite different during the Battle of Monmouth. It was June of 1778, and it was hot— over 100 degrees Fahrenheit.

Even people who don't know about the historical significance of Monmouth know about Molly Pitcher, who supposedly brought water to the sweltering troops and took over her wounded husband's cannon. Molly Pitcher may be largely myth (although "Molly Pitcher's Well" does appear on some maps), but the heat and the importance of the battle are reality. On June 18, British troops left Philadelphia and headed for New York. On June 19, George Washington led his troops away from Valley Forge to chase the British. On June 28, 20,000 British soldiers were camped on or near the Freehold–Mount Holly Road; the much smaller Continental Army was camped at Manalapan Bridge, and in Englishtown, 5,000 more American troops under the command of General Charles Lee were ordered to attack the rear of the British Army. Lee surrounded the British troops as they were getting ready to leave their camp, then realized during the fighting that the British were preparing to come back and attack his forces. He ordered a retreat, which was intercepted by Washington, who ordered the troops to continue fighting. The main battle took place that afternoon, in fields and wood lots in what was then a well-established farming community with hayfields, pastures, orchards, and homes. It ended late that night, as the British resumed their journey south. The battle marked something of a turning point in attitude as much as military standing, since the Continental Army had been able to hold off a much larger British army on open ground without depending upon the guerilla tactics that had led to success in some earlier battles.

Monmouth Battlefield State Park (437 Freehold Road, Manalapan Township, 732-462-9616) does its best to give visitors a sense of what happened on June 28, 1778. The main entrance to the park is off Business Route 33, just west of Freehold. In July 2000 the state park service was in the process of restoring the area to its eighteenth-century appearance; in the centuries since the battle, woods have grown up where open fields once were. Brush was being cleared to re-create the pastures and fields that set the scene for the battle, and trees were to be planted to re-create the woodlots of the period.

History aside, this is a serviceable recreational state park. It has picnic tables, charcoal grills, water fountains, and restrooms, as well as playground equipment and an open field for games and kite flying—also ample parking. There are also twenty-five miles of old roads, paths, and trails for hiking, biking, horseback riding, and, when there's snow, cross-country skiing and snowshoeing. The park is open year-round, dawn to dusk, and the visitor center is open daily from 9 AM to 4 PM.

Although the architecture of the visitor center is contemporary and rather institutional, there are excellent, informative exhibits. The first thing you see when you enter is a panoramic photograph of the area that's visible just in back of the center. A numbered key explains what happened at several of the spots, adding a great deal more interest to what would otherwise be just a pretty view of fields and a low hill. There are also maps showing the hour-by-hour progress of the battle, as well as a display of military and everyday Revolution-ary-era artifacts (shoe buckles, musket balls, and a screwdriver, for example) that were excavated around the battlefield under the su-pervision of park authorities. On the last weekend of June each year, a reenactment of the battle takes place at the park.

The Craig House, one of the farmhouses that witnessed the battle, is on the far side of the battlefield from the visitor center and is accessible off Route 9. It has been restored and refurnished and is open on Sunday afternoons.

Just around the corner from the entrance to the state park is **Battleview Orchards** (91 Wemrock Road, Freehold, 732-462-0756). Part of Wemrock Road is lined with orchards; that's a scenic advan-tage and has the added benefit of giving some idea of what parts of the area must have looked like in 1778. (In fact, the state leases part of Monmouth Battlefield State Park to farmers for agricultural use.) More to the point for day-trippers is what's growing in the orchards. Battleview is a good destination for those who like to pick their own apples and pumpkins. What sets it apart from many other fine pick-your-own farms is that Battleview also grows peaches and nectar-ines, and at the height of the season, generally late July through early September, you can pick your own. Even when the pick-your-own sections are closed, Battleview sells its own peaches and nectarines, some as early as the beginning of July. Battleview Orchards also sells baked goods such as pies and cookies, as well as other produce.

Not far from Monmouth's main battlefield, on Tennent Road just north of the intersection with Route 522, is **Old Tennent Presbyte-rian Church**, built in 1751. The small, white building is at the top of a low hill and is topped by its original weathervane, which is, in fact, several decades older than the church itself. The church is surrounded by a large cemetery, parts of which are quite new. Closer to the church, the inscriptions on many of the older stones are so weathered that they are barely legible. Some of the older gravestones are those of Revolutionary War soldiers who died at the Battle of Monmouth. On the side of the church, near the entrance, is a plaque put up by the local chapter of the Daughters of the American Revolution in 1901; it commemorates "the patriots who fought at the Battle of Monmouth

Walter Choroszewski

Old Tennent Presbyterian Church

on Sabbath, June 28, 1778." The church, which still has a congregation and is open for Sunday service, is not primarily a tourist sight. The graveyard is open daily, however; and you can peek through the windows at the church's dignified interior and appreciate the historic surroundings in peace and, usually, solitude.

If your visit to Monmouth Battlefield State Park has put you in a recreational frame of mind, you may want to drive over to the Monmouth County Park System's **Turkey Swamp Park** (Georgia Road, Freehold, 732-842-4000). It has a seventeen-acre lake where you can boat and fish; in winter, ice conditions permitting, it's used for skating. Canoes and paddleboats are available for rent during the summer. Turkey Swamp also has an archery range and miles of trails, as well as playgrounds and picnic areas.

Freehold

Freehold has several identities. It was the center of agricultural Monmouth County for decades, and although the region is now suburban, the town's long Main Street still has the feeling of a local market town with a good mix of businesses (antiques, collectibles, shoe store, copy store, pharmacy, dry cleaning, restaurants). Dunkin' Donuts and Colombo Yogurt are in a beautiful pink stucco building that dates from 1872. **Federici's** (14 East Main Street, 732-462-1312), right in the center of town, has lots of outdoor tables for good-weather dining, and its thin-crust pizza is consistently rated as among central New Jersey's best. In business since 1921, Federici's is open daily for lunch and dinner.

Both west and east of town, Main Street (Route 537) is tree-lined, with lovely nineteenth-century houses, some with intricate gingerbread trim. The First Baptist Church, just outside the business district, is a very pretty white-frame building with gray trim. Freehold is the town where Bruce Springsteen grew up; the sign on Route 537 that thanks motorists for "visiting our hometown" is a reminder of Freehold's place in American popular culture.

Freehold Raceway (Routes 33 and 9, 732-462-3800) is another reason that people know Freehold. The Raceway is the oldest daytime half-mile harness-racing track in the country. It features live standard-bred harness races for trotters and pacers from August through May and is open seven days a week and six nights (closed Monday evenings) year-round for thoroughbred and harness-racing simulcasts from tracks throughout North America. Admission is free every afternoon and all day Sunday and Monday, with free parking in the evening for the simulcasts.

Freehold Raceway has a long history. In 1853, the Monmouth County Agriculture Society was formed to hold an annual fair with harness racing in Freehold, and in 1854 the society rented from Hudson Bennett the ten-acre plot of land that is now the site of Freehold Raceway. The society bought more land later in the 1850s, and in the late 1870s the raceway's half-mile track and grandstand were built. Financial problems led to the demise of the Monmouth County Agriculture Society in 1888, and the track was unused for several years after that. The Freehold Driving Club was formed in 1895 and leased the track for $174 a year. The club disbanded in 1909 and was replaced by the Freehold Driving Association, which rebuilt the track. For about a decade the annual fair continued to be the main event, but in 1917, a major, five-day meet was held at the track. The grandstand was rebuilt in 1923, and the Freehold Driving Park offered both a week of trotting races and a week of running races. For several years attendance dwindled, and in 1936, Harry Gould, a sportsman from Bergen County, bought the track, which he reopened as the Freehold Trotting Association. He did not want to be involved in gambling, however, and sold the track in 1941 to a contractor from Maplewood, who ran the track. Several changes in ownership occurred over the following decades, but racing continued.

In 1946, Freehold started a twenty-four-day pari-mutuel meeting, and in 1960 the raceway was sold again, reportedly for $5 million. It prospered through the early 1960s and was purchased by Gibraltar Pari-Mutuel in 1965. The racetrack was rebuilt in 1967 to allow for eight horses instead of six to start behind the starting gate. In 1970, the grandstand was enclosed to permit year-round racing. The grandstand and dining room were destroyed by fire in May 1984, but simulcast racing featuring races from the Meadowlands resumed in July of that year. After another change of ownership, a new grandstand and dining room were built in 1985. In 1990, the then-new owner, Wilmorite, Inc., opened the Freehold Raceway Mall across the street from the track. There were several more changes in ownership, but Freehold Raceway continues to offer both live and simulcast racing.

Leaving Freehold

If you continue on Route 537 leaving Freehold and traveling toward Colts Neck, you will soon come to the intersection of Route 34. **Delicious Orchards** (Route 34, Colts Neck, 732-462-1989; www.deliciousorchards.nj.com) is just around the corner, with the **Berry Farm** (Route 34, Colts Neck, 732-294-1989) tucked neatly behind it, to make this Colts Neck crossroads a major magnet for foodies.

Although Delicious Orchards opened decades ago as a simple farm market, it has since developed way beyond that. It is certainly an excellent source of produce; the room where corn and tomatoes and other summer vegetables are sold is always bright and busy, and the corn is sweet and fresh. The big room where fruit is sold usually has a better-than-average choice of varieties, with useful explanations, like "Black Diamond Plums have red flesh, Black Plums have amber flesh"—particularly helpful if your family looks upon red-flesh plums as a special treat, as mine does.

The key thing about Delicious Orchards for many people, however, is that you enter this super market through the bakery department. And what a bakery department it is. The shelves on either side are lined with relatively straightforward items like Danish pastries and cookies. The counters beyond are where temptation really lies.

The first counter sells cream pies: the Key lime pie is wonderful, but so is the chocolate cream pie; there are also éclairs, and sometimes little blueberry tarts in what is described as "light custard." There is also a pie counter, followed by a bread counter and bordered by strategically placed tables selling things like fully baked, fully freezable baking powder biscuits. After the bakery, you can make your way to a dairy case/prepared food/meat counter area. And beyond that, the produce rooms await you. There's more: there are shelves of condiments, salad dressings, candy, and coffee; if shopping at your regular neighborhood market seems dull, you could buy almost all your week's food here, or you can be virtuous and just buy fruits and vegetables. To whatever degree you want to be tempted, Delicious Orchards makes it easy to eat well; lots of fruit, lots of vegetables, lots of milk and cheese, and always something special for dessert.

Delicious Orchards opened in 1911 in what was then a farming and horse-breeding community. After World War II the business shifted from a wholesale operation to a retail one. In 1959, then-owner Carroll W. Barclay started selling apples at a roadside stand, and the next year he built a 1,200-square-foot stand. Product lines expanded from there, with cider and apple pie, and eventually much more. The bakery operation expanded in the 1960s; citrus fruits were soon added, along with cheeses (more than 150 kinds by now). The store size more than doubled by 1982. The bakery began to sell cookies, doughnuts, and custom cakes; grocery items and dozens of varieties of coffee and tea were added, along with candy and gift baskets.

The Berry Farm is best described as being in back of Delicious Orchard's employee parking lot; there is a sign nearby identifying Berry Farm parking. This is a highly seasonal, purely pick-your-own operation. The last time I was there, on a weekday afternoon in blackberry season, a man in a hurry came along, asked if there were any picked berries for sale, and was ready to leave when he discovered there were not. But the woman in front of me on the cash-register line was accompanied by several little girls who had finished their picking, and she offered to sell him a pint of their berries; they were happy to go pick more. He took their place in line, paid for the berries, and went happily on his way, while they went happily back to the fields. The Berry Farm also grows red raspberries and black raspberries; the autumn raspberry season is my favorite. Be sure to call before you go to ascertain which berries are in season and to be sure that the berry fields will be open for picking.

More Food

If your visit to Delicious Orchards has made you hungry for a meal before you get home, you may be in luck. A branch of one of the state's most popular seafood restaurants is virtually across the street. **Ray's Seafood** (Route 34, Colts Neck, 732-303-1339) is open Tuesday through Friday for lunch and daily for dinner.

Chapter Sixteen

Warren County, Starring Belvidere

There is a billboard at the side of Route 46, just where you turn onto county road 620. It invites you to visit "Victorian Belvidere, New Jersey's best-kept secret." In a way, I want to keep this secret to myself. Ever since the quiet, early-fall day in 1986 when my husband and I packed our six-year-old son and eight-month-old daughter into the car, turned on the radio to listen to a Mets game, and found ourselves about an hour later parked on a street along the perimeter of the Belvidere Green, I have thought of Belvidere as a treasure to be discovered.

Belvidere is the kind of place you visit not to do anything in particular, but for the sake of the overall experience. If my traveler's reminiscences appeal to you, then Belvidere is a destination to put on your own itinerary, and when you visit it, your day will unfold in its own way. Keep in mind, too, that although walking along the historic streets of Belvidere may appeal mostly to adults, there are several ways to turn a trip to Warren County into a very family-friendly outing. These variations are covered later in this chapter.

On my most recent trip to Belvidere, coming from Hope along a county road that I thought led to Belvidere, I found myself approaching it from Route 46. Fortunately, Route 46 in Warren County bears very little resemblance to the congested, overdeveloped divided highway familiar to residents of Passaic, Essex, and eastern Morris Counties. It's a pretty road, running, surprisingly for an east-west thoroughfare, along the Delaware River in places. When I came to the sign, I turned off Route 46 onto Warren County 620 South, pleased at the prospect of returning to an even narrower, more winding highway. I wasn't completely sure I was headed toward Belvidere, but the standard blue-and-white sign pointing to the Warren County Library seemed promising.

After missing the cross street that should have taken me to the courthouse square and finding myself gazing at a sign warning me I was now leaving scenic Warren County, I turned around, checked the map, and finally figured out how to get downtown via Hardwick Street. I reached Greenwich Street and admired wonderful Victorian houses. As I drove along Fourth Street and turned up and down Mansfield and Hardwick Streets, I was impressed by how close to downtown these beautiful streets are; they have the air of a thriving nineteenth-century small town, almost like an idealized 1930s movie set version of a turn-of-the-century American town.

Third Street after Mansfield was beautiful, with brick and stone Victorian houses. My goal was to do a self-guided walking tour around the green, but first I walked along Third Street, admiring the houses, trees, lawns, and porches, even the ferns. Each house and each yard seemed to have something special; the houses at the corner of Third and Knowlton Streets were especially impressive, because each one was so different from its neighbors. Along the way on Third Street, I saw a turquoise-plum-and-pink house (it had a for-sale sign in front of it, so the color scheme may have changed by the time you see it, but it would be a very appealing house no matter what the color), an olive one, white ones. The street scene was utterly seductive; the sun was shining after a rainy morning, and there were small children in costume apparently on their way to or from a school program. You don't have to go to Main Street at Disney World to feel as though you are time-traveling in a perfect America.

I turned back along Third Street and walked past a house on Hardwick Street whose front porch was guarded by two stone lions.

I walked past the courthouse, which was built in the 1820s and renovated in the 1950s, and reached Veterans' Place, part of Second Street,
at the next corner. Dedicated on November 11, 1998, it's a quiet spot
with shiny new memorial tablets for Warren County's casualties from
World War I through the Vietnam War. Belvidere is the kind of place
where you expect to see a Civil War monument on the town square,
and Veterans' Place, honoring those who served in later wars, is part
of that continuum.

Incidentally, the Warren County Library, the destination indi-
cated by all those blue-and-white signs, is just off the square. It's a
beautiful Italian Revival building, tan with dark-brown brackets under the roof. What a treat it would be to use a library that looks like
that for homework research and routine book borrowing.

There is one time of year when you can do more than admire
Belvidere's homes from the sidewalks. The town holds annual Victorian Days, traditionally scheduled for the weekend after Labor Day.
The Victorian Days include historic house tours and "porch and garden tea parties," as well as arts and crafts exhibits, children's activities, and more. Tickets for the house tours are sold in advance, as
well as on the weekend itself; check local newspapers for details, or
call or write the Victorian Days Committee (PO Box 1134, Belvidere
17823; Belvidere Recreation Coordinator, 908-475-4124).

In addition to county offices and lawyers' offices in some of the
buildings around the square and near the courthouse, Belvidere has
several streets with shops and other commercial activity. They are
not the reason to go to Belvidere, but once you are there, they are
worth a stop. After my courthouse square walk, I drove back to Water Street and turned down Market Street (its name changes to Greenwich Street) to take another look at the business district, where **Uncle
Buck's Diner** (2 Market Street, 908-475-3668) overlooks a little waterfall and shares the block with other establishments. At Pequest
Plaza across the street a grooming salon for pets reminds romantically minded visitors that this is a real-life town; a hardware store
just beyond the plaza reinforces that idea. The **Country Gate Play-
house** (114 Greenwich Street, 908-475-1104) presents live theater
year-round in what was once a movie theater. The intersection of

Warren County Courthouse

Greenwich and Front Streets has been a commercial crossroads for a long time.

Perhaps the most enchanting shop on this street is **The Painted Lady** (16 Greenwich Street, Belvidere, 908-475-1985). I had noticed it on my way in to town, because the building itself was so prettily maintained and there was a beautiful old lace dress in the window, worn by a mannequin designed to look like a bride. The whole window display was lovely and the dress was a striking centerpiece for it. The Painted Lady, divided into several delightful rooms, sells antiques and collectibles. Prices are not low, but everything in the shop is nice. Items for sale include upholstered Victorian furniture, marble-topped tables, elegant old china, collectible models of cars and trucks, and a selection of Victorian-style new stationery and greeting cards.

Around the corner on Front Street are other places of business, including at least three eateries. The **Pequest River Book Company** (316 Front Street, 908-425-1303) is a wonderful combination of several kinds of stores. Downstairs it sells books (with an especially cozy children's book section), greeting cards, pottery, and other gift items. Upstairs, it sells more gifts, including Caswell-Massey products. To top it all off, there's a very welcoming three-table café. After ordering my Mediterranean salad and iced tea at the counter, I sat at one of the tables and looked out the window at the other buildings. It was very pleasant and friendly, and the salad was delicious. Even if you don't plan to buy books or gifts at the shop, the Pequest River Book Company is well worth a stop for the gracious service and good food. Down the street are **Thisilldous Eatery and Ice Cream** (320 Front Street, 908-425-2274), which is also an inn, and the **Corner Deli** (324 Front Street, 908-425-3902). Whatever your mood or taste in food and ambience, you won't go hungry once you find Front Street. And if the weather is good, you can take your food back to the nearby green and picnic.

Farm Food (and Drink)

A visit to **Matarazzo Farms** (10 Doe Hollow Lane, Belvidere, 908-475-3872; www.matarazzo.com) is always a treat. Matarazzo Farms is located on Route 519 north of town, and in the fall you can pick your own apples or pumpkins there. The farm market sells produce, pies, cookies, and specialty items.

The **Four Sisters Winery at Matarazzo Farms** was added to this agricultural tradition in 1981, when wine grapes were planted among the other crops. Located in the federally designated Warren Hills viticultural area, the Four Sisters Winery offers public tours to help visitors understand both the grape-growing and wine-making processes. There are also wine tastings. The winery has won a number of regional, national, and international awards for red, white, rosé, and fruit wines. Named for family members, the fruit wines include Sadie's Apple, made from several varieties of late harvest apples; Cherry Melissa; Robin's Raspberry; and Strawberry Serena. The Four Sisters Winery is open daily from April through December and every day except Wednesday from January through March.

Hope

Wonderful as Belvidere is, it is by no means the only place to go in Warren County. Northeast of Belvidere is the even older and equally unspoiled Hope. If you are coming to Hope via Route 80, you may be pleased or dismayed, depending on the state of your gas tank, to discover that the Hope exit (Route 521) is undeveloped; it has no gas station. Signs direct you to the Land of Make Believe as well as to Hope, which seems like a nice pairing.

Founded by Moravians in 1769, the town wanders gently for several blocks in each direction from the crossroads of Routes 521 and 519. It is on the state and national registers of historic places, and its most notable features are the dignified stone buildings that are remnants of the Moravian settlement of the late eighteenth century. The town was very quiet when I visited on a weekday morning in the spring. Hartung's store was open, selling a wide variety of items, including the *Wall Street Journal*. Established in 1937, Hartung's announces its services and products in old-fashioned brown lettering contrasting crisply with a background of white paint scalloped to resemble curtains: dairy products, ice cream, luncheonette, newspapers, candy, and, unsaid of course, atmosphere. The small Hope

Historical Society, which is open on summer weekends, was closed, however. High Street is lined with well-kept old houses, most of them of wood, and it was very peaceful that day. The side-street crossroads of Walnut and Cedar Streets was even more peaceful, almost dreamy, with an old and beautiful stone house almost completely hidden behind a tall hedge. The last time I visited Hope, the **Schade Tree** (Walnut Street, 908-459-9011), a workshop of traditional arts such as pottery, ceramics, candle making, and weaving, was announcing its opening. The Schade Tree occupies space in the Long House, which once housed women of the Moravian settlement. Several realtors and antique/collectible shops seem to make up to bulk of the business on High Street. A number of the large Moravian-built structures are now used for businesses such as banking and insurance but are still very dignified and impressive. On Route 521 just south of the crossroads are two very similar stone houses that apparently remain residential; interestingly, one is labeled "Moravian 1776," the other "American 1776."

A guided walk thorough Hope may be the best bet for people with a deeper interest in history and architecture. You can pick up a self-guided tour map at the **Village Café** (3 Millbrook Road, 908-459-4860); **Help Our Preservation Effort,** or HOPE (908-459-9177), offers guided walking tours of the town on Saturday mornings June through October. The tours leave from the Inn at Millrace Pond.

The atmospheric **Inn at Millrace Pond** (Route 519, Hope, 908-459-4884) is set on twenty-three acres just outside the center of Hope. The inn includes three historic buildings: the landmark pre–Revolutionary War gristmill, the miller's house, and the wheelwright's cottage. Dinner is served daily in the inn's highly rated restaurant and overnight accommodations are available in seventeen distinctive guest rooms. The Inn also hosts conferences and weddings and other private parties. Nearby are the **Hope Chest** (3 Millbrook Road, 908-459-4348), which sells home and garden items, and the Village Café, with a picture window overlooking a brook. This little back section of Hope is very pleasant, well worth the short walk from the center of town.

The **Land of Make Believe and Pirate's Cove** (Route 611, Hope, 908-459-9000) has been a popular seasonal destination for families for more than forty years. About a mile out of Hope, it is open weekends from the Memorial Day weekend through the second weekend in June and open daily from the third Saturday in June through Labor Day. It is also open on the weekend after Labor Day. In May and June it hosts school trips on weekdays; no group trips are permitted after June 30. Nestled against a wooded hillside, the Land of Make Believe has the look of a country fair, with glimpses of striped tents, colorful rides and activity areas peeking through the trees. There is a picnic grove as well as refreshment stands, gift shops, a water park, and a variety of rides. Popular attractions include Blackbeard's River, a river-tubing adventure for the whole family; the life-size Buccaneer Pirate Ship, with nets and water slides; Pirate's Cove Wading Pool and Slides; and the Black Hole, a ride for parents and children eight years and older. Other activities include a maze, a carousel, the Enchanted Christmas Village, and Old McDonald's Farm, with live farm animals, as well many more rides and games. Parking is free.

Oxford

Southeast of Belvidere, and accessible via narrow, scenic back roads, Oxford was a very early industrial center. From the mid-eighteenth century through the mid-twentieth century it was an iron-mining town; iron products were also made in Oxford. From Belvidere, Oxford Street leads to the **First Oxford Presbyterian Church,** at the corner of Routes 519 and 623 South. It's a brick building a little larger than a one-room schoolhouse, with delicate white woodwork at the eaves.

On the hill just above downtown Oxford is the **Oxford Furnace** (Washington Avenue at the corner of Cinder Street, 908-453-4381). It's labeled as Oxford Furnace 1, Oxford Historical District Site 4: construction started in 1741, first blast 1743, blown out 1884. It looks like a giant stone chimney, which, in a way, is what it was. Site 3 is the Grist Mill, built in 1813; it became the Colonial Methodist Church in 1913 and is next door to the furnace.

The disadvantage to approaching Oxford from Belvidere is that you miss the first, striking view of **Shippen Manor** (8 Belvidere Avenue, 908-453-4381), a lovely stone house set on a hill above Oxford's present-day downtown. Shippen Manor is just across Belvidere Avenue from the furnace. Built in 1754, the manor was home to the Shippen brothers, who owned the ironworks. Now the home of the Warren County Cultural and Heritage Commission, it is open for tours the first and second Sunday of each month.

There's more to Oxford than history and iron mining. The **Pequest Trout Hatchery and Natural Resource Education Center** in the **Pequest Wildlife Management Area** (605 Pequest Road, Oxford, 908-637-4125) is a deservedly popular destination, especially for fishing enthusiasts, school trips, and families. It's easy to get to from the Oxford Historic District, but if you would like to picnic at Pequest, pick up food at one of the shopping areas along Route 31 south of Oxford. To get to Pequest from Oxford, take Route 31 North to Route 46 East. This part of Route 46 is still very rural, a winding two-lane road with very few buildings of any kind and lots of trees and other greenery. Across from the entrance to the fish hatchery is a long, low hill that gives the area a sheltered feeling.

The parking lot just inside the entrance is for a fishing area, although the sign identifies it as the Pequest River Trout Conservation Area. Trout are available here throughout the legal fishing season, but the area is closed to fishing on Fridays. The waters also are home to catfish and eels. A few yards from the end of the parking area, which has several spots marked for handicapped drivers, are two handicapped-access fishing areas reachable by a gravel path. They are level, graveled areas with a benches and railings; each rail has a dip in the top rail so that a person seated in a wheelchair would be able to fish comfortably without the rail getting in the way. The Pequest River is lovely here even if you don't fish, and these spots are pleasant sitting areas. In late spring, with birds singing, wildflowers in bloom, and the air very sweetly scented, they provide a momentary refuge for anyone who wants to sit and contemplate the river and the surroundings.

Continuing along the access road will take you to the hatchery and the education center. The latter has a wildlife exhibit, information brochures, an auditorium where a video about the hatchery is shown, and rest rooms. To get from the education center to the hatchery for a self-guided tour, follow the green fish painted on the sidewalk. The tour of the nursery building is from the outside looking in; public access to the hatchery areas is restricted to "prevent the introduction of parasites or disease," according to the hatchery brochure. Explanations of the various stages of nursery life are displayed at large windows through which you can see the incubators and the tanks. Each year the facility produces more than half a million trout—brook, brown, and rainbow. After they reach the appropriate size (about ten and a half inches), they are stocked in about two hundred bodies of water that are open to public fishing. From the nursery building, you can continue to follow the green fish to the open-air raceways, where fingerling trout three to four inches long live until it is time for them to be stocked. The major stocking season runs from mid-March to May, but some stocking is also done in the fall.

The Pequest Butterfly Garden and a picnic grove are down a bank from the raceways. The Butterfly Garden is a habitat designed to attract butterflies by providing food, water, shelter, and space. The brochure available at the education center told me more than I had ever known about butterflies, although I visited Pequest too early in the spring to see any of the inhabitants.

A Natural Resource Trail starts behind the picnic area and has numbered sites along its route. You have to cross Pequest Road to follow most of it. You will then pass sites such as a lime kiln, a fallow field, a forest, several information stops, and an observation blind before the trail loops back. In addition to being informative, the trail is a very pleasant walk.

Chapter Seventeen

Reservoirs and River Cities: Round Valley and Spruce Run, Phillipsburg and Easton

I had heard about the reservoirs and seen the signs on Route 78 for years, but until recently I never quite found my way to Round Valley and Spruce Run. Now that I have been there, I know they are both worth a trip, whether you decide to spend the entire day near the water, or just stop by for a restorative hour or two as part of a trip to another destination, such as Flemington or the Phillipsburg/Easton area. Water and weather conditions permitting, the Round Valley and Spruce Run Recreation Areas are places to swim, boat, camp, picnic, camp, or simply gaze out at the water, hills, and sky and enjoy the day. Neither is a natural body of water, but each provides ample water recreation and open public space. If you don't have your own Hunterdon County estate with a large pond and rolling fields, you can happily share these parks with fellow taxpayers.

Round Valley Recreation Area (Lebanon/Stanton Road, Lebanon, 908-236-6355) is jointly managed by the New Jersey State Park Service, the Division of Fish, Game and Wildlife, and the New Jersey Water Supply Authority. Perhaps the key thing to know about Round Valley Reservoir is that it's a beautiful lake surrounded by hills. The park access road is just off Route 22, but soon after you turn onto it you know you are far way, at least psychologically speaking, from the bustling Route 22 of eastern New Jersey.

The reservoir itself is the result of the 1958 Water Supply Law and Water Bond Act, whose purpose was to help the state meet increasing demand for water and recreational facilities. The recreation area was opened to the public in 1977; an earth dam separates the swimming area from the main reservoir so that water levels in the swimming area remain constant. The reservoir, more than 180 feet deep, is the deepest lake in the state. Although swimming is allowed only when lifeguards are on duty, the recreation area offers many other opportunities for outdoor fun. There are three picnic areas, with restroom buildings; the picnic areas are especially appealing because they offer plenty of shade, thanks to both trees and shaded shelters. If summer appears suddenly in early May or comes back for a surprise visit in early November, the picnic areas make especially pleasant lunchtime spots. Paved paths along the lake, though not exactly rustic, are nice. Light fixtures topped by big, white-glass globes probably provide ample light at dusk, but they look a little awkward and urban in daylight.

Scuba and skin diving are allowed from April through October, depending on water temperature. The boat-launch ramp accommodates sailboats, canoes, and motorboats of up to ten horsepower. Trout are stocked in the reservoir each year, and fishing is permitted, though you must abide by the posted regulations. Waterfowl hunting by boat is permitted in season. There are more than one hundred campsites, all accessible only by foot or boat and open from April through November. In winter, when snow cover is sufficient, there is a designated sledding hill, and the trails and slopes throughout the recreation area make for excellent cross-country skiing.

If your picnic lunch was eaten a long time ago and you'd like to enjoy a meal someone else has prepared, the surroundings at the **Cokesbury Inn** in nearby Lebanon will allow you to hold on to the get-away-from it-all mood of Round Valley. Lebanon's main street parallels Route 22, but the buildings along the street are mostly old and attractive wooden houses, and the Cokesbury Inn fits right in.

Spruce Run Recreation Area (1 Van Syckel Road, Clinton, 908-638-8572) is also a joint project of the Park Service, the Water Supply Authority, and the Department of Fish, Game and Wildlife. Spruce Run Reservoir was one of the first water-supply facilities built by New Jersey, and the recreation area was opened in 1973. A sign that I saw announcing "7 wooded sites for sale" just before the entrance to the recreation area didn't seem to bode well for open space, but once you turn down the driveway and are safely on the way to the information building or the picnic areas, the feeling of escape from the city returns. The recreation area covers about 600 acres, including nearly 1,300 acres of water surface.

The beach is bigger at Spruce Run than at Round Valley (note, however, that there have been recent summers when swimming has not been permitted). The beach is staffed by lifeguards in summer, and adjacent to the beach is a large complex (open seasonally) that includes changing areas, rest rooms, showers, a first-aid station, and concessions selling food, beach supplies, and other items. The architecture, especially the conical roofs of the various buildings and the concrete patios between the buildings, is not exactly sensitive or in keeping with the surroundings, but the services are certainly convenient. There are basketball hoops set up just behind the large parking lot across from the beach and concession area.

Even in spring before the water-recreation season starts, people come to walk, bicycle, and picnic. Note that there are charcoal grills at the picnic areas, so you can eat more than peanut-butter sandwiches or cold chicken. There are seven picnic areas at Spruce Run, all with rest rooms and many with open space nearby for field games.

Sailing, motor boating, canoeing, fishing, and windboarding are permitted twenty-four hours a day, and you can rent dry storage space for your boat from April through October. There is also a boat-rental concession (908-638-8234). (Both Round Valley and Spruce Run have warning-light systems that blink when winds are blowing at twenty-five miles per hour or more; all activities on the reservoir must stop when the wind reaches that speed.) The Division of Fish, Game and Wildlife stocks Spruce Run with trout, northern pike, and hybrid striped bass, and fishing is popular both at the reservoir and along its two main tributaries, Spruce Run Creek and Mulhockaway Creek. Waterfowl hunting is permitted in season from points below the high-water mark. In winter, conditions permitting, cross-country skiing, ice fishing, and ice boating are popular activities. Seventy campsites are open from April through October.

River Cities

Look at all the strollers. They cluster at the entrance to the interactive section of the main exhibit area of the **Crayola Factory®** (Two Rivers Landing, 30 Centre Square, Easton, 610-515-8000; www.crayola.com). If you have small children who love their crayons (and chalk, markers, Silly Putty, and arts and crafts in general), it will be hard to justify omitting this colorful place from your trip, even if it does mean crossing the Delaware and venturing—just barely—into Pennsylvania. You don't really get to see the factory floor, but you do get to see a lot of Crayola products, and a special-for-visitors crayon-manufacturing display facing a marker-manufacturing display. At the drop of a giant token, each visitor gets a free marker and a dainty box of crayons. Think of it as a compact indoor theme park rather than a factory tour and you will have a perfect destination for a toddler, a preschooler, and a not-too-much-older sibling who will enjoy reading about the history of crayons and colors. The Crayola Factory® itself consists of a floor of interactive exhibits and activities, such as the Color Garden, the Light Zone, and the Creative Studio; special events and workshops are also part of the attraction. Although the Crayola Factory® may interest children who have completed kindergarten or first grade, they may feel a little self-conscious surrounded by all those strollers and the very young preschoolers who ride in them; children any older may feel out of place, though deep down they may not find it boring. The visit will almost certainly awaken your family's desire to own more Crayola products, offered at the Crayola Store® next door (610-253-3703). It sells T-shirts, stuffed animals, and accessories, as well as a major collection of arts-and-crafts supplies produced by Binney and Smith, the makers of Crayola products.

The **National Canal Museum** occupies the two floors above the Crayola Factory® at Two Rivers Landing. Given the specialized subject matter, this could be a museum geared toward history-minded adults, but, perhaps because it shares the building with a museum that is designed solely for young children, the Canal Museum instead seems to be geared to a young audience. The information in the exhibits is presented in simple language, in what seems to be an effort to make it accessible to eight-to-twelve-year-old visitors. There are several interactive exhibits illustrating how canal locks and planes work; the most interesting exhibits focus on the history of canals as a form of transportation and show the life of people working and living along them.

The Lehigh Canal was an important part of Easton's history, and the Canal Museum is just part of the city's canal-related activities. The ground floor of Two Rivers Landing houses the visitor center of the Easton-area National Historic Corridor, and the exhibits there give a general overview of Easton's history and economy. For greater focus, head for **Hugh Moore Park** (610-559-6613), off Lehigh Drive and across the Lehigh River. Occupying land once owned by the Lehigh Coal and Navigation Company, this city park parallels the Lehigh River and is devoted to the preservation and interpretation of canal and industrial history; you can see a restored segment of the Lehigh Canal and visit the Locktender's House Museum. Rides on a mule-drawn canal boat are available in season, and you can also make reservations for a cruise that includes the experience of being lowered on a lock of the Lehigh Canal. Open from dawn to dusk, Hugh Moore Park has picnic tables, grills, and biking and hiking trails, including a three-and-a-half-mile paved bike path. Canoes and paddleboats are available for rent at the canal boat boarding area.

In addition to its emphasis on canals and crayons, Easton is an appealing city. On first sight, the area around Centre Square looks like a picture-perfect small city, the kind illustrated in reading and social studies textbooks of the 1950s and 1960s. The square is highlighted by a large Civil War monument and ringed by solid-looking masonry buildings. The buildings house a reassuring range of businesses; although there are antique shops and galleries, this seems to be a city that has avoided both decay and boutique overload.

Just across the river from Easton is **Phillipsburg**, a city on the edge of New Jersey, a name on countless Route 22 signs, the long-ago terminus of the Morris Canal. Founded before Easton, Phillipsburg never came to dominate its region as Easton did. When you drive along Phillipsburg's long Main Street, the city seems less formal than Easton in its layout, lacking a major central area, but rich in nineteenth-century architecture. There is ample parking at meters along Main Street, and Phillipsburg is definitely worth a stop if you are interested in old houses, old cities, and the economic history that led to their construction. There were a lot of factories and jobs in Phillipsburg once, and the town's architecture and layout reflect that past. Several historical markers along Main Street provide a context for the buildings. There are handsome rowhouses, and even a brownstone, complete with historical signs. Detailed wood trim on a corner building and the precision of a law firm's restored green-and-white building add to the charm of these blocks. Close to the river, several buildings, not yet fixed up, are intriguing. One, with a massive brick foundation, rises from the curve of the street. The old stone buildings near the former railroad station are especially appealing.

Food

In Easton, you can find a variety of restaurants, specialty food shops, and takeout food stores on and near Centre Square. You can get everything from doughnuts and ice cream to pizza, Chinese food, and steak; there is even a McDonald's Express right at Two Rivers Landing. If you'd rather stop for a meal before or after your visit to Easton, there's a family-friendly **Cracker Barrel Country Store** off Exit 15 of Route 78, east of Phillipsburg (6 Frontage Drive, Clinton, 908-713-9205).

Chapter Eighteen

Frenchtown/Stockton/Lambertville: Year-Round Delight

The stretch of central New Jersey along the Delaware River is one of my favorite places. Maybe that's because it's just far enough from my home to make a good but not overwhelming day trip, a perfect distance and direction for a trip straight out on Route 78 followed by a scenic diagonal meander down one of the triple-digit roads. (Happily, it's a convenient trip from most other parts of the state, too.) It's discovered enough—I hate to say touristy—to provide varied shopping and browsing in towns like Lambertville and Frenchtown, but not yet boringly standardized in its offerings. It has a high concentration of good restaurants in several towns and several price levels, and it's widely known for being pretty— Pennsylvania's more famous Bucks County is just across the river, after all. Although the surrounding countryside is accented by beautiful rolling hills, the roads that run parallel to the river are flat enough for easy bike riding, and the Delaware River itself invites canoeing, kayaking, and rafting. There's lots of open space, but the region is dotted with houses and settlements, as well as a concentration of wineries, many of them open to the public at certain days and times.

If you start at the northern end of this trip, you may find yourself getting off Route 78 at Exit 7, where there is a giant truck stop, with trucks that look even larger as they pull out of the parking lot than they do when you are next to them on the highway. As soon as you leave the area around the exit, the surroundings change. Old houses, cornfields, hayfields, and the town of Bloomsbury, near the exit, are everything a start to a drive in the country should be. Once a mill town, Bloomsbury, on the banks of the Musconetcong River, now looks very peaceful as you drive through it.

If you like to visit wineries, this is where you should take one of your detours and follow the signs to **King's Road Vineyard** (Route 579, Asbury, 908-479-6611; www.kingsroad.com), three miles out of Bloomsbury, up a curving road into the hills. There is some residential development in the fields, but the views are still pretty much unspoiled, and there's a tiny, old cemetery surrounded by a stone wall shortly before the entrance to King's Road. The vineyard is open for tastings and tours at specified times; call for hours and days.

It's easy to get lost as you wind your way north and west from Bloomsbury, but eventually most roads will lead to the Delaware River. If you want to continue your winery tour, you are not far from **Alba Vineyards** (269 Route 627, Finesville, 908-995-7800), which is also open to the public several days a week. A barn built in 1805 houses the winery and tasting room, as well as the Musconetcong Art Gallery, which displays the work of local artists. Concerts are also held at Alba Vineyards: in winter, they take place in the gallery, and in summer they take place under the grape arbor outside the barn.

If you would like to keep exploring, follow signs to Riegelsville, then follow the narrow old road right along the river. The road, with old houses built close to the bluff on one side, has a forgotten feel; the patchy pavement parallels overgrown railroad tracks, but the scenery is spectacular. Riegelsville is tucked away on the river, and a small bridge leads to Pennsylvania. It does not have the recently-fixed-up look of the towns farther south, but it's very appealing all the same.

From Riegelsville, the road turns away from the river. Then there's a sign for **Milford** that sends you to Old River Road, which is also Route 627, past more narrow houses, old tracks, and industrial buildings. Milford is something of a surprise. In the early 1800s, the town had three mills and a ferry; ferry service stopped in 1842, and now a bridge connects Milford to Pennsylvania. Many of the houses are built close together near the river, and sharp angles in the narrow road make it seem as though you are driving in an English village with streets laid out well before the automobile age. Quiet and out-of-the-way as it may seem, Milford has an active downtown, with a liquor store, beautiful stone bank, stationery shop, hair salon, and more. In addition, Milford is the home of a well-regarded restaurant, the **Milford Oyster House** (17 Bridge Street, 908-995-9411). It features seafood and homemade desserts and is open for dinner Wednesday through Sunday.

Going south from Milford on 627, the bluff above the river is still high, but not quite as steep. Every now and then, a road cuts through the hill, connecting the riverbank with the outside world, and the wider roads on the other side of the hill. Eventually, River Road reaches Frenchtown; you realize you are on the outskirts of someplace fairly substantial because there are more houses close together. At first they look quite uniform, like workers' housing, although some have imaginative color schemes, but closer to downtown there are more elaborate houses.

Frenchtown is smaller than Lambertville, but its Bridge Street is full of intriguing stores and restaurants, and there is a little spillover to Race Street and neighboring areas. Before the Revolutionary War, a ferry crossed the Delaware River from Frenchtown, and there were mills in the area. Frenchtown was a mill and industrial town through the middle of the twentieth century; grain was shipped via the Delaware and Raritan Canal and then via the Delaware-Belvidere Railroad; other industry included making wagon wheels, peach baskets, and furniture. Frenchtown prospered throughout the nineteenth century, and it's that period that shaped its architecture; it's full of houses in a variety of styles, from simple to ornate.

Many of the shops focus on home decorating and antiques. A number of them are especially fun to peek into, including **WoodsEdge Antiques** (36 Bridge Street, 908-996-7185), a simple, elegant store that sells equally elegant American antiques, including folk art and quilts. At **10 Bridge Street,** in a wonderful Italianate building that once housed a bed-and-breakfast, there are several interesting shops, such as the Studio, Civilian, and Fluxus, selling clothing, gifts, and decorative accessories. The **Chisel and Quill Studio** (4 Race Street, 908-996-0591) is a woodcarving, painting, and sign shop that's also worth a look.

Food possibilities are almost as varied as shopping options. The **Frenchtown Inn** (7 Bridge Street, 908-996-3300), known for delicious contemporary American and French food, provides a gracious setting for dinner. It's also a fine place to have lunch in the same gracious setting but at a more casual time of day. The **Race Street Café** (Race Street, 908-996-3179), featuring interesting salads and eclectic entrées, is also a popular lunch and dinner destination. Last time I was in Frenchtown, I ate lunch by myself at the **Bridge Café** (8 Bridge Street, 908-996-6040). It was a beautiful weekday in late October, and the informal restaurant, which overlooks the river, was more than half full, pretty busy for a weekday in a quiet, small town. In addition to enjoying the food, I enjoyed watching the other people, about half of whom looked surprised to find themselves in such a pretty place in New Jersey.

Delaware and Raritan Canal State Park

The defining feature of this stretch of the Delaware Valley, in addition to the scenery and towns themselves, is the narrow seventy-mile-long park that runs along the river and the Delaware and Raritan Feeder Canal. Originally, the feeder canal was intended to bring water to the main Delaware and Raritan Canal, but later it was also used for canal boats and barges. The growth of railroads made both the main and the feeder canal less useful; the canal's last profitable year was 1892, but it stayed in operation until 1932. The state took it over, and in 1972 the canal and its structures were added to the National Register of Historic Places. Sixty miles of the canal became a state park in 1974. The section from Bull's Island to Frenchtown was added in the 1980s, and the trail system became a

National Recreation Trail in 1992. It is deservedly popular with walkers and bicycle riders.

There are fishing-access and boat-launch points off Route 29 from Frenchtown south. Fishing is permitted in both the river and canal, subject to Division of Fish, Game, and Wildlife rules. Trout are stocked in parts of the canal, and bass, sunfish, perch, and pickerel are available year-round, according to the park brochure. Canoes, kayaks, and other small boats are permitted on the canal, and you have to portage at the locks and at some of the bridges. Only electric motors are allowed on the canal, but there are no motor restrictions on the river.

Frenchtown is a good place to park if you'd like to walk or bike along the feeder canal trail; there's a parking lot off Bridge Street. Another good place to park and explore is **Bull's Island Natural Area**, about ten miles south of Frenchtown. Bull's Island has a picnic area, a park office (609-397-2949), and a campground. It also is the site of a pedestrian bridge that crosses the river to Pennsylvania. Although it's perfectly possible and very enjoyable to walk across the other bridges in the area, there's something especially appealing about this bridge, which is quite formal looking, just like a traditional vehicle bridge. It has a concrete walkway, cables suspended between tall vertical posts, and the profile of a real bridge. People of all ages look particularly cheerful as they stroll across.

Just north of Stockton, **Prallsville Mills Historic District of the Delaware and Raritan Canal State Park** is another point of special interest. It is a nineteenth-century mill complex that includes a sawmill, a gristmill, and a linseed oil mill. Historic significance aside, it's very pretty. Although it is part of the park, it is operated by the Delaware River Mill Society (609-397-3586). Concerts, art exhibits, and other programs—even weddings—take place here.

From Frenchtown, it's eleven miles to Stockton and fourteen to Lambertville. Going south, as soon as you pass the Prallsville Mills complex, you are in **Stockton**, known, among other things, for the **Stockton Inn** (1 Main Street, 609-397-1250), whose wishing well figured in a Rodgers and Hart song. The inn building dates to the 1700s, and even if you don't stay there overnight or eat there, you can see the wishing well. The business street that leads to the river is considerably shorter than Frenchtown's Bridge Street, with several restaurants and shops and some very nice houses. **Atrio Café** (515 Bridge Street, 609-397-0042) serves creative American food. **Meil's** (Bridge Street, 609-397-8033) serves both traditional American fare and Pennsylvania Dutch specialties.

Bring Your Bike

This section of the Delaware Valley is perfect for bike riding. The feeder canal path is good for family bike riding. Route 29 itself is slightly less scenic, but it does offer some views of the river and has wide shoulders on both sides, good for adults or older children. The roads in the hills just off the river are beautiful and not heavily traveled by cars, but you have to enjoy going up and down hills, and because they are narrow, winding, and sometimes steep, they're probably not a good choice for rides with children.

River Road, the section of Route 627 that runs close to the river north of Milford, with the steep hill rising directly above the road on the inland side, offers the best views of the river, as well as a feeling of extraordinary seclusion. It is paved but very bumpy. The near-cliff makes an almost spooky contrast with the bright, wide-open space on the river side. The road is very narrow—there are places where two cars cannot pass each other, and there are occasional cut-outs in the road where a car can pull over to allow another to pass. This means that nobody travels very fast on River Road, so it lends itself to bike riding as long as you are careful about the bumps.

Once a busy ferry site, then an industrial center, and later New Hope's quiet, undiscovered neighbor, **Lambertville** has been a star for years, as glamorous as, and perhaps a little less trite, than New Hope, attracting crowds of shoppers, antiquers, diners, and browsers. Change keeps coming to Lambertville. It's still a place people go for antiques, but some of the familiar places are gone, and new favorites are bound to appear; for example, the 5 & Dime, once known for its North Union Street store selling mid-twentieth-century toys and collectibles, now does business only on-line. The shop it occupied is now **Generations** (40-42 North Union Street, 609-397-5051), selling furniture and decorative items, not GI Joes. There are so many antique shops in Lambertville that you can't avoid them; the concentration extends far beyond Union and Bridge Streets to the smaller side streets such as Coryell and Church. There are large centers, such as the **People's Store** (corner of Union and Church Streets, 609-397-9808), a forty-dealer coop, and smaller, more specialized shops such as **Lovrinic Antiques** (15 North Union Street, 609-397-8600), with its fine eighteenth- and early-nineteenth-century American and English pieces. Although Main Street isn't as scenic, it does have its share of shops, including **David Rago Antiques** (333 North Main Street, 609-397-9374), which specializes in twentieth-century decorative arts. Tucked away on many of the streets are dozens of other antique sellers, as well as tempting shops selling books, flowers, and clothes.

And then there are the restaurants, which provide another reason to visit Lambertville. One favorite is **Full Moon** (23 Bridge Street, 609-397-1096). It's a crowded and cozy breakfast/lunch/dinner place, filled with plants and offering menu choices that sound good, may be good for you, and also taste good. **Lambertville Station** (11 Bridge Street, 609-397-8300) is fun for children, because it's in a restored Victorian railroad station. It serves American food and has a children's menu. It's open daily and is right on the canal. As you stroll along Church Street, one of the prettiest of the side streets off Union Street, you will come across the **Church Street Bistro** (11½ Church Street, 609-397-4383). It serves French country food in a tucked-away setting. For something seemingly quite removed from the Delaware River, there's the highly regarded **Ota-Ya Japanese Restaurant** (21 Ferry Street, 609-397-9228), with an extensive menu featuring teriyaki, sukiyaki, tempura, sushi, and sashimi. A romantic way to end a day in Lambertville is to have dinner (reservations recommended) at **Anton's at the Swan** (43 South Main Street, 609-397-1960). It serves creative American food in a building that dates to 1879.

Lambertville extends for blocks north and south, but only for a few blocks east from the river; like the state park that runs along the river, the town is linear. If you turn off Main Street (Route 29) and cut west on Perry Street or one of the other streets toward the northern end of town, then drive down Union Street, you will see a wonderful array of houses, too, not just shops. (Don't wait until you reach Bridge Street to park; spots on Union Street are metered, and although empty spots are easy to find during the week, they are at a premium on weekends.) There are little row houses that must once have been home to mill and factory workers; there are elaborate Victorians, and elegant hybrids. Almost all are perfectly maintained or restored, with carefully chosen color schemes and pretty gardens. Even if your focus is not on shopping, Lambertville is a great place to walk and admire buildings. It's almost a surprise to realize that one of the buildings on Main Street is the Lambertville Public School; it's a reminder that this is a real place, not a re-created village fantasy.

Lambertville was the hometown of James Wilson Marshall, who discovered gold at Sutter's Mill in California, sparking the 1849 gold rush. His boyhood home, built in 1816, is now a museum operated by the Lambertville Historical Society (62 Bridge Street, 609-397-0770).

If your main goal is to walk around Lambertville and enjoy the sights, it doesn't matter when you go. But if you want to go shopping or choose your Lambertville meal from the full range of restaurants, don't go too early in the day, and avoid Mondays and possibly

Tuesdays, when many businesses are closed. While some shops are open daily, others are on more limited schedules, and many do not open until late morning or early afternoon.

If you missed the wineries at the northern end of this trip, there's one you can visit on your way out of Lambertville via Route 202. **Unionville Vineyards** (9 Rocktown Road, Ringoes, 908-788-0400; www.unionvillevineyards.com) isn't far from Route 202 as you drive north; it is on an old farm that started as an orchard, became a dairy farm, and then made the transition to grapes. The exit, for Wertsville Road and the Ringoes business district, is well marked, and there's a sign for the vineyard. It is open for tours and tastings; call for hours.

Raven Rock and **Rosemont** are two tiny settlements that in their way epitomize the appeal of this area. Raven Rock is just a few old, narrow, stone buildings built up against the hillside on one side of Route 29, near Bull's Island. Rosemont, which has lovely houses and wide views of the hills and valleys around it, is perched on a ridge above Route 29; there's a signpost for it on Route 519, the road that goes uphill directly opposite the entrance to the Bull's Island parking lot. It's the kind of place that makes you just want to stand in the sunshine and admire the world around you.

Chapter Nineteen

Trenton to Titusville: Good Weather, Bad Weather, Past, and Present

This is the Delaware Valley trip for families. It's not that the State House and State Museum aren't interesting for adults, or that Washington Crossing State Park isn't a pretty state park, or that a family couldn't have a wonderful time biking or strolling along the old Delaware and Raritan feeder canal near Stockton, but the attractions on the Trenton–Titusville stretch of riverbank are especially well suited to children of varying ages. What elementary-school kid doesn't know about Washington's midnight boat ride across the Delaware to Trenton? What third-grader wouldn't like to go to a professional baseball game, albeit a minor-league one? And who doesn't enjoy a trip to a working farm with a nostalgic note of history to set it apart from the others?

Even the most avid booster of New Jersey will probably admit that Trenton isn't one of the region's great state capitals. Trenton doesn't have the intimate charm of Vermont's Montpelier, or the multifaceted dazzle of Boston. All the same, every state capital has its living lessons in government, its special historic sites, and its own unique reasons to be visited, and Trenton is no exception. It has lots of history, and a fair share of historic buildings.

Where to start? The **New Jersey State Museum** (205 West State Street, Trenton, 609-292-6464) is one possibility. Admission is free and it's indoors, so weather is never a factor—unless it's just too nice a day to spend indoors, which is a good problem to have when you have planned a family excursion. The State Museum is one of those big, multipurpose places that you can walk through quickly or spend some time studying in more detail. It focuses on both art and nature, with some history thrown in. Exhibits include decorative arts, paintings, Native American artifacts, archaeological items, and the first dinosaur excavated in America. The planetarium adjacent to the museum presents shows on weekends for the public and for school groups during the week. The museum is closed Sundays and public holidays.

Another weather-neutral site, but one with more limited visiting hours, is the **State House** (Tour Office, West State Street, 609-633-2709). It is the second-oldest state capitol building in continuous use. Tours are free and give you a chance to see the Senate and Assembly chambers, caucus rooms, and the Governor's Reception Room, although not the governor in person. The tours, which last about an hour, are offered on Tuesday, Wednesday, and Friday from 10 AM to 3 PM and on Saturday from noon to 3 PM; tours are also available Monday through Saturday in July and August. You can also tour the **State House Annex**. One of the highlights of the hour-long tour is the stained-glass skylight, which was made at Wheaton Village in Millville and includes representations of various cultural and geographical New Jersey icons. Nearby, in the Department of State buildings, battle flags used by New Jersey battalions and regiments during the Civil War are on display in a specially designed and lighted gallery; it is open daily from 9 AM to 5 PM and admission is free.

Not far from the state building complex are several nongovernmental monuments and sites. The recently restored **Old Barracks Museum** (Barrack Street, 609-396-1776; www.barracks.org) is one of those pre–Revolutionary War buildings we have a tendency to take for granted in this part of the country. Built in 1758, it was one of several constructed in New Jersey to shelter troops during the French and Indian Wars, and it accommodated 300 soldiers in 22 barracks rooms. It served as an American military hospital during the Revolutionary War, as well as housing Hessian and British prisoners of war and Continental soldiers at various times. Among the rooms you can see are the surgeon's office and a hospital room. The Old Barracks Museum has an active interpretive program, with exhibits specially geared to school groups and school-age visitors. It is open from 10 AM to 5 PM daily except for Thanksgiving, Christmas Eve, Christmas, New Year's Day, and Easter.

Not far from the central Trenton attractions is one of the legendary pizza destinations of New Jersey, **DeLorenzo's Tomato Pies** (530 Hudson Street, 609-695-9534).

It is easy to forget, amid the institutional architecture and somewhat shabby bustle of downtown, that Trenton is a place with a Revolutionary War pedigree—in fact, there were two Battles of Trenton. The first followed Washington's famous December 25 crossing of the Delaware. His surprise attack on the Hessian soldiers serving the British had been planned for 5 AM on December 26, 1776, when the Hessians would supposedly still be asleep following Christmas night festivities, but the American troops did not arrive in Trenton until several hours later, so they faced a more wide-awake enemy. Despite this, the Americans were able to overpower the guards, capture artillery, and capture nearly 1,000 Hessians. The battle, relatively bloodless as it was, gave the Americans a psychological boost and was considered a decisive point in the war. The Americans returned to the Pennsylvania side of the river later in the day, then crossed back to the New Jersey side a few days later. The British sent several thousand troops to stop the Americans from continuing on their way in New Jersey; General Cornwallis and his men arrived on January 2, 1777, and attacked the Americans, who were camped at Assunpink Creek. The Americans were able to repel the late-day attack, but Washington reportedly believed they would not be able to hold off a more concerted attack, and after consulting with his officers led the Americans to Princeton via a back road. The cold had frozen the muddy road enough to make it possible to transport artillery relatively efficiently. Washington and his army left quietly at night, leaving behind burning campfires and a few men, so the British would not realize that the large part of their quarry had escaped. The Americans went on to overpower the British at Princeton on January 3.

The 155-foot-tall **Trenton Battle Monument** (intersection of Warren and Broad Streets and Brunswick, Pennington, and Princeton Avenues), dedicated in 1893, marks the spot where the Americans opened fire at the first Battle of Trenton. There is a viewing platform, reachable by elevator; the monument is staffed part-time by rangers from Washington Crossing State Park (609-737-0623); call for open days and hours.

An even older vestige of Trenton's past is the **William Trent House** (15 Market Street, 609-689-3027). Built in 1719, it is the oldest surviving building in the city. Originally a summer estate, it is now city property and is furnished primarily with items from the late seventeenth and early eighteenth centuries. The Trent House is open daily from 12:30 PM to 4 PM.

Trenton is more than a place to observe government and dip into distant history. It also has a long and varied past as an industrial center. Before I ever set foot in Trenton, I used to pass the famous "Trenton Makes, the World Takes" sign when I traveled back and forth between Philadelphia, where I attended graduate school, and my parents' home in New York. I later learned that Trenton indeed made many things. John A. Roebling of Brooklyn Bridge fame had a wire mill here, where the steel cable that was used in the Brooklyn Bridge was manufactured. Lenox Pottery was based in Trenton, and many other types of pottery were made there as well. Once, Trenton was a center of the cigar-making trade. It was also an active port. There are still sections of Trenton that bustle with activity other than the public business of government that is now the city's economic mainstay.

One of the most distinctive is **Chambersburg**, the traditionally Italian neighborhood south of Route 1. Like Newark's Ironbound, it has a low-rise, gently weathered look and is known for its restaurants. Among the popular Italian eateries in the area are **Baldassari's Roebling Pub** (801 South Clinton Avenue, 609-396-9411); **Diamond's** (112 Kent Street, 609-393-1000); **Marsilio's** (541 Roebling Avenue, 609-695-1916); and **Sal De Forte's** (200 Fulton Street, 609-396-6856).

On the southern edge of the city, along the Delaware, **Mercer County Waterfront Park Stadium** is a lively place during the baseball season, when the Trenton Thunder (the AA Eastern League, Northern Division affiliate of the Boston Red Sox) play at Samuel J. Plumeri Sr. Field (1 Thunder Road, off Route 29, 609-394-3300; 609-394-8236; www.trentonthunder.com). The stadium, built in 1994, seats more than 6,600 people, and the team plays from April through early September. Nearby, the vast restaurant **Katmandu** (Waterfront Park, 609-393-7300) is a year-round place to go for entertainment, food, and drink. Housed in the former Cooper Iron Works building, it has a noticeably contemporary air, thanks in part to its lively tropical decorating theme. Katmandu's appeal combines several worlds: there's a children's menu, a separate bar, deejay and dancing at night, and outdoor dining when the weather permits. And it's close enough to the state office complexes to be a popular weekday lunchtime destination, too.

Washington Crossing State Park

Washington Crossing State Park (355 Washington Crossing-Pennington Road, off Route 29, Titusville, 609-737-0623), a few miles north of Trenton, is where the Continental soldiers crossed the Delaware River from Pennsylvania early on the morning of December 26. After arriving at what was then known as Johnson's Ferry, they began their short, cold march to the city. Washington Crossing is one of those pretty state parks that is both historic and recreational; even if nothing famous had happened here, its nearly one thousand acres would be a lovely place for a walk or a picnic. There are nature trails; you can ride a horse or a bicycle, and, if there is enough snow, go cross-country skiing or snowshoeing. The park is also known for its wildlife habitat; migrating birds rest and nest in its stream and ravine, and some species spend the winter in the park, so it's a good place for bird-watching in any season. Fishing is permitted. In summer, there's a music and drama festival in the park's open-air theater (609-737-1826).

The events of 1776 do, of course, play a major role in shaping the atmosphere of the park. Perhaps its best-known special event is the Christmas Day reenactment of the river crossing. But even if you choose another day for your trip, there's no lack of history to catch up on. The Johnson Ferry House, an eighteenth-century former farmhouse and tavern, was owned by Garret Johnson, who farmed nearly 500 acres and operated a ferry service across the Delaware. Washington and his officers may have spent some time here on Christmas night. Local period pieces in the keeping room, bedchamber, and textile room are similar to the furniture used by the Johnsons from 1740 to 1770. There is also an eighteenth-century kitchen garden and an orchard of period fruit trees. The house is open Wednesday through Sunday, year-round, and there are living history demonstrations on weekends. For schedules and other information call 609-737-2515. Another of the park's historic homes is the Nelson House (609-737-1783), open in summer and operated by the Washington Crossing Association of New Jersey. The Swan Historical Foundation Collection (609-737-9303) at the Visitor Center contains nearly 900 Revolutionary-era artifacts used by soldiers of both sides. It is open Wednesday through Sunday year-round.

Living History

Visiting Washington Crossing State Park is one way to keep the past alive. Another way, and one that also is especially fun for children, is to visit the **Howell Living History Farm** (101 Hunter Road,

Titusville, 609-737-3299). Once you turn off Route 29 and take the side road to the farm, you may feel that you have traveled back a century. The farm, operated by the Mercer County Park Commission since 1984, was worked for more than 250 years and has been restored to the way it would have looked in the earliest years of the twentieth century. On weekend there are organized activities—including popular perennials such as sheepshearing, haying, maple sugaring, and hayrides. Even when there are no special activities, the self-guided tour of the farm buildings and grounds is very rewarding, peaceful for adults and enlightening for children. Among the sights on the tour are the beehives, fields, including a pasture complete with grazing animals, a sheep barn, a chicken house, the main barn, an apple orchard, an icehouse, and the farmhouse itself.

Howell Living History Farm is open from late January through November, Tuesday through Saturday; it is also open on Sundays from April through November. Call for hours and special events.

Fiddler's Creek Farm (Hunter Road, Titusville, 609-737-0685) is nearby; it specializes in curing and smoking pork and poultry. Eating the very tasty products may not be quite what you or your children will want to do right after seeing the cute pigs and chickens at Howell Living History Farm, but it's definitely worth a stop, and you will enjoy the treats later. Fiddler's Creek is open Monday through Friday from 8 AM to 5 PM.

Chapter Twenty

Burlington and Points South: History and Trees

Route 541 between the Turnpike or I-295 and Burlington is heavily developed with strip malls (not to mention the Burlington Center Mall) and fast-food stops. That makes your arrival in Burlington itself all the more a treat. **Burlington**, on the Delaware River, is old and interesting, New Jersey's own little Colonial Williamsburg. It was settled by Quakers in the late 1600s and thrived as a port and as the capital of West New Jersey. When East and West New Jersey were united in 1702 it served as co-capital, with Perth Amboy. The historic district includes a number of streets around the center of the town that are lined with centuries-old buildings. You should be able to find a parking spot either on High Street or in the large parking lot near the river. If you are in the riverside parking lot, walk past Café Gallery to High Street. You will be facing a row of lovely old brick buildings, including Temple B'nai Israel. The building, originally a private home, dates back to 1801. Temple B'nai Israel, formed in 1907 and one of the oldest congregations in southern New Jersey, purchased it in 1916.

The brick sidewalks and three-story brick structures of the 200 block of High Street set the mood quickly. Walk away from the river and turn onto West Union Street or stop at the corner to admire the display of old soda bottles and ice-cream makers in the window of Ummm Ice Cream Parlor on High Street. You may also want to take an introductory peek at the map of Historic Burlington that is posted in the little park at the corner of West Union and High Streets. West Union Street is tree-lined; the buildings are almost uniformly old and beautifully maintained. You will pass the 1864 brownstone housing the **Library Company of Burlington** (23 West Union Street, 609-386-1273), chartered by King George in 1757. The library's interior is as charming as its exterior, with a large Palladian window across the back wall providing both light and atmosphere. Lush gardens are visible between and behind many of the houses on this block, making the walk a special treat at times of year when greenery and flowers add to the scenery.

Turn toward the river at Wood Street for more beautiful houses. The **Revell House**, built in 1684, is a little brick building that was home to Thomas Revell, who was the first clerk of the Burlington Court and later served on the West Jersey Council. The elaborate brick house at the riverfront is called "**The Cottage.**" Built in 1872, it was the home of a young Civil War officer who later served as minister to Spain. If you make a left on Riverbank you will get to the corner of Talbot Street, where you can see the **Shippen House**. Peggy Shippen, who summered at the house, married Benedict Arnold. If you simply reverse your route along Wood Street from the river, just beyond West Union Street you will come to the house where the family of General Ulysses S. Grant spent the last days of the Civil War. Beyond that are the graveyards of the **Friends' Meeting House** and **St. Mary's Church**. Continuing to the corner of Wood and Broad Streets will take you to **Old St. Mary's**, a simple stucco building dating from 1702, and identified as the "mother parish of New Jersey." New St. Mary's is just down Broad Street. Designed by Richard Upton and completed in 1854, this elegant brownstone church was one of the first cruciform buildings in America, and the churchyard is very peaceful and beautiful. Burlington is known for having active railroad tracks still running down Broad Street; the trains go at a walking pace for safety reasons. You may have the odd experience of standing with your back to an early eighteenth-century church while you watch a short freight train roll by, and feel that you still have many decades to go before you catch up with the twenty-first century. To return to High Street, either walk along Broad Street or, to maintain the mood of tranquility a bit longer, go back to Wood Street and walk through the Friends' cemetery or along Smith's Alley to High Street.

If you would like to see more, the **Burlington County Historical Society** (457 High Street, 609-386-4773) operates several houses as museums in the 400 block of High Street; call for hours. One of these was the birthplace of James Fenimore Cooper; another was the home of Captain James Lawrence, a War of 1812 naval officer remembered for the phrase "Don't give up the ship."

Mount Holly doesn't have the Delaware River as a backdrop, as Burlington does, but, as the county seat, it has its share of historic buildings. The imposing brick houses along the northern stretch of High Street are a signal to think about parking. I was lucky enough to get a spot right on High Street in front of the historic Burlington County Jail, designed by Robert Mills in 1808. It was the first fireproof building in the United States and remained in use as a prison until 1965; it is now a museum. This is a good starting spot for a small walking tour. The old Burlington County Courthouse is just down the street. This lovely white-painted brick building, dating from 1796, has an especially graceful cupola. If you continue to Garden Street and make a left, you will pass the Friends' Meeting House and graveyard. The first Meeting House was built in 1716; the present building dates from 1775, and the British used it as a commissary in 1778.

A stroll down Buttonwood Street, left off Garden, will take you past a range of old houses; the local chapter of the Daughters of the American Revolution has placed markers on some houses, identifying dates of construction and original owners. The corner of Buttonwood and Broad is especially attractive, and there are several houses sporting colorful paint and very inviting porches on the block of Broad Street that leads back to High Street. At the corner of High and Broad you will have a view of the half-dozen or so brick mansions that lie north of the courthouse. Walk along High Street toward Ridgeway and you will see three more striking houses across the street. At Ridgeway Street there is a picture-perfect Queen Anne–style brick house whose DAR marker says it was built in 1880.

If you decide to take a longer walk, or find a second parking space, you can see some of Mount Holly's oldest buildings, which are down the hill from Garden Street. Off High Street at 35 Brainerd Street is **Brainerd School**, founded in 1759 and used as a school until 1848. The **John Woolman Memorial** (99 Branch Street, 609-267-3226) is named for a local Quaker who was an early antislavery advocate; he built this house for his daughter in 1771. Beyond the High Street/Mill Street commercial district, on Park Drive in Mount Holly Park, is the 1712 **Shinn Curtis Log Cabin**. Another house had been built around the cabin, which was rediscovered in 1967 when the newer house was demolished to make way for a road-widening project. The cabin was moved from its original location and is now operated by the **Mount Holly Historical Society** (609-267-8844).

Food

Ummm Ice Cream Parlor (236 High Street, 609-387-9786), tempting Burlington passersby "since 1982" according to its window sign, opens at noon seven days a week. Not only does it have a nostalgic window display, it also has old-fashioned green tables with bentwood chairs, as well as a high counter just right for enjoying a sundae. If you can't have dessert because you haven't eaten yet, **Café Gallery** (219 High Street, Burlington, 609-386-6150) can solve that problem. This French restaurant, which is also an art gallery, is open Monday through Saturday for lunch and dinner and for brunch on

Sunday. Route 541 between Burlington and Mount Holly is densely packed with fast-food and family-style restaurants. Downtown Mount Holly offers a number of eating options, too. These include the eclectic **C. J. Muffins** (64 High Street, Mount Holly, 609-267-0025) and the atmosphere-rich **Robin's Nest** (2 Washington Street, Mount Holly, 609-261-6149). It is open daily for lunch and Wednesday through Sunday for dinner.

More Towns and Trees

A zigzag trip from Burlington to Haddonfield on a series of state and county roads takes you through classic—and not always pre-possessing—New Jersey industrial scenery. It also gives you tantalizing glimpses of the Delaware River and ample opportunity to drive or stroll through pretty towns and enjoy lovely tree-arched streets and roads. Once you have explored Burlington in as much detail as you wish, you can start your drive by taking High Street away from the river. Follow the signs to Route 130 South and then to Beverly Road, which is Route 543 South. After you go through a deep cut-stone underpass, you'll pass some nice nineteenth-century houses. Trees arch over the road.

The first town you go through, Beverly, is old, quiet, and tree-lined. There are great views of river from the narrow streets off Beverly Road; some of these streets are dead-end and hard to turn around on, but the effort is worth it for closer looks at the views. Once you pass the center of town the road becomes less attractive, with more open space and fewer interesting houses. Incidentally, although the road is still 543, its name changes to Warren Street in Beverly and becomes Burlington Avenue once you get to Delanco. You can drive right along the river in Delanco by turning right on Lilac Lane and then left on Delaware Avenue. The river is magnificent here, and the houses facing it are elegant. Note, however, that stopping and standing are forbidden along this street. Take Willow Street back to 543, which becomes Pavilion Avenue when you cross the Rancocas Creek bridge into Riverside. As you bear right, it becomes St. Mihiel Drive, flat, bleak, and industrial, with railroad tracks on one side and miscellaneous structures and empty lots on the other—interesting, in a way, because it is what people who don't know New Jersey think the whole state looks like. And then you get to Riverton, and everything changes.

The street is now Broad Street, the trees are healthy again, and the houses are beautiful. Take Main Street toward the river, following signs for the historic area. You can circle around town, to the river, along Bank Avenue, away from the river on Cinnaminson or Garfield, then left on East Broad Street, and then south on Route 603, which at this point is called Riverton Road. Or you can park along one of the pretty streets and wander, getting a closer look at the beautifully maintained houses in varied styles. Lippincott Street and Carriage House Lane are rewarding, as are the numbered streets that run parallel to the river. Once you are back in your car, you will find that Riverton Road, on the far side of Broad Street, is also beautiful. In addition to lovely tree-lined stretches, there are impressive newer residential areas as you approach Moorestown. Go left briefly on Bridgeboro Road and then right on Westover, Golfview, and Stanwick, and you will get to East Main Street, Moorestown. If you go straight instead of taking the left on Bridgeboro, you will be on Chaster Road, which is lined with big houses and old trees and takes you to approximately the midpoint of Main Street. Whichever route you choose, the gently aged brick buildings and historic aura of Moorestown are worth the trip. As you drive west through Moorestown, Main Street becomes Kings Highway (Route 41). If you want to continue your trip, you will find there is nothing picturesque about this stretch of road except its name, but it does lead to **Haddonfield**, whose historic downtown is gracious, with tree-lined streets and tempting stores that quickly make you forget Kings Highway.

This all sounds great for grownups who like to drive around, look at scenery, and go for quiet walks. What if it rains? What if this is a family trip? Two very child-friendly possibilities present themselves at the southern end of this trip; both charge admission.

The **Garden State Discovery Museum** (16 North Springdale Road, Cherry Hill, 856-424-1233) offers fifteen hands-on exhibits geared toward children aged two through ten. Visitors can climb a rock wall, bandage a wounded teddy-bear, "shop" at the farm stand and "cook" at the Discovery Diner, and more. There is also a gift shop and a snack area. The Discovery Museum is open Tuesday through Sunday. The **New Jersey State Aquarium** (1 Riverview Drive, Camden, 856-365-3300) houses local and tropical species of sea creatures. Among its exhibits are a shark tank, a penguin tank, an outdoor seal pool, and a 760,000-gallon open ocean tank, as well as interactive exhibits. The aquarium is open daily. The terrace overlooking the Delaware River is an added attraction, though not for a rainy day.

More Food

Assuming you have made the trip south, either for scenery and pretty towns or for children's activities, you may be in the mood for a meal without having to return to Burlington or Mount Holly. There is something for everyone in Camden County. Kings Highway has a fair share of chain restaurants, including an **Outback Steakhouse** (230 Lake Drive East, or Route 38, Cherry Hill, 856-482-1350). If you would prefer local flavor, **Ponzio's** (7 Route 70, Cherry Hill, 856-428-4808) is one of those diners everyone in the area knows about. It has been in business since 1964 and is, as you would expect, open daily. **La Campagne** (312 Kresson Road, Cherry Hill, 856-429-7647) is perhaps even more widely known—same town, different style. It is a French restaurant with a reputation for excellent food. Housed in a building that dates from the 1830s, it is open Tuesday through Friday for lunch, Tuesday through Saturday for dinner, and Sunday for brunch. **Al Khimah** (Pine Tree Plaza, 1426 East Marlton Pike, or Route 70, Cherry Hill, 856-427-0888) offers something a bit different—Moroccan food, belly dancers on Friday and Saturday nights, and a children's menu. It is open daily from 11 AM to 11 PM.

Chapter Twenty-one

Sandy Hook and the Bayshore

There's something festive and exciting about getting off the southbound Garden State Parkway at exit 117 and seeing Keansburg's light-blue water tower that welcomes one and all to the Bayshore. The sky seems wider than in it does in the northern inland counties, the land definitely looks flatter (unexpected, since it is the highest part of the Shore), and even now there's something hauntingly 1940s about some of the stretch of small commercial buildings along Route 36, especially in the Port Monmouth/Leonardo area. The obvious attraction is that in summer, Sandy Hook, New Jersey's own section of Gateway National Recreation Area, is an amazingly close beach spot for residents of northern New Jersey. Yes, it gets very crowded; sometimes the parking lots close surprisingly early on weekend mornings because they are filled to capacity. But the beaches are beautiful, wide and sandy and with those views of the New York skyline and the bridges that remind you what a spectacular place New Jersey is for viewing the wonders of the city.

As you approach the Bayshore, you have to be alert to all the intriguing little signs that will tempt you off Route 36. This stretch of road lends itself to wandering and exploring without a major goal in mind, but it also offers a number of specific attractions. For example, if you are interested in a drive and an unfamiliar destination rather than a day at the beach, follow the signs for Bayshore Waterfront Park and the Belford Seafood Co-op. The **Belford Seafood Co-op** (901 Port Monmouth Road, Belford, 732-787-6509) is at the end of the road, very industrial-looking, with buildings painted pale green. It is not a quaint Maine fishing village, but a working seafood terminal, with a retail seafood shop and restaurant called the Catch of the Day, where you can enjoy very fresh seafood both indoors and out. Both are open seven days a week.

Just off the road that leads to the Seafood Co-op is **Bayshore Waterfront Park**, part of the Monmouth County Park System and worth a stop. From the park's parking lot, you can see a rather tall old white house with a mansard roof and little third-floor dormers; it's not hard to imagine smugglers, pirates, or spies of past centuries walking along the road in front of that house. But the real attraction is just beyond the parking lot. As soon as you walk to the sandy top of the little hill—or dune—at the entrance to the beach, you are greeted by the view: the Verrazzano Bridge, the bay, very blue on sunny days, Staten Island, the Manhattan skyline. The day I was there, I also saw two large gray ships anchored off a spit of land in the middle distance. I later learned they were navy ships loading ammunition off the Navy Weapons Station at Earle.

Leonardo State Marina (102 Concord Avenue, Leonardo, 732-291-1333) has a launch ramp and offers daily transient berths as well as seasonal berths and monthly transient berths. In 2000, the fee for a daily transient berth was seventy-five cents a foot for vessels forty feet or less in length and a dollar a foot for vessels longer than forty feet. The daily launch ramp fee was nine dollars.

Going back to the main road from Belford will soon lead you to another jughandle turn, this one for the Atlantic Highlands business district. **Atlantic Highlands** has a nice downtown; it is something of a small town classic, in fact. Restaurants and shops line First Street, the town's main street, which runs perpendicular to the bay. The

Walter Choroszewski

Keeper's house and lighthouse, Sandy Hook

Skipper's Shop (35 First Avenue, 732-872-0367), which sells boat equipment and supplies, fits right in with the mood of the waterfront. If you are hungry, **Memphis Pig Out** (67 First Avenue, 732-291-5533), popular for barbecue, doesn't fit the nautical theme but is worth a visit. It opens at 1 PM on Sundays, but not until 4 PM the rest of the week. For light refreshment from late morning on, you might consider the **CTC Emporium,** 79A First Avenue (732-291-9696). This smoke-free café serves a wide variety of tea and coffee, as well as desserts and gifts.

The key feature of town, of course, is the waterfront, pleasantly bustling even in spring. The full-service marina and launch ramp is run by the **Atlantic Highlands Municipal Marina** (Municipal Harbormaster, 732-291-1670). The adjacent recently refurbished waterfront park, with a promenade, parking (ample off-season), seating areas, and public restrooms, is very appealing. Definitely not a boardwalk, the promenade is urban in style, with black iron railings, boat-shaped planters mounted on the rails, and handsome streetlights. It's a very welcoming place to spend some time looking out at the bay and the masts of the boats. If you turn your back to the bay for a few minutes, you will also get a great view of several large, old houses with turrets and lots of windows for gazing across the park through the forest of masts to the water.

And if you want to spend a few hours on the water, you'll be pleased that a number of half-day fishing boats are based along this waterfront at the end closer to town; rates and departure times are posted. Atlantic Highlands is close to a number of excellent fishing grounds and is home to one of the state's largest fleets of party and charter boats, so you will have plenty of choices.

Views and History

There's no need to wait for summer to visit the Bayshore. Choose any day when the air is clear enough to see a few miles into the distance and the temperatures are comfortable enough for you to enjoy being out of doors. The trip works well from north or south, but I prefer to start from the north. Leaving the waterfront in Atlantic Highlands, make a left to go south along County Route 8, Ocean Boulevard. After driving along several miles of winding road and enjoying peeks at dozens of lovely well-kept houses and gardens on both sides of Ocean Boulevard, you will be at the top of a bluff.

The incredible panorama at **Mount Mitchell Scenic Overlook** is right off Ocean Boulevard just before it rejoins Route 36. With its shaded Japanese-style pillared seating areas and picnic tables set on a grassy area behind the parking lot, it is both restful and dramatic. As one of the designated points of interest along the New Jersey Coastal Heritage Trail, it's nicely annotated, with maps mounted at the edge of the overlook, and informative text along with the mounted maps. The Coastal Heritage Trail, incidentally, was established in 1988 to highlight for visitors and residents the natural and cultural sites along New Jersey's coast; it is divided into five regions: Sandy Hook, Barnegat Bay, Absecon, Cape May, and Delsea.

The view from Mount Mitchell, more than 250 feet above sea level, stretches from New York to Sandy Hook and beyond. It is extraordinary, an eye-catching beginner's lesson in what makes the Bayshore special. I was gratified to see a car with Massachusetts license plates parked at the overlook on a sparkling spring afternoon, and the presumed owner of the car sitting on one of the benches admiring the New Jersey vista.

If you're hungry and want to take a break before doing more exploring, you don't have to go far. Down the road from Mount Mitchell is the **Hofbrauhaus** (301 Ocean Boulevard, Atlantic Highlands, 732-291-0224). As you might expect, its emphasis is on German music (an oom-pah band) and food. It has both a liquor license and a children's menu, so although it is not bargain-priced (adult entrées are in the $17 to $20 range), you could make it part of a family outing as well as a grown-up treat. It opens at noon on Saturdays and Sundays, 4 PM the rest of the week.

When you return to Route 36 heading east, you will be on your way to Sandy Hook. (You will also see signs for what is perhaps the Bayshore's best-known restaurant, the very popular seafood restaurant, Doris and Ed's.) Just before the turn for Sandy Hook, there is a sign for **Twin Lights Historic Site** (Highlands, 732-872-1814), which is home to a rather special lighthouse—a romantic-looking stone structure with two towers. The road that leads to Twin Lights is narrow and steep, and the residential neighborhood around it is very attractive. If you get lost, as I did the first time I tried to find Twin Lights, you may well decide that you have to move to this part of the Bayshore right away and live in one of those houses with a hillside garden and a view of the Bay.

The Twin Lights of the Navesink Light Station, perched on a headland above Raritan Bay, were built by the federal government in 1824, although there was probably a lighthouse on the site as early as the mid-eighteenth century. The first Fresnel lenses to be used in the United States were installed at the Twin Lights in 1841, and the present structure was built in 1862. The two towers are connected by the keeper's quarters and storage areas. Although the Navesink Light Station was decommissioned in 1949, a sixth-order light (the least bright of the six Fresnel lenses) still flashes from the North Tower from dusk to dawn as a symbol and reminder of the site's past importance.

In addition to the two stone towers and a red-brick domestic-style building with the date 1862 prominently displayed below the roof, there is also a brick powerhouse, which contains an exhibit about what makes lighthouses bright. The star attraction is the ten-ton Fresnel lens that once shone from the South Tower. The building's beautifully maintained white-tile interior and wood ceiling add to the historic atmosphere.

After you leave the powerhouse, especially if the weather is good, you may be tempted just to explore the grounds, which include several shingle-covered stands with buttons you can push to hear programs about various Twin Lights and Shore subjects. There's a historic marker for Marconi Tower, where in 1899 Marconi himself installed the antenna mast for the first wireless telegraph installation in the United States; only the concrete foundations for the tower's guywire supports remain now. You may want to peek inside the life-saving station, which was moved to Twin Lights from Spermaceti Cove at Sandy Hook in 1954 and now houses a boat collection. Beyond the Marconi Tower, on the water side of the main building, there are benches for sitting and enjoying the vista. From here, Twin Lights looks like a brownstone fortress.

Inside the main building, a museum contains exhibits about lighthouses and the United State Life Saving Service. There are great pictures of old lighthouses and life-saving stations, as well as fine views of the museum's bay side. You can top off your visit to the museum with a climb up an old-fashioned iron spiral staircase to the top of the North Tower. Back in the lobby, a gift shop sells a nice selection of Dover coloring books with sea themes, books for both children and adults about lighthouses and shore life, and key rings, pens, notepads, and other souvenirs.

Twin Lights is operated by the New Jersey Department of Environmental Protection, Division of Parks and Forestry. A donation is requested for admission to the museum, but there is no set fee. The site is open year-round, with more extensive hours from Memorial Day to Labor Day than during the rest of the year.

Just south of Twin Lights is the turnoff for **Sandy Hook,** the barrier beach peninsula at the northern tip of the Shore. This part of **Gateway National Recreation Area** (732-872-5970; www.nps.gov/gate) is open year-round, and there is no admission fee most of the year; you do have to pay between Memorial Day Weekend and Labor Day. Lifeguards are on duty at the ocean-side beaches from mid-June through Labor Day. Sandy Hook has a lot to offer year-round, however, and although history and vistas are certainly key ingredients, there's really something for everyone here.

The Sandy Hook Visitor Center at Spermaceti Cove is open all year, and hiking trails begin at the Visitor Center. You can pick up brochures at the Visitor Center, check the list of special activities, and spend some time at the detailed life-saving exhibit. When I was there on a beautiful spring Saturday, the featured attractions were a walk on Old Dune Trail, and visits to the Historic House and Officer's Quarters at Fort Hancock. (Incidentally, Sandy Hook, like Bayshore Waterfront Park, is designated as a carry-in/carry-out park. Kiosks at the entrances to the parks are well supplied with bags to make it easy to take picnic trash or other throwaway items back out with you, a nice way to keep the parks cleaner and more attractive.)

Except for designated shorebird nesting areas, the ocean beaches are open for walking, too. Because the area is so flat, it's wonderful for bike riding in the off-season when there isn't too much auto traffic. It can be windy, however, making the ride more challenging than you might expect. Because Sandy Hook is several miles long, you can certainly spend an afternoon bike riding, stopping along the way to picnic and explore historic and natural sites. Because there are so many parking areas, you can also ride short loops, or park midway out Sandy Hook and ride to Fort Hancock. If you'd prefer a more stationary pastime, you can fish at any unguarded beach during daylight hours, or purchase a permit for night fishing at the visitor center.

A large part of the history of Sandy Hook is military and navigational, and whatever brings you to Sandy Hook, you'll notice a lot of structures. In colonial days, Sandy Hook was strategically important because of its position at the entrance to New York Harbor, and the passage through Sandy Hook Channel was treacherous. The dazzlingly white tower of Sandy Hook Lighthouse is probably the most prominent structure around, by virtue of its height, but that is not its only impressive attribute. The brick walls of the lighthouse are enormously thick, to support its height, and the closer you get, the more massive it appears. When Sandy Hook Lighthouse was built in 1764, it was a vital beacon. Now, it is not just the oldest of New Jersey's nineteen lighthouses but the oldest operating lighthouse in the United States. A restoration project was completed in mid-2000, and the lighthouse is open for public tours, primarily on weekend afternoons.

The buff-colored brick buildings clustered around the lighthouse are part of Fort Hancock. A temporary fort was built at Sandy Hook during the War of 1812, and a permanent fort was begun in 1859, although it was never completed. Between 1874 and 1919, the army tested weapons at Sandy Hook, and a number of gun batteries were built in the 1890s. The first thirty-two residential buildings date from about the turn of the twentieth century, and by the 1911 Fort Hancock had a YMCA, library, school, chapel, and other services and businesses for soldiers and their families. The post reached its peak population of more than 18,000 in 1945 and was deactivated in 1950. It was reactivated for antiaircraft defense in 1951, then deactivated again in 1974 and transferred to the National Park Service.

Approaching Fort Hancock you are greeted by a long row of large, tan brick houses with spacious green-painted front porches with views across Sandy Hook Bay to the mainland. This is Officers' Row, part of a plan drawn up in 1896 that called for thirty-two brick buildings, to include officers' quarters, bachelor officers' quarters, barracks, a hospital, a guardhouse, post headquarters, a quartermaster storehouse, and a bakery. There aren't many trees, but otherwise it looks much like a well-preserved small town, minus the commercial storefronts. History House, a lieutenant's quarters built in 1898, is open on weekend afternoons; so is the Fort Hancock Museum, built in 1899 as the post guardhouse. Other buildings and areas such as an 1894 mortar battery are also open to the public at various times. Schedules vary by season, so call park headquarters before visiting the lighthouse and other places of historic interest at Sandy Hook.

Food

The town of Highlands, just outside Sandy Hook, offers several possibilities for eating. The most famous is **Doris and Ed's** (348 Shore Drive, Highlands, 732-872-1565), a great way to finish off a day at the beach in any season. For something a bit simpler, two well-established spots to consider are the **Clam Hut** (Bay Avenue, Highlands, 732-872-0909) and **Bahr's Landing** (2 Bay Avenue, Highlands, 732-872-1245).

Heading south on Route 36 will lead you to several places to eat, including **Something Fishy** (140 Ocean Avenue, Sea Bright, 732-747-8340) and **McLoone's** (816 Ocean Avenue, Sea Bright, 732-842-2894), which is known for sunset views, grilled fish, and Sunday brunch.

Sandy Hook in Summer

In summer, the beaches are the great attraction, crowded on weekends but very family-oriented and well served by food concessions, changing rooms, and rest rooms. If you are out for a day with your children, however, you may want to avoid Gunnison Beach. About a decade ago, when I couldn't get a parking space in my usual Sandy Hook parking area because I had left home late with my four-year-old and eleven-year-old, I accidentally discovered that Gunnison is a clothing-optional beach. It's a fine choice if it *is* your choice, but a little disconcerting when you settle down on the sand and gradually realize that the people around you don't seem to be wearing any bathing suits.

When It's Chilly, or Someone Is Bored

If you need a child-centered activity, or the weather isn't great, or you happen to be heading west from the Shore anyway, there are several attractions just inland. You can reach them by turning at Sea Bright, going past the large, elegant homes of Rumson, and gradually entering suburban reality. These not-quite-Shore destinations will make a cloudy day more enjoyable—and there's nothing wrong with enjoying at least one of them in the sunshine either. **Holmdel Park**, on Longstreet Road in Holmdel (732-946-2669), part of the varied Monmouth County Park System, offers pleasant picnic areas, marked trails, and a lake stocked for fishing. What makes it special, however, is **Longstreet Farm** (732-946-3758). This nine-acre living history farm is maintained to reflect farm life in the late nineteenth century. (The farm is actually much older than that, with part of the house dating back to the mid-eighteenth century.) Some of the home's furnishings belonged to the Longstreet family. Children will especially enjoy regularly scheduled events such as sheepshearing and wool spinning.

If peering at farm animals isn't what your family has in mind, the **Monmouth Museum**, on the campus of Brookdale Community College (Newman Springs Road, Lincroft, 732-747-2266), may be more inviting. It is a child-friendly place with programs on art, science and nature, and history and culture. Its Becker Children's Wing is geared to children ages seven to twelve, and its Wonder Wing is for children six and under. Nearby, at **Eastmont Orchards** (Route 537, Colts Neck, 732-542-5404), you can, depending upon season, pick your own apples, peaches, or pumpkins, another nice way to punctuate the day. There are horse farms on this stretch of Route 537, so children (or adults) who like horses, and the open fields and rail fences that go with them, will especially enjoy the drive.

Deep Cut Park (Red Hill Road, Middletown, 732-671-6050), another Monmouth County property, isn't so much for children as it is for dedicated gardeners and those who enjoy other people's gardens. Its specialized gardens include a rock garden, a rose garden, a butterfly and hummingbird garden, and an azalea walk, as well as greenhouses. It is open all year, and the paths are pleasant to walk on even when the gardens are winter gray.

A Detour for Antiques

If you are heading north after a day at Sandy Hook and feel the need for just one more stop, **Keyport** may be your place. **Red Bank** is also a great place for one more excursion—or a day in its own right if you want to go all out antiquing. Even if you don't want to stop at the antique centers in these two towns, they make good walking, with interesting architecture and an appealing range of stores, although Red Bank's downtown is larger and more varied.

Keyport is just off bustling Route 35. It still looks like the fishing port it once was, and you may view some of its buildings as a bit more than charmingly timeworn. Small Victorian cottages give the side streets on the edge of town a distinctive appearance, and one large brick house with a cupola adds a dramatic highlight to the domestic streetscape. Many of the storefronts of Keyport's red-brick downtown now display antiques and collectibles rather than the array of current everyday items they once did. There are also several multidealer antique centers, including the **Keyport Antique Emporium** (46-52 West Front Street, 732-888-2952) and the **Keyport Antique Market** (17-21 West Front Street, 732-203-1001). The latter, housed in the former J. J. Newberry store, has 25,000 feet of space, a balcony, and a basement; exploring the layout is something of a nostalgia trip in itself.

Red Bank, with a population slightly over 10,000, feels like a city, especially when you enter it from the south after passing through the upscale Shrewsbury highway-based mini-mall zone on Route 35. Red Bank, at the mouth of the Navesink River, was an active port through much of the nineteenth century, and it has a compact masonry-building downtown to reinforce its image as a product of that era. It also has a huge antique center, spread out in several buildings and complemented by several smaller centers interspersed throughout the same neighborhood near the riverfront. Two of the three buildings that make up the **Antique Center of Red Bank** (195B West Front Street, 732-741-5331, and 195 West Front Street, 732-842-3393) share a parking lot. Building III, at 226 West Front Street, 732-842-4336, is just across the street. Because there are so many dealers—about 150 in three buildings—there is almost more merchandise to browse than you may want to take in during one visit.

Chapter Twenty-two

Long Branch to Toms River: The Shore for All Regions

As the shoreline starts to run south rather than east, the Garden State Parkway takes on a different feeling, and the towns along the way seem to fit more snugly into their strip of ocean-tinged land. This stretch of the Shore is within feasible day-trip reach of virtually any part of New Jersey. It has appealing year-round communities and quintessential beach towns, an idyllic, unspoiled barrier-beach state park, and an equally unspoiled in-from-the-shore state park with intriguing historical attractions. In some parts of it you can catch glimpses of the World Trade Center's twin towers, while in other parts you feel as close to the mid-nineteenth century as to the early twenty-first. It has boardwalks, dazzling architecture, and pockets of urban grittiness almost within sight of palatial residential neighborhoods. Signs pointing you along circuitous routes to the Garden State Parkway abound, as do Coastal Evacuation Route signs that lead more directly to the desired destination. However and whenever you navigate this region, in or out of the season of ice-cream cones and lifeguards, it's worth visiting for natural and historic and cultural attractions.

To me, the highlight of this stretch of Jersey Shore is **Island Beach State Park** (Seaside Park, 732-793-0506). There are lots of other

Walter Choroszewski

Island Beach State Park

beaches, of course, run by town or county authorities, and lots of amusement parks and rides and towns full of restaurants and other attractions, but there is only one stretch of unspoiled barrier beach, and that's Island Beach State Park. In fact, it is one of the few undeveloped barrier beaches on the Atlantic Coast. When you want to go to a beach that doesn't have a town behind it or a boardwalk adjacent to it, this is a great choice. Enough other people know about the park to make getting there on a beautiful summer beach day a bit of a challenge. Like Sandy Hook, the park closes when its parking lots are full. You have to get there early in the day in summer. When the swimming season is over, the park remains open, because it is a terrific place for fishing, bird watching, and nature walking. The road that runs through the park is level enough to be a pleasant bike ride, too, but you can't see much from the road: the dunes, grasses, and low-lying but dense trees and shrubs limit the views of water. Water views are best appreciated by walking the designated trails and boardwalks.

I am still a little surprised by the sharp contrast between the communities just north of Island Beach State Park and the peace and determinedly preserved natural quality of the park itself. In Seaside Park, you can rent surfboards, wet suits, and boogie boards; at Island Beach State Park, you can be alone in a thicket of tall grass. And to be fair, you can appreciate the park all the more after driving through the rapidly developing and commercialized stretch of Route 37 West that takes you to the bridge across Barnegat Bay and to the barrier island that is anchored on the north by Point Pleasant Beach and on the south by Island Beach. Although the bridge across the bay isn't especially attractive in itself, the view from the bridge across the open water, with the barrier beach in the distance, is a delight at any time of year.

The 3,000-acre state park, which was once a separate island, is at the southern end of the barrier island; Barnegat Lighthouse is just across the inlet from the tip of the park and the island. At various times in its history, Island Beach was inhabited by fishermen and members of the United States Life Saving Service; it was in the early stages of development as a luxury resort under the ownership of Henry C. Phipps, an Andrew Carnegie associate, when the stock market crashed in 1929. It was used as a site for army aircraft rocketry experiments during World War II. In 1953, the state bought Phipps's estate of more than 2,600 acres to preserve the natural beauty and open it to the public for recreation; the park opened in 1959. Admission fees are in effect year-round.

The park is divided into three zones: the Northern Natural Area, the central recreation zone, and the Southern Natural Area. The recreation area is where the swimming beaches—that is, Ocean Bathing Units—are. The natural areas contain sand dunes, tidal marshes, and freshwater wetlands. The Northern Natural Area is the place of most limited use: fishing and beach walking. The Southern Area also accommodates picnicking, sunbathing, fishing, and nature study. In the section just north of Barnegat Inlet, scuba diving (register at the park office before your first dive each year) and underwater fishing are allowed. There are a number of short but pleasantly secluded self-guided nature trails in the Southern Area. The air is very sweet and the vegetation is surprisingly varied. There are interpretive centers in each of the park's three areas, and scheduled tours and activities from spring through fall. Flies can be a problem except at the central swimming area.

One of the pleasant and easy walks is Fishermen's Walkway, the wide, handicapped-accessible boardwalk that leads to the mobile sport fishing area (where, by permit only, you can drive your four-wheel-drive vehicle to the beach to fish). It also leads to a wheelchair surf fishing area.

Back in the Real World: Outside the Park

You don't have to live in New Jersey very long before Seaside Heights and Bay Head become part of your vocabulary. The **Seaside Heights** boardwalk is a classic of the genre, with all the usual games and rides and things to eat and drink. A number of the attractions are vividly advertised as being open year-round. The purple flowers, purple letters, and red-white-and-blue wall of **Lucky Leo's Arcade** (215 Boardwalk, 732-793-1323) are eye-catching. The **Water Works Amusement Park** (at Sherman Avenue, 732-793-6501) is one of the more action-oriented highlights, with slides and tubes that make you go very fast, while the **Casino Pier** carousel (732-830-8374) is a more traditional ride.

If amusement parks don't amuse you, there are great year-round opportunities for walking along the boardwalk, with beach views on one side and varied residential and commercial clusters on the other. Many of the retail businesses (even bakeries and supermarkets) are seasonal, though. As you head north toward **Mantoloking**, the houses become more interesting, large and elegant; parking becomes more limited, the number of restaurants and day-tripper attractions decreases, but the beaches and the boardwalks-for-walking remain. If you just want to admire beach-town architecture and enjoy the feeling of being at the Shore, this is a fine off-season destination. **Bay Head** has a lovely, settled feeling. Of course, you can buy a beach pass and simply enjoy the sand and water in summer, but you can also stroll through the town and enjoy its ambience, as well as browsing at the very appealing **Fables of Bay Head** (410 Main Avenue, 732-899-3633). Fables sells a creative combination of things, including beautiful wood furniture, pretty stationery, candles, and ice cream. The **Grenville Hotel and Restaurant** (345 Main Avenue, 732-3100) is one of those casually elegant places that serves creative American food. It does have a children's menu, but it's a place grownups particularly will relish. It's closed Monday and open for lunch and dinner most other days, and for brunch on Sunday. It is owned by Renault Winery and features Renault wines.

Bay Head leads nicely into **Point Pleasant Beach**, a town that combines a solid downtown commercial district with several appealing antiques centers and one of the best boardwalk/beach areas around. Starting with the beach, the focus is on Jenkinson's. **Jenkinson's** (300 Ocean Avenue, 732-892-0600; www.jenkinsons.com) offers everything you might want in the way of beachfront entertainment, from the beach itself to an aquarium, a candy store, three miniature-golf courses, restaurants, summer concerts on the beach, and rides and games. The aquarium, arcade, gift shops, and candy store are open all year. Exhibits at **Jenkinson's Aquarium** (Ocean Avenue and Parkway, 732-899-1212) include a local saltwater fish tank containing carnivorous fish. It also boasts an open ocean shark tank and a coral-reef fish exhibit. Other attractions include African black-footed penguins, alligators, harbor seals, and touch tank animals, such as small sharks, lobsters, crabs, and urchins.

The **Point Pleasant Antique Emporium** (Bay and Trenton Avenues, 732-902-2222; 800-322-8002) is one of several large, well-developed antiques centers in town. Two full floors and a gallery house more than 100 dealers, including some who specialize in certain types of items, such as kitchenware, vintage clothing, and books.

Another tempting aspect of Point Pleasant Beach is its wide variety of eating places. **Hoffman's Donut Shop** (509 American Legion Way, 732-892-3472) sells many kinds of wonderful doughnuts. **Hoffman's Ice Cream** (804 Richmond Avenue, 732-892-0270) sells homemade ice cream (there's also a branch in Spring Lake). For more substantial fare, **Europa South** (521 Arnold Avenue, 732-295-1500) is a popular destination for Spanish cuisine. **Southern B-B-Que Ribs** (Washington Avenue and Route 35, 732-899-7427) is a child-friendly place for great barbecue. **Spikes Seafood Restaurant and Fish Market** (415 Broadway, 732-295-9400) and **Red's Lobster Pot** (57 Inlet Drive, 732-295-6622), which is open seasonally, are hot spots for fresh seafood.

Heading north from Point Pleasant Beach on the mainland, you will approach some of the Shore towns that everyone knows and some love. They all have beaches, most have boardwalks (either for walking or for spending money on), and many of them also have distinctive personalities and make them places you might want to visit even when it's not beach weather.

Spring Lake (for beach and other information, call 732-449-0577) is full of beautiful houses and a year-round shopping district. It was developed in the late nineteenth century as a seaside resort, and its large rambling houses illustrate its affluent past and equally affluent present. Hotels are the dramatic highlights of some of the beach blocks; the enormous Essex and Sussex Hotel was still under renovation in late 2000, but its presence is spectacular even as work in progress.

Belmar is another quintessential beach town, full of rides and bars, parking meters, and, in season, people. **Bradley Beach** is a great beach destination, too. And then there's **Ocean Grove**, with its wonderful gingerbread cottages, its history as a Methodist camp meeting site, its Auditorium, and its jarring proximity to Asbury Park, which after years of hope and dreams of renewal, still is most notable for an empty beachfront, tall buildings with boarded-up windows, glimpses of a deserted downtown, and the Stone Pony.

Ocean Grove is a delight; you glimpse it as you drive toward it around one of its two lakes, the shape and color of the houses immediately announcing that this is not a standard seaside strip. Now a National Historic District, **Ocean Grove** was founded in 1869 by Dr. William B. Osborn. He, along with twelve other Methodist ministers and thirteen laymen, formed the Ocean Grove Camp Meeting Association. Ocean Grove, like other camp meeting sites, was a place for open-air religious revivals; the tents that were used at first gave way to permanent structures. Most of Ocean Grove was built before the nineteenth century turned into the twentieth.

As you drive or walk the streets of Ocean Grove, you can still see narrow, peaked-roof cottages whose dimensions clearly reflect those of the nineteenth-century tents. The ornate architecture and overall charm make a nice afternoon's walk, despite the occasional shabby house. Even the small streets just north of Fletcher Lake are charming, with tiny houses one-room across, adorned with little bits of gingerbread. The homes in the heart of Ocean Grove, for example, on Broadway, are generally larger. Near Pilgrim Pathway on Webb Avenue, there are some especially decorative houses. Even the tree-lined commercial Main Avenue maintains the mood, as well as having a good range of shops and eateries. The **Raspberry Café** (60 Main Avenue, 732-988-0833) is more than a pretty name; it serves good sandwiches, salads, and fruit smoothies. If you are in town at dinnertime, consider waiting in line at **Moonstruck** (57 Main Avenue, 732-988-0123), a very popular purveyor of Italian fare in casual, upscale surroundings.

The **Great Auditorium** (800-773-0097), completed in 1894, was the site of large camp meetings in its earlier days. It is still used for Sunday services in summer, as well as for secular cultural events, notably concerts by a wide range of performers from Enrico Caruso to the Preservation Hall Jazz Band. For more information about Ocean Grove's history and its lively present, you can get in touch with the Ocean Grove Camp Meeting Association, 732-775-0035; www.oceangrove.org.

As you drive away from Ocean Grove toward the "Welcome to Asbury Park" sign, the world changes. A mud-colored lake separates **Asbury Park** from Ocean Grove; a faded Thom McAn sign signals the edge of the business district of what was once a thriving little city with solid-looking buildings. Even a parking deck was in ruins when I visited in September 2000. A drive along Asbury Park's Ocean Avenue doesn't turn up much to celebrate, although the Convention Hall, less desolate than its neighbors, is a beautiful brick building with interesting multicolored trim.

The moment you go north across Deal Lake, cheerfulness returns. **Deal** and **Elberon** look more than comfortable; they look rich. Here again are streets you can wander to admire the architecture; some of the oceanfront Deal houses are so large they look like hotels. Elberon is actually the southern tip of Long Branch. Some may think **Long Branch** is a bit built up for a long-established seaside resort and a bit shabby for an up-to-date one; it did, after all, suffer damage to both property and pride after a major pier fire in 1987. It may not have the elegance of Deal or the charm of Ocean Grove, but it has relatively little of the desperate emptiness of Asbury Park; it's a nice compromise between idyllic little Shore town and big Shore city.

Long Branch's history as a resort dates to 1788, when Philadelphians came to vacation there; it flourished through the nineteenth century as a seaside resort. Monmouth Park racetrack in nearby Oceanport and rail connections to New York, were added attractions. President Grant had a summer house on Ocean Avenue; President Garfield died here in September of 1881 after having been shot earlier in the summer. Presidents Rutherford B. Hayes, Benjamin Harrison, Chester A. Arthur, William McKinley, and New Jersey's (and Virginia's) own Woodrow Wilson also spent time in Long Branch.

It's not surprising, then, that one of the best-known present-day attractions in Long Branch is **Seven Presidents Oceanfront Park** (Ocean and Joline Avenues, 732-229-0924). Run by the Monmouth County Park System, this is a well-maintained, nearly mile-long stretch of public beach. In addition to swimming, it has fishing and picnicking facilities as well as playgrounds.

If you don't have a car or don't like to drive, this stretch of the Jersey Shore will be particularly appealing, since it is accessible by **NJ Transit's North Jersey Coast Line** rail service (for schedule information, call 800-772-2222 in northern New Jersey and Mercer County; 800-582-5946 in southern New Jersey; www.njtransit.state.nj.us). Bay Head is the southern terminus of the route, and there are stations all along this stretch of coast, including Point Pleasant Beach, Bradley Beach, Long Branch, and Allenhurst, to name just a few.

History and Hiking at Allaire

If you are looking for a diversion that doesn't depend on sunbathing or water activity, **Allaire State Park** (Parkway exit 98, Farmingdale, 732-939-2371) is well worth considering. First of all, it is pretty. Add the park's history as a center of the nineteenth-century bog-iron industry and it becomes more unusual. **Allaire Village** (732-938-2253), many of whose buildings survive, serves as a living museum year-round, though it is most active on weekends from Memorial Day through Labor Day.

The park's **Pine Creek Railroad** (732-938-5524), established in 1952, is, according to the state's brochure, the "only live-steam, narrow-gauge train" ride in New Jersey. The railroad was intended to illustrate the three-foot-gauge railroads that made it easier to build rail lines in mountainous areas. Since 1963, the railroad has been the principal exhibit of the New Jersey Museum of Transportation, which also displays several railroad structures on the grounds, including buildings from Spring Lake and Manasquan. Trains operate on a one-and-a-half mile, twelve-minute route on weekends and holidays from April to mid-October, with daily service added in July and August.

When my son was a toddler, we occasionally went to Allaire State Park and rode the Pine Creek Railroad, or pushed his stroller along the gravel paths of Allaire Village. Those things are still great attractions for other families, but the village is also a delight for adults who are not accompanied by children. The gravel paths may be a little rough on strollers or wheelchairs, but they are fairly firm and should be manageable.

Allaire Village was first developed as Williamsburg Forge in the 1790s and was known as Howell Furnace through the early 1800s. James Allaire, after buying the property in 1822, developed the site over the next decade or so, constructing brick row houses and commercial and industrial buildings, including a general store, blacksmith shop, gristmill, and bakery. Allaire Village thrived through the 1830s, until 1848, when the charcoal-powered furnaces ceased to operate as a result of competition from coal and high-grade iron ore from Pennsylvania. Subsequently, the village began to decline. James Allaire died in 1858, and the estate was left to his son, Hal Allaire; when he died, Benjamin Harrison, his friend as well as a former President of the United States, paid off the back taxes and sold the estate to Arthur Brisbane, at the time a well-known editor for the Hearst newspaper chain. Under Brisbane's ownership, the village and estate were put to various uses; the general store was used as an inn, the carpenter shop as a restaurant. The Monmouth Council of Boy Scouts used the site as Camp Burton until 1937. Brisbane's widow deeded the property to the state in 1941, and in 1957 a nonprofit corporation started to raise funds to restore the village.

The remaining buildings, surrounded by lawns and shaded by trees, are surprisingly gracious. Short trails lead from the central village to the massive blast furnace and the mansion. Paintings of several vanished buildings help fill in the outlines of the village's past life. The building that once housed the enameling furnace is now used for special exhibitions. When I visited in autumn of 2000, this beautiful structure of white-painted brick, which was built in two parts and dates from 1828 and 1834, was the site of an excellent exhibit of photographs showing the village as it was from the late 1800s to the mid-1900s. At the time it was not yet known whether this exhibit would become permanent; if it is still there, it is well worth a visit.

On weekends, the bakery and general store are open for business. The former sells cookies, pastries, breads, cakes, and tarts, as well as cookbooks and mixes; the latter sells eighteenth- and nineteenth-century reproductions, including pottery, candles, glassware, tinware, and toys. Special events are scheduled throughout the year, and the visitor center is open daily.

Elsewhere in the 3,000-acre park there are hiking and multi-use (hiking, biking, and equestrian) trails. The trails, open sunrise to sunset, are beautiful enough to make you feel that you are on your own private estate. Nearby stables rent horses to visitors. Not far from the visitor center is a nature center, staffed from Memorial Day to Labor Day. The Manasquan River runs through the park and is stocked annually with trout. It is also popular with canoeists. The Village Mill Pond is designated specifically for fishing by children under fourteen.

Just down the road from the entrance to Allaire State Park is **Spring Meadow Golf Course** (Atlantic Avenue-Route 524, Wall Township, 732-449-0806), a public golf course.

Farther Inland: Great Adventure(s)

My daughter, Rebecca, loves roller coasters and other rides that make people scream with what they insist is gleeful fear. It is a helpful coincidence that she attends a school that makes an annual end-of-school excursion to Great Adventure. When I picked her up at school after the June 2000 trip, I asked her what she had liked best, and she answered, "Everything."

If you like theme parks, that will probably also be your reaction to **Six Flags Great Adventure and Wild Safari** (Route 537, Jackson, 732-928-1821; www.sixflags.com). This entertainment complex now has three attractions: Great Adventure Theme Park, Wild Safari, and Hurricane Harbor, a water park that opened in May 2000. You can buy separate tickets for each park, or combination tickets for the theme and safari parks or theme, safari, and water parks. Great Adventure and Wild Safari are open daily from mid-May through Labor Day, weekends through the end of October. Wild Safari is only open from 9 AM to 4 PM, but Great Adventure opens at 10 AM and stays open well into the evening. Hurricane Harbor opens for Memorial Day weekend and the first weekend in June and is then open daily from mid-June through Labor Day. It opens at 10 AM and closing hours vary. Children under forty-eight inches tall get into Great Adventure for half price, and there are more than 40 rides for children 54 inches and under.

Six Flags offers an abundance of guest services. Guest Relations provides ride accessibility information for guests who use wheelchairs. A limited number of strollers, wheelchairs, and electric vehicles are available for rent on a first-come, first-served basis. The park takes credit cards, has an ATM machine, and accepts checks with appropriate identification. Pets are not permitted at any of the attractions, but free boarding for pets is provided. There are baby-changing areas in all women's rest rooms and most men's rest rooms, and although you cannot bring in your own food or beverages, there's a wide range of food choices available for purchase, with both indoor and outdoor dining: you can choose from pizza, mozzarella sticks, hamburgers and hot dogs, Mexican food, salads, and, at the new Wok & Roll near Skull Mountain, Chinese food. There's no shortage of ice cream, candy, and cold drinks, either. You will also have ample opportunity to buy souvenirs, as well as necessities that you somehow forgot, including sunscreen, bathing suits, and ponchos. Six Flags Great Adventure also presents concerts and special events throughout the season; call for schedules and other information.

Great Adventure Theme Park features more than 100 rides, shows and attractions in nine themed lands. Each ride at the theme park posts height, weight, size, and health rules for riders. There are many combinations, and a child of any size will find ample rides to choose from. We used to make family trips to Great Adventure. At first we headed for Bugs Bunny Land, which features nearly 20 miniature versions of larger park rides and interactive attractions. I remember coaxing my son, then six or seven years old and small for his age, to ride the little airplanes that soared gently above our heads while his little sister, Rebecca, watched longingly from her stroller. Now Bugs Bunny Land has been joined by Looney Tunes Seaport™, at the other end of the theme park. It offers young children more than a dozen rides and interactive attractions, including Yosemite Sam's Flight School™ Flying airplanes, Daffy's Deep Diver™ submarine in motion, the Bugs Bunny Fun Factory™ soft play area, and Koala Canyon, a half-acre water play area for children under 54 inches tall.

Great Adventure's Saw Mill Log Flume, a free-flowing water ride with a forty-foot drop, is a step beyond these rides. It is a wonderful ride for a hot day. Rebecca, now tall enough to enjoy Great Adventure on her own, recommends it as refreshing, not scary. She also lines up for the River Rapids for white-water thrills—whether you get wet on River Rapids depends which side you sit on. Great Adventure has eleven roller coasters, and they are the main attraction for many visitors. Rebecca's hit parade includes Medusa™, the world's first floorless coaster; the Great American Scream Machine, a seven-loop steel roller coaster; Rolling Thunder, a traditional wooden roller coaster that, paradoxically, Rebecca describes as the scariest; Batman the Ride®, an inverted, outside looping steel roller coaster—your feet hang down; Batman™ and Robin™: The Chiller, a "linear induction looping steel roller coaster" (it goes backward); and Skull Mountain, which has the added appeal of being indoors, in the dark. Stuntman's Free Fall isn't a roller coaster, but it is very popular; it lets you fall thirteen stories for four and a half seconds.

My favorite part of Great Adventure has always been **Wild Safari,** a 350-acre wildlife preserve that is home to nearly 1,200 animals—57 species—in simulated natural habitats. You can have absolutely no interest in amusement-park rides and still have a great time at Wild Safari. Seeing the animals is fun; a giraffe's long neck and towering height are always an amazement. I enjoy the 4.5-mile drive, the largest drive-through safari outside Africa, according to Six Flags. It features rare, exotic and endangered animals such as Siberian and Bengal tigers, African elephants, giraffes, southern white rhinoceros, anubis baboons, lions, peacocks, and flamingos. Cute little monkeys scamper all over slowly passing cars as if cars were part of their natural habitat. There is a guided tour bus through Wild

Safari if you are worried about the monkeys' claws scratching your car. Seating on the bus is first-come, first-served.

Hurricane Harbor, the newest attraction at the Six Flags complex, occupies 45 acres, 22 for the water park and 23 for parking. Like the Great Adventure theme park, it has a number of thrill rides but does not neglect families with younger children. Finding the right experience is largely a matter of observation and common sense. The Blue Lagoon wave pool contains nearly a million gallons of water, with three- to five-foot rolling waves that last nine minutes. Its depth ranges from one to six feet. Hurricane Harbor's tubing "river" is 2,150 feet long, just under 3 feet deep and approximately 17 feet wide; it features a number of special effects, including waterfalls and rapids. Families and other groups can ride a large round raft, capacity up to six people, down two paths: Big Bambu and Reef Runner; one is comparable to level 3 white water, the other is gentler. There are speed slides for body sliding, three 50-foot-tall tube slides, and four coaster slides. Discovery Bay is a family activity lagoon featuring an interactive family water playground with 4 slides, 75 water gadgets, climbing nets, tipping buckets, and a child-size wave pool.

Beyond Six Flags

You won't have to go far from the theme parks for a change of pace. **Six Flags Factory Outlets** (Route 537, Jackson, 732-833-0680) is a relatively new outlet center and a pretty good one. Just down the road from the entrance to Great Adventure, it has more than seventy stores, including the Gap, J. Crew, Nine West, OshKosh B'Gosh, and Black & Decker. What's more, it has a Harry and David outlet and a food court that includes Chinese food, pizza, pretzels, and a New York–style deli.

For something completely different, head slightly south of Six Flags to **Cream Ridge Winery** (145 Route 539, Cream Ridge, 609-259-9797; www.creamridgewinery.com). It opened in 1988 and makes white, red, and blush wines, as well as an appealing selection of fruit wines. For several years in a row its cherry, plum, and cranberry wines have won the Governor's Cup, the highest award given to a wine in the state of New Jersey. Cream Ridge also makes raspberry wine, rhubarb wine, apricot wine, peach-nectarine wine, and Almondberry, a blend of raspberry and white wine with almonds. Visits to Cream Ridge include wine tastings, and the winery's hours of operation are 11 AM to 5 PM daily. Cream Ridge also offers a number of special events each year, which are posted on its Web site.

Chapter Twenty-three

Barnegat to Great Bay: Long Beach Island and More

It always amazes me that there is only one bridge to Long Beach Island. The island extends roughly from Exit 69 of the Parkway down to Exit 52, but the only place to cross Barnegat Bay to reach LBI is from Exit 63, where Route 72 stretches tantalizingly to the east. The bridge arches across the bay and there you are on the island, with the beacon of Barnegat Light and the architectural wonders of Loveladies to your north and the sub shops, ice-cream stands, and seafood emporiums of Brant Beach and Beach Haven to your south.

Although most people think of LBI as a place to have a house, or have friends who have a house, the island boasts miles of great beaches, free street parking (though not necessarily on the dead-end beach blocks) in most of the towns, and the reasonable daily beach fees that are a somewhat underappreciated part of modern New Jersey life. While LBI may not be the beach day trip of choice for North Jersey residents—it's a little far when your main goal is just to get there and stretch out on the sand with a blanket and a book—it is within easy reach for lots of other people. And there's something about being on an island that sets the day apart.

If beach time is your main reason for a trip to LBI, deciding where to spend your day is largely a matter of whim and available parking spaces. And you never have to worry about bringing anything in the way of food or other supplies, because Long Beach Boulevard, particularly from Surf City down, is a bustling retail strip that blends beach ambience with downtown shopping in an essence-of-Shore-town way. The absence of standard-issue boardwalks keeps the beaches feeling like beaches rather than amusement parks; the presence on or near Long Beach Boulevard of assorted miniature-golf courses, game arcades, and the varied attractions of **Fantasy Island** (320 West Seventh Street, Beach Haven, 609-492-4000) means that you, or more likely your children, can have a change of pace if the sand and water begin to seem monotonous or clouds roll in before you're ready to head home.

Beyond the Beach

Although Long Beach Island owes its fame to its beaches, it does have other attractions. At the northern tip of the island is **Barnegat Lighthouse State Park** (Barnegat Light, 609-494-2016). This thirty-two-acre park is the home of Barnegat Lighthouse, the cheerful red-and-white landmark that looks out over Barnegat Inlet, Long Beach Island, and Island Beach State Park. Its vantage point was long regarded as a major "change of course" point for vessels bound to and from New York; they depended on the lighthouse to help them avoid shoals. Strong currents and shifting sandbars added to the challenge of navigating the Jersey Coast. The lighthouse tower is 165 feet tall; the first light on the site was built in 1835. Although admission to the park itself is free, if you want to climb the 217 steps to the top of the lighthouse you will have to pay a fee; the lighthouse is open daily in summer and on weekends in spring and fall. The view from the top is spectacular, but the view from the ground is pretty good, too.

Although Barnegat Lighthouse State Park is compact, it is more than a place to see a lighthouse. It has a picnic area, and a thousand-foot concrete jetty for fishing. The picnic area and the jetty are accessible to people with disabilities. Anglers can catch striped bass,

Walter Choroszewski

Barnegat Lighthouse State Park

bluefish, summer flounder, winter flounder, and black bass, among
other creatures. The jetty is also a fine walkway and a great place to
sit and watch the sea. In spring and fall, the park is a good spot for
watching migrating birds. There is also a short nature trail that leads
through the last remnants of maritime forest in New Jersey. The forest is dominated by black cherry, eastern red cedar, and American
holly, and migratory birds use it as a resting and feeding area when
they travel to and from breeding sites.

Not far south of Barnegat Light rise the elegant angles and masses of homes in Loveladies and Harvey Cedars. This affluent community is known for its eye-catching contemporary architecture. Even if you don't have friends who live there, it's worth a drive along Long Beach Boulevard, or a stroll up and down the street. Tilted windows, arched windows, pastel trim, and shingled geometric shapes give the townscape a playful look. Other houses are somewhat more conservative in design, with shingles, flat-topped towers, and big windows to make the most of the views. There is an annual Seashore Open House Tour, traditionally scheduled for the first Wednesday in August. It benefits the **Long Beach Island Foundation of the Arts and Sciences** (120 Long Beach Boulevard, Loveladies, 609-494-1241). The Foundation is a nonprofit organization that sponsors events and activities such as arts and crafts festivals, entertainment, and adult and children's classes.

Toward the other end of the island is the **Long Beach Island Museum** (Engleside and Beach Avenues, Beach Haven, 609-492-0700), housed in the former Holy Innocents' Episcopal Church, built in 1882. The museum is owned and operated by the Long Beach Island Historical Association; its exhibits reflect Long Beach Island life in the late 1800s and early 1900s. The museum is open daily in summer and on weekend afternoons in May and September. Hours vary, so call before you plan to go. In addition to its regular exhibits, the museum hosts events such as crafts shows, Monday-night lectures, other educational and cultural activities, and twice-a-week walking tours through historic Beach Haven.

The Mainland

It isn't always beach weather, even in summer and even at the Shore. The stretch of mainland across the water from Long Beach Island offers several alternatives for off-season or gray-day activities—though they're equally enjoyable in good weather. **Tuckerton Seaport** (120 West Main Street, Tuckerton, 609-296-8868;

www.tuckertonseaport.org), which opened in 2000 and is still a work in progress, is a re-created village whose structures represent the crafts and trades of the Barnegat Bay region. Boats, tools, and decoys are on display; there are also demonstrations and workshops. Tuckerton Seaport is open daily; the admission fee for adults is $8; senior citizens pay $6; children six through seventeen $4; children under six are free.

Moving inland from Parkway Exit 52 will take you toward the varied attractions of Wharton State Forest. Depending upon your interests and the weather, you can head for ample outdoor recreation activities or for the historical display of Batsto. **Wharton State Forest** (609-561-0024) is so large that it occupies parts of three counties—Atlantic, Burlington, and Camden. In fact, with more than 110,000 acres, this vast area in the heart of the white-cedar and pitch-pine forests of the Pinelands is the largest single tract of land within New Jersey's state park system. There are two visitor centers, one toward the northern section of the Forest at Atsion Recreation Area and the other at Batsto Village. This part of the state, and Wharton State Forest in particular, is rich in beautiful waterways for boating and fishing. Canoeing can be idyllic on the Mullica, Batsto, Wading, and Oswego Rivers (the park offices have a list of nearby businesses where park visitors can rent canoes); a boat launch at Crowley Landing gives motorboats (electric power only) access to the Mullica River. There is swimming from a sand beach at Atsion Lake (Route 206, Shamong Township, 609-268-0444) and picnicking at several formally designated sites.

Covering about 25,000 acres, **Bass River State Forest** (Stage Road, New Gretna, 609-296-1114) is small only when compared to Wharton. It was acquired by the state in 1905 for public recreation, water conservation, and wildlife and timber management. It offers swimming, boating, and fishing at 67-acre Lake Absegami, which was created in the 1920s. There are a number of hiking and riding

trails, including a trail that goes through the pine-and-oak woods
of the Absegami Natural Area. The much larger West Pine Plains
Natural Area, which covers more than 3,000 acres, is a naturally
stunted forest, known colloquially as the Pygmy Forest. It is an
extremely rare environment and supports pine and oak trees whose
canopy height is as low as four feet.

Although Wharton State Forest has hundreds of miles of unpaved roads for biking and horseback riding, hiking is its special
attraction. That's because of the Batona Trail, which runs for about
fifty miles through Lebanon, Wharton, and Bass River State Forests.
Begun in 1961 by the Batona Hiking Club, the trail is now jointly
maintained by the club and the State Park Service. This wilderness
trail is largely level, though there are some rolling hills and wet areas. It has a number of access points, so you can cover as much
ground as you wish in a day's hike, as well as experience unspoiled
sections of the Pinelands, from wildlife to blueberries to historic place
names. The paved roads at the edges of Wharton State Forest also
lend themselves to biking; they are level, not heavily traveled, and
have shoulders, albeit narrow ones.

Batso Village, at the southern edge of Wharton State Forest, is a
former bog-iron and glassmaking industrial center that flourished
from 1766 to 1867. The approach to Batsto is very pretty, a mix of
woods and fields. At the visitor center (609-561-3262), be sure to
pick up a brochure about the village; it includes an annotated map,
which will make your walk through the grounds much more interesting. You may also want to walk through the excellent historical
exhibit at the visitor center to get a sense of why Batsto was significant. You will see everything from cannonballs to nineteenth-century clothes to a re-created furnace, and the exhibits provide a very
helpful context for exploring the village, which doesn't really come
to life if you visit during the week when there are no demonstrations
going on. I had not realized, for example, that bog iron was readily
available before the American Revolution, or that the little streams

and rivers of the Pinelands were strong and quick enough to provide the waterpower necessary for the bellows of the iron furnaces.

Although Batsto was founded in 1766 and supplied items such as camp kettles as well as munitions to the Continental Army during the Revolution, the Batsto that has survived is much more recent. Its preserved buildings primarily reflect the life that existed in the village in the late nineteenth century, when Batsto was the property of Joseph Wharton, an industrialist from Philadelphia. Batsto had continued to produce pig iron, cast-iron water pipes, and other specialty items through the middle of the 1800s; when the iron industry collapsed, production switched to window glass, but by the late 1860s that industry also was in decline. Wharton bought Batsto and originally intended to dam the waterways and sell the water to Camden and Philadelphia. When that plan did not succeed, he instead developed Batsto as an agricultural community and forest-product manufacturer; cranberries became a major crop at this time. The village brochure describes the Batsto of this period as Wharton's gentlemen's farm, and when you look at the layout of the village and the dominance of the thirty-plus-room Italianate mansion where he lived, that seems like a fair description. Mansion tours are scheduled several times a day. Sign up at the visitor center, where the schedule is posted; there is a small fee for the tours.

Walking past the mansion over the wooden bridge that spans the Batsto Lake dam takes you to a village street lined with very small, plain wooden houses where the workers lived; a few of them are open and furnished to illustrate various aspects of village life. The waterpowered gristmill is, as you would expect, beside the dam on the way to the village houses; it ground and processed several grains in addition to wheat. The flour was sold at the nearby general store, which is now one of the livelier buildings on the site, with Mason jars, weighing instruments, colorful spools of thread, hanging baskets, and other period details. Demonstrations of the gristmill in action are scheduled on weekend afternoons. The value of a family trip to Batsto probably depends on how close you live to it and how interested you are in local history. Although it illustrates a significant aspect of New Jersey history, Batsto is one of many restored or re-created villages. It is certainly worth a visit if you are in the area, but it may not warrant a special day trip from far away.

Renault Winery

Heading away from Batsto toward the Shore, you will come to a sharp junction with Route 563 South, which leads surprisingly quickly to Egg Harbor City; just before Egg Harbor City, you can turn left onto Moss Mill Road (also called 561 Alternate) and find yourself following signs to the **Renault Winery** (72 North Bremen Avenue, Egg Harbor, 609-965-2111; www.renaultwinery.com). You can also approach it from Egg Harbor City by taking Route 30 toward the Shore and turning off the highway at the sign—and the giant champagne bottle.

The Historic Renault Winery has been there since the 1860s. Turning into the winery's driveway, you will be greeted by vineyards on one side and old wooden wine vats on the other. The casks are huge. Tours and tastings are offered year-round, but September and October, when the grape harvest and winemaking take place, are the best time to visit; the rest of the year you see the surroundings without the activity. Renault is a very down-to-earth place despite the glimpses of the several reception rooms (a new ballroom, the Vintage Room, the Wine Cellar) available for weddings and other special events; the end-of-tour wine tasting (for visitors aged twenty-one and older) takes place in a wood-paneled barroom that feels like a cozy basement recreation room. Serious wine people may raise their eyebrows when introduced to the vineyard's unique blueberry champagne, but the champagne is part of the experience, and it really does smell like blueberries. Renault sells its wines at an on-site gift shop and directly to restaurants but doesn't distribute through retail outlets anymore. The winery's Garden Café is open for lunch Monday through Saturday; the winery's well-regarded Renault Gourmet Restaurant, for which you need reservations, is open for dinner on Friday, Saturday, and Sunday and for brunch on Sunday.

Chapter Twenty-four

Atlantic City:
The Expected and
the Unexpected

Long before Atlantic City became a casino city, it was a popular multipurpose resort. The first boardwalk was not completed until 1870, but construction of the Camden and Atlantic City Railroad, whose purpose was to bring people and their money to Atlantic City, began in 1852. A railroad company engineer planned the city's layout and assigned the ocean names to the streets that were to parallel the beach. Most of them, like the cross streets named after states, have become part of the American consciousness because they are Monopoly® names: low-price purple Baltic, valuable yellow Atlantic and really valuable green Pacific, mid-level orange New York, and many more.

The first amusement pier was built in 1882, and decades later, in the 1930s, the piers and the convention center defined the place. The 2,000-foot-long Steel Pier at the Boardwalk and Virginia Avenue featured three diving horses—with riders—that jumped into a pool of water three times a day; the 1,700-foot Million Dollar Pier at Arkansas Avenue boasted a house, compete with conservatory, shrubbery, and garden; Steeplechase Pier, at Pennsylvania Avenue, started out as a playground pier and became a fishing and yachting center when it was rebuilt after a 1932 fire. The Heinz Pier (think ketchup) showed model kitchens, among other "educational" displays, and the Garden Pier, the newest of the piers, specialized in public entertainment, with regular boxing and wrestling matches and occasional summertime opera. The beach and Boardwalk were backed by tall hotels, with the blocks behind them punctuated by restaurants and shops.

Time passed and tastes changed. Atlantic City declined over the years, as people traveled farther for their vacations and the hotels and piers languished. State-authorized casino gambling was supposed to turn everything around. The first casino opened in 1978, and there has been a lot of tearing down and building up since then. Now, Atlantic City is once again a leading tourist destination. Only hotels with at least 500 rooms can apply for casino licenses, and the big-name entertainment the hotels offer is an added temptation to stay at least one night.

All the same, Atlantic City remains an extremely popular day-trip destination. Day-trippers are big business at the casinos. After all, Atlantic City is a few hours away from any part of New Jersey—not to mention New York City and Philadelphia. Drivers be warned: although there is some metered street parking, it is hard to find a convenient and comfortable parking space that isn't related to the casinos. The casinos have large self-park garages just off the Boardwalk, with variable but reasonable daytime rates. The catch is that you have to be either a hotel guest or a casino customer to park in one. If you don't want to drive, the casinos and bus companies throughout the state make it easy to travel to Atlantic city by bus. In addition to locally provided bus service from many New Jersey towns, New Jersey Transit, Greyhound, and Academy provide scheduled service to Atlantic City from the Port Authority terminal at Forty-first Street and Eighth Avenue in New York City. The Atlantic City Municipal Terminal is located at Michigan and Atlantic Avenues near all major hotels. There is also train service: NJ Transit's Philadelphia–Atlantic City Rail Line (800-AC-TRAIN/228-7246) runs thirteen trains daily between Philadelphia's Thirtieth Street Station and the Atlantic City Rail Terminal, with local stops. Free shuttle service is available between the Atlantic City Rail Terminal and all casinos.

Walter Choroszewski

Boardwalk, Atlantic City

The Casinos

Harrah's (777 Harrah's Boulevard, 609-441-5000; 800-2-HARRAH/353-7724) and **Trump Marina Casino Hotel** (Huron Avenue and Brigantine Boulevard, 609-441-2000; 800-966-6608) are at the northern end of the city, with direct access to the water. Most of the casinos, however, are concentrated along the central Boardwalk. All offer a variety of games. Slot machines are a universal, of course; blackjack has its serious players; baccarat and roulette share a glamorous image, traceable to at least one James Bond movie and countless other cinematic moments. The **Atlantic City Hilton Casino Resort** (Boston and the Boardwalk, 609-347-7111; 800-231-8687) is the southernmost casino. The more central **Caesars Atlantic City Hotel Casino** (2100 Pacific Avenue, 609-348-4411; 800-345-7253), with its evocation of ancient Rome, is an impressive sight. The **Claridge Casino Hotel** (Indiana Avenue at the Boardwalk, 609-340-3400; 800-257-5275) promotes itself as friendlier than its larger neighbors, and it offers a good selection of lower-stakes tables to match its smaller size. The **Tropicana Casino and Resort** (Brighton Avenue and the Boardwalk, 609-340-4000; 800-843-8767) has a glass-enclosed elevator to delight the young or brave. **Trump's Taj Mahal Casino Resort** (1000 Boardwalk at Virginia Avenue, 609-449-1000; 800-825-8888) boasts elephants outside and crystal chandeliers inside.

Lucy the Elephant, or Lucy the Landmark, as I think of her, is only a few miles south of the Taj Mahal, in Margate City. Lucy is a building in the shape of a sixty-five-foot-tall elephant. You can see the Atlantic City skyline as you cross the marshes to get to Margate. It's a seemingly different world, though. Signs along the way warn you to watch for turtles crossing roadways; the billboards on the way in to Margate advertise religious congregations, and once you cross the toll bridge you are in a heavily developed town of homes and houses of worship, with prosperous-looking businesses on the main streets. Brown landmark signs point the way to Lucy (9200 Atlantic Avenue, Margate City; 609-823-6473). She has been there since 1881 but has recently been spruced up, with a colorful observation platform in the shape of a howdah. You enter through her hind legs and go upstairs for a view. There is a small parking lot right at her feet, and Lucy is open for visits daily in summer and weekends in spring and early fall; she is closed November through March. The fee in summer 2000 was $4 for adults, $2 for children.

Outside the Casinos

While the casinos have brought Atlantic City its most recent wave of prominence, there is a lot more to the city and its environs than slot machines, blackjack tables, and glittering nightlife. The Boardwalk is still bustling. The beach is free. The Garden Pier houses the **Atlantic City Art Center** (Boardwalk at New Jersey Avenue, 609-

347-5837). It features monthly exhibits by national and regional art-ists/artisans and is open daily. Also on the Garden Pier is the **Atlantic City Historical Museum** (609-347-5839), with displays about the Atlantic City of old. There is a **Ripley's Believe It or Not Museum** at New York Avenue and the Boardwalk (609-347-2001).

There are other places to explore. As I drove north on Pacific Avenue, behind the casinos, heading for the White Horse Pike, I saw something that came as a nice surprise. Ahead of me, in an empty lot at the corner of Rhode Island Avenue, rose a lighthouse, a classically shaped, black and pale-yellow tower. It is **Absecon Lighthouse** (609-449-1360), with a reconstructed keeper's house snuggled up against it. The lighthouse, designed by George Meade of Civil War fame, was built in 1857 and is open to visitors. The tallest of New Jersey's lights, it still has its original first-order Fresnel lens. There are boat rides, too. **Atlantic City Cruises, Inc.**, at Historic Gardiner's Basin (800 North New Hampshire Avenue, 609-347-7600), offers daily skyline, marine mammal, and calm water cruise adventures. Weather and season permitting, you can also take in a minor-league baseball game, watching the **Atlantic City Surf** (609-344-8873), who play within the Atlantic League. At the edge of town is the **Ocean Life Center** (New Hampshire Avenue and the Bay, 609-348-2880; www.oceanlifecenter.com), a marine science attraction with aquariums, touch tanks, and interactive exhibits.

If you don't have a car or don't want to use it for little trips within the city, you will be glad to know that jitneys run round-the-clock every day of the year. The thirteen-passenger minibuses travel the length of the city and stop at most major Atlantic City attractions, notably the casinos. The jitneys originate on Pacific Avenue, one block from the Boardwalk. Stops are located on the corner of every route and have color-coded signs so you can figure out which jitney to ride to your selected destination. For more information, call 609-344-8642.

Food

You certainly won't go hungry in Atlantic City. Each casino hotel has multiple restaurants encompassing a wide range of styles and price ranges. There are, among many other offerings, delis and Italian restaurants, barbecue places and cafés, as well as serious (and pricier) restaurants. **Le Palais** at Resorts Casino Hotel (1133 Boardwalk at North Carolina Avenue, 609-340-6400) is highly regarded for its décor and contemporary French food. It serves Sunday brunch and dinner Wednesday through Sunday. **Capriccio**, also at Resorts (609-340-6457), is an upscale Italian restaurant with tableside singers and house-made pastries. **Peregrine's** at the Hilton (609-347-7111) is another of the more ambitious establishments, with an extensive wine list and contemporary menu. It's open for dinner Thursday though Sunday, and jackets are required. At **Bacchanal** at Caesars (800-CAESARS/223-7277), costumed Roman characters entertain at dinner. There are two dinner seatings Wednesday through Sunday, and Sunday brunch is also served; dress is casual but reservations are required.

Several blocks inland from the Boardwalk and south of where the Expressway comes into town is one of the city's gastronomic landmarks. At the **White House Sub Shop** (2301 Arctic Avenue, 609-345-1564), you can get cheese steaks, sausage sandwiches, an assortment of cold subs, and they all are delicious. There are a few booths if you want to eat on the premises, and a good ticket-number system to keep things fair among the takeout orders (you can also phone ahead). More good news: there's free parking for White House customers and Ducktown shoppers in a lot diagonally across the street from the sub shop.

You can find good food in a sit-down setting away from the casinos, too, though you will need to call ahead for hours and table availability. (Some don't take credit cards, so check on that too before you go.) Among the popular restaurants outside the casinos are **Chef Vola's** (111 South Albion Place at Pacific Avenue, 609-345-2022); **Dock's Oyster House** (2405 Atlantic Avenue at Georgia

Avenue, 609-345-0092), family-owned since the late 1800s; and **Little Saigon** (2801 Arctic Avenue at Iowa Avenue, 609-347-9119).

North of the City

Just a couple of miles from Atlantic City is the **Marine Mammal Stranding Center** (Brigantine Boulevard, Brigantine, 609-266-0538; www.mmsc.org). Since its founding in 1978, this private nonprofit organization has responded to more than two thousand calls for stranded whales, dolphins, seals, and sea turtles. Whenever possible, the animals are brought back to the Center for rehabilitation and eventual release. The Marine Mammal Stranding Center is the only organization in New Jersey authorized to rescue and rehabilitate stranded marine mammals and sea turtles. Rehabilitation can last up to several months and cost thousands of dollars for a single animal; donations and membership fees support the facility and help care for the animals.

The center's museum, also known as the Sea Life Education Center, was dedicated in 1986. It is housed in a 1930s Coast Guard boathouse that was brought from the north end of Brigantine and renovated in 1984 by the Bell Atlantic Telephone Pioneers. The museum features twenty-five life-size replicas of marine mammals and fish, all found or stranded in New Jersey waters. Educational displays explain the hazards faced by marine animals that ingest ocean debris. There is also a "Please Touch" display of marine mammal bones. The museum gift shop is a major source of rescue center funding; it sells T-shirts, coffee mugs, jewelry, children's books and games, and stuffed animals, among other items.

The **Mariott Seaview Resort** in Absecon is a peaceful hotel not far from Atlantic City. Long known for its golf facilities, it now has the added amenity of an **Elizabeth Arden Red Door Spa** (609-404-4100) at its Fairway Villas condominium complex just down

Route 9 from the main hotel. It isn't a drop-in sort of place, but it does offer a variety of beauty services, and you might want to plan ahead for a stop at this 12,000-square-foot center, whose facilities include heated outdoor Jacuzzis, an indoor lap pool, relaxation rooms, therapeutic steam rooms, and seventeen rooms for facials and other treatments. For non–hotel guests there is a minimum fee of one hour of spa service.

A few miles north of Atlantic City on Route 9 are several other places that make worthwhile destinations in their own right or side trips from Atlantic City. The **Noyes Museum** (Lily Lake Road, Oceanville, 609-652-8848; www.noyesmuseum.org), just off the highway, is a wonderful place both architecturally and culturally. Southern New Jersey's only private, not-for-profit art museum, it features nineteenth- and twentieth-century American fine and folk art from the mid-Atlantic region, and is especially well known for its collection of vintage bird decoys. It mounts ten to twelve exhibits a year in spacious galleries that extend out from a dramatic central area.

The museum was founded by Ethel Marie Noyes and Fred W. Noyes, Jr., who formed the Mr. and Mrs. Fred Winslow Noyes Foundation in 1973, the year before they sold the Historic Towne of Smithville to the American Broadcasting Companies, providing the financial backing for establishing a museum. Mrs. Noyes died in 1979, but development of the museum continued, and the Noyes Museum of Art opened to the public on June 4, 1983. Although the museum is open year-round, it has relatively limited hours: Wednesday through Sunday, 11 AM to 4 PM. Be sure to call before you go to check any changes in the schedule. The general admission fee for adults is $3, $2 for people over age 65 and ages 12 to 18. Admission is free for children under age 12. Fridays are free for all visitors.

The Noyes Museum is just up (or down) the road from the **Edwin B. Forsythe National Wildlife Refuge** (Great Creek Road, Oceanville, 609-652-1665). The refuge encompasses more than 43,000 acres of coastal habitat, mostly salt meadow and marsh; the refuge includes more than 6,000 acres of undeveloped barrier beach and 5,000 acres

Photograph courtesy of the Noyes Museum

Shorebird decoys from the permanent collection of the Noyes Museum

of woodlands. Even at the main entrance, near the Noyes Museum, you get a sense of space and peace, as well as a chance to see tremendous numbers of birds and other wildlife (the refuge is located in one of the Atlantic Flyway's most active flight paths). Most of the public-use sections are at the refuge's Brigantine Division headquarters area in Oceanville and are open from sunrise to sunset. (The Barnegat Division is farther north.) Human use of the refuge is not free; there is a $4 entrance fee. One of the favorite parts of the refuge for many people is the eight-mile wildlife drive; there are also several foot trails. The refuge suggests spring and fall as the best times for wildlife viewing. Seasonal waterfowl and deer hunting are permitted in some sections of both the Brigantine and Barnegat Divisions, and there is a boat ramp at Scotts Landing in the Brigantine Division.

The **Historic Towne of Smithville** (609-652-7777; www.smithvillenj.com) has undergone a number of changes since being sold to ABC. It is a collection of old buildings clustered around a green; the Smithville Inn, which was once the centerpiece, closed for a while and has since reopened. Smithville is primarily a shopping destination, with dozens of shops, such as the **Cook's Corner** (609-748-9030), the **Candle Shop** (609-652-0440), and an outpost of the **Tomasello Winery** (609-652-2320) to make you feel that you've gone for a ride in the country. There are several restaurants in addition to the Inn.

Chapter Twenty-five

Cape May: City and County, Buildings and Beaches

What is there to say about Cape May? It's charming, historic, and scenic. It offers sandy beaches, whale-watching excursions, side trips to lighthouses and a tranquil state park. Cape May City itself is filled with restaurants, shops, and wonderful nineteenth-century architecture. The two-lane roads west of town are great for bicycle riding. Cape May is a deservedly discovered treasure. People love it—and they love to visit it. A sunny Saturday in September may be a peaceful time in Stone Harbor or Long Beach Island, where you may even have trouble finding an ice-cream shop open for business. But in Cape May, the season doesn't end with Labor Day. The trick is to figure out a time to visit when the bridge that takes you past the piers and boats into town will not be lined with cars moving slowly (or not at all) toward the narrow streets of Cape May City.

Cape May is as much about history and houses as about being a resort. People from Philadelphia and points south, as well as New Jerseyans, have been coming to Cape May for a long time. Its hundreds of late-Victorian buildings are relative newcomers to the scene; the town and its cape have served as a resort since decades before the Civil War. As you walk the streets, you know you are part of a long series of people who have come here for sun, sand, peace, and entertainment.

Although Cape May no longer looks much like Nantucket, that classic gray-and-white whaling island/town off the coast of Massachusetts, its origins are not as different as present-day appearance suggests. Whalers settled in Cape May in the seventeenth century, as they did in Nantucket. By the early 1800s, steamships were bringing people from Philadelphia to Cape May in search of sea breezes. Rail connections followed within decades. Presidents visited. Seaside hotels were built. In 1878, a major fire destroyed much of Cape May, and the frilly, gingerbready replacement buildings provide a charming setting for a Cape May sojourn. Because Cape May became less popular in the early 1900s, the replacements were not replaced; new development had moved north to Atlantic City.

To get a sense of where you are and where you will be going, stop first at Cape May's **Welcome Center** at the corner of Lafayette and Jackson Streets (407 Lafayette Street, 609-884-9562). If you are arriving from the north across the bridge, the Welcome Center is hard to miss. The Center has a small parking lot with half an hour's free parking as well as three hours' paid parking, and better yet, it has a wealth of brochures and maps for self-guided exploring.

Bustling **Jackson Street**, home of restaurants and inns, is highly decorative; **Columbia Avenue** is another particularly rich lode for those in search of architectural treasures. A self-guided tour map will keep you on track. It will also give you an opportunity to admire decorative exteriors such as that of the **Mainstay Inn** (635 Columbia Avenue and the **Southern Mansion** (720 Washington Street). The **Emlen Physick Estate** (1048 Washington Street, 609-884-5404) en-

Photograph courtesy of Mid-Atlantic Center for the Arts

The Emlen Physick Estate

joys what is perhaps the highest profile of all the Cape May architectural gems. The circa-1880 mansion that is the estate's centerpiece is
believed to have been designed by Frank Furness, one of the re-
nowned architects of the day. The house, administered by the Mid-
Atlantic Center for the Arts, is now open to the paying public as a
house museum displaying Victorian furniture, toys, clothing, and
other items. Not only is the house itself interesting, with more than
a dozen authentically restored rooms of exhibits, but there are several appealing shops on the premises, including the Sun Porch Museum Shop, which sells period-style jewelry, toys, and decorative
objects, as well as books. Twinings Tearoom at the Physick Estate
(609-884-5405, ext. 138; reservations required), located in the Carriage House across from the main house, serves "tea luncheons" and
"elegant afternoon tea." The set menus include a variety of tea sandwiches, including cucumber with mint butter, smoked salmon with
dill and cream cheese, and egg salad with watercress. Naturally, there
is a selection of teas, and the adjoining Gallery Shop sells tea and
tea-related accessories, including a delightful assortment of teapots.

Incidentally, the Emlen Physick Estate is a few blocks away from the Jackson/Decatur/Washington Square commercial concentration, and it has a parking lot. If you prefer to take a more compact walking tour of just one set of streets, you can always drive over to the estate afterward.

For organized tours, turn your attention to the **Mid-Atlantic Center for the Arts,** or MAC (for information, 609-884-5404; for tickets, 800-275-4278; www.capemaymac.org). You should have no difficulty finding a tour to join. The Washington Street Mall Information Booth on Ocean Street is the usual starting point. Even during the off-season there are weekend tours and events; the schedule is busier in summer. Be sure to call ahead if you want to plan your visit around a tour, since schedules vary by time of year and day of the week.

MAC's trolley tours may be the best and most general way to get to know the town. There are also guided walking tours through the Historic District, an "Inns and Outs of Cape May" tour that combines a one-hour walking tour of the Historic District with a visit to two landmark houses, a "Great Estates" tour that goes to the Emlen Physick Estate and the Southern Mansion, and many more. MAC sponsors or co-sponsors special events throughout the year. The October Victorian Week, which features historic house tours, Victorian fashion shows, brass-band concerts, and many other tempting activities, is one of the highlights. Two weekends' worth of Spring Festivals feature garden tours, demonstrations by Wheaton Village glassblowers, and entertainments such as nineteenth-century dance workshops and an antiques and collectibles show.

Not only does MAC provide insight and guidance regarding Cape May's buildings, it also can help you find an alternative to driving and parking. Several times a day, **Cape May Seashore Lines** will take you through Cape May County, with stops at the Cold Spring Station and the 4-H Fairgrounds as well as the Cape May City Terminal. **Cold Spring Village** (Seashore Road, 609-884-1810) is an open-air living history museum that operates from late May to September. The buildings were gathered together and brought from other places in the area to create the semblance of a southern New Jersey village of the nineteenth century; costumed interpreters demonstrate period trades and crafts.

Beyond the Buildings

Cape May is so charming it's easy to forget why it became a resort in the first place. Easy, that is, until you find yourself on Beach Drive, with a wide expanse of sandy beach visible from the sidewalks, and block after block of hotels on the inland side of the street. Beach passes are needed in season, but the beach is beautiful at any time of year and provides an intriguing, timeless contrast to the densely packed buildings that surround you less than one block inland.

This is a place that also tempts you to get out onto the water and gives you many chances to do so. From May to September, MAC (609-884-5404 or 800-275-4278) and the Cape May Whale Watchers co-sponsor several **Delaware Bay lighthouse cruises** as well as a **World War II history cruise**. The former take you past seven lighthouses (Brandywine Shoal, Abandoned Light, and Cross Ledge, to name a few), some of which are visible only from the water; the latter takes you past bunkers, gun emplacements, and lookout towers. The Cape May Whale Watch and Research Center (1286 Wilson Drive, Cape May, 609-898-0055; www.capemaywhalewatch.com) runs **whale- and dolphin-watch cruises** from April to December. For a trip that combines birdwatching with sea travel, there's the **Salt Marsh Safari Cruise** aboard the *Skimmer.* It sails from Miss Chris Marina (Second Avenue and Wilson Drive, Schellenger's Landing, Cape May, 609-884-3100; www.skimmer.com).

The **Cape May–Lewes Ferry** (609-889-7200; www.capemaylewesferry.com) may be part of a longer coastal journey for some travelers, but it also makes a great day trip. The ferry sails several times a day year-round, so if you just want to spend some time on the water traveling the seventeen miles between New Jersey and

Delaware, you can do that at virtually any time. Several seasonal
foot-passenger travel packages are also available. Prices include
round-trip ferry and shuttle transportation to and from ferry terminals. For example, from June to September, the Historical Lewes Tour
leaves from Cape May and gives you the opportunity to visit the
Lewes Historical Society Complex, the Cannonball Complex maritime museum, and the *HMB DeBraak* exhibit at the Zwaanendael
Museum. In July and August, the DiscoverSea Shipwreck Tour takes
you on a treasure tour to Fenwick Island; sights include shipwreck
artifacts and a restored lifesaving station.

Two miles from Cape May City, **Cape May Point State Park** (Cape
May Point, 609-884-2159) has everything a peninsula-tip park should
have. The Cape May Lighthouse, the most visible marker at the park,
is smoothly painted in a bland shade of tan (its original color). At
first glance, it's not one of the most picturesque lighthouses at the
Shore, but it is very visible and has a lot to offer visitors. The Mid-
Atlantic Center for the Arts is at work here too, having undertaken a
restoration and interpretation program. Paying visitors can climb to
the top of the 157-foot-tall structure and get a panoramic view of the
Atlantic Ocean and the Delaware Bay. In season, visitors are greeted
by actors playing the couple who, in the 1920s, were the last keepers
of the lighthouse.

Another interesting piece of history at the Point is the World
War II bunker clearly visible from the shaded pavilion close to the
parking lot and visitor center. During the war, the park area, not yet
a park, was a coastal defense base and bunkers were built in 1942 to
protect against possible attack. The Cape May Point bunker, originally 900 feet inland, is now in the water as a result of coastal erosion. The museum in the interpretive center at the park has a fascinating but sobering photographic blowup illustrating the extent of
erosion all around the Point, as well as other interesting and informative displays.

On a more cheerful note, Cape May Point is a birders' paradise;
most of the park has been designated as the **Cape May Point Natural Area**. The area is a resting and feeding place for migrating birds
and monarch butterflies; it also has a noteworthy population of

dragonflies. At the parking-lot edge of the Natural Area, a Wildlife Observation Platform provides an especially good vantage point for viewing the fall migration of birds and butterflies. Three colorfully blazed trails, including a half-mile barrier-free self-guiding boardwalk nature trail, lead through the marshes. They are lined by yellow flowering plants (in September, at any rate) as tall as people, and by enormously tall grasses called phragmites, explained in one interpretive sign as a kind of weed that forces out natural flora and diminishes the habitat for the birds and other fauna of the area.

The two-lane road leading from Cape May City to Cape May Point State Park has broad shoulders in both directions and is very flat. Unsurprisingly, it is a popular bike route. Not only is it a short and easy ride between town and park, but the winding streets of Cape May Point just outside the park are attractive, with lovely old buildings—notably the tiny Carpenter Gothic St. Peter's-by-the-Sea, an Episcopal church built for the Centennial celebration in Philadelphia in 1876 and soon afterward moved to Cape May Point. It has since moved several more times, first to be closer to the water for the cooling breezes, then farther inland to escape the encroaching sea. Nearby are both appealing Victorian houses and interesting contemporary homes. There is also a nature area where you can walk along a fenced path to a jetty.

Although Cape May City itself is often too congested for leisurely bike riding, it has potential if you manage to find a time when there is less traffic. If you don't want to bring your bike to Cape May, rentals are available; check at the Welcome Center for brochures.

Sunset Beach (Sunset Boulevard, Cape May Point, 609-884-7079), just down the road, is known for Cape May diamonds, to be found both on the beach and at the nearby gift shops, and for the concrete ship *Atlantus*. The "diamonds" are quartz crystals that have washed down from the upper Delaware River and traveled over thousands of years to the sea. The *Atlantus* is a relic of the World War I steel shortage, when the United States Shipping Board planned an emergency fleet of thirty-eight concrete ships. Twelve concrete ships were put into service, and construction was begun but not completed on two others. The *Atlantus* was launched in November 1918, about a week after the Armistice, at Wilmington, North Carolina, commissioned in June 1919, and served for a year as a government-owned but privately operated commercial coal steamer in New England. Along with other members of the "Concrete Fleet," the *Atlantus* was decommissioned in 1920; it was stripped after a salvage company bought it. In 1926, it was towed to Cape May by a company that wanted to start a ferry service from Cape May to Lewes, Delaware. While work was being done to prepare the ferry route and channel, the *Atlantus* broke loose of her moorings during a storm in June of that year and went aground. Attempts to free the ship were futile.

Food and Other Fun

Cape May is more than sights, sea, and sand. There is a lot of food, both to walk around with and to sit down and enjoy. It starts with the scent of fried clams that perfumes the air near the South Jersey Marina on the way into Cape May. It teases you with the displays at Morrow's Nut House, with locations on the Boardwalk and on the Washington Street Mall, where a bag filled with a quarter pound of the deluxe mix makes a nice snack, or lunch if you tell yourself nuts are full of protein. Laura's Fudge Shop, on the Washington Street Mall and at Washington Commons at Ocean Street, sells fudge, chocolate-dipped fruit, and the ubiquitous Shore treat, saltwater taffy; the multi-location Fudge Kitchen will also tempt you with sweets, including hand-dipped chocolates as well as fudge. **Dry Dock Ice Cream Bar and Grill** (1440 Texas Avenue, 609-884-3434) is popular for burgers and grinders as well as ice cream treats. The

Cape May branch of **Uncle Bill's Pancake House** (Beach and Perry Streets, 609-884-7199) will feed your family three meals a day. And then there are the heavy-duty, well-known Cape May eateries. **The Mad Batter** (19 Jackson Street in the Carroll Hotel, 609-884-5970) doesn't just serve the wonderful breakfasts its name suggests. It also serves a variety of contemporary and regional American food for lunch and dinner. Jackson Street is full of interesting building and people, and a meal at the Mad Batter is part of the experience. **Axelsson's Blue Claw** (Ocean Drive, Lower Township, 609-884-5878), which offers a serious seafood dining experience, is open for dinner Thursday through Sunday. **The Lobster House** (Fisherman's Wharf, Schellenger's Landing, 609-884-8296) is another classic Cape May dining spot; its hours vary seasonally, but its quality is consistent, and you get a value-adding view of boats and water. Two well-regarded destinations for Italian food are **Frescos** (412 Bank Street, 609-884-0366) and **Cucina Rosa** (301 Washington Street Mall, 609-898-9800). Among the elegant restaurants enjoying statewide reputations for fine and creative food are the **Washington Inn** (801 Washington Street, 609-884-5697), the **Ebbitt Room** at the Virginia Hotel (25 Jackson Street, 609-884-5700), and **410 Bank Street** (410 Bank Street, 609-884-2177).

The Beaches: The Wildwoods and Points North

Although Cape May brings to mind images of Victorian mansions and wonderful restaurants, it encompasses much more than one town. Starting at Wildwood—really **the Wildwoods**, since Wildwood, North Wildwood, and Wildwood Crest are separate yet related entities—and heading up the Shore, Cape May County is home to towns that virtually define the Shore for thousands of people, especially people from Philadelphia. If you drive through Avalon in September, when the weekends are still lively but many stores and places of refreshment are closed, you are likely to see a "Go Eagles" sign outside a tavern.

Walter Choroszewski

Amusements on the boardwalk, Wildwood

Traveling north out of Cape May, you can go directly onto Ocean Drive. After you have paid the first of several tolls that will allow you to travel on the bridges of Ocean Drive, you will be in Wildwood Crest. Then comes Wildwood, home of countless now-classic mid-twentieth-century motels, wide, free beaches, and an essence-of-Shore boardwalk. The free beaches are a key to Wildwood's identity, and especially important for day-trippers, although you will have to find a parking space—and pay for it—at meters or in lots. Wildwood attracts tens of thousands of visitors daily in search of summer fun. Unlike Cape May, Wildwood is primarily a summer place, although the quiet, relatively unpeopled streets have a certain mystique out of season; many of the business are only open seasonally. The board-walk amusement parks are one of the signatures of Wildwood. **Morey's Pier and Theme Parks** (609-522-3900) is a massive pres-ence, really three parks with several major roller coasters, waterparks, go-cart tracks, and more. **Dinosaur Beach Adventure Theme Park** (Poplar Avenue and Boardwalk, Wildwood, 609-523-1440; www.dinosaurbeach.com) offers its share of thrill rides, including the Crazy Mouse roller coaster with spinning cars. **Park Place** (5000 Park Boulevard, Wildwood, 609-522-4400) has elaborate miniature-golf courses, batting cages, a roller rink, and an arcade. Bicycle rent-als are an appealing option for day visitors.

The Wildwoods keep their visitors busy and have information centers (Boardwalk at Schellenger Avenue, Wildwood, 609-522-1407; Rambler Road at the beach, Wildwood Crest, 609-522-0221; and 22nd Street and the Boardwalk, North Wildwood, 609-729-8686) to help visitors figure out what to do; they are open daily in summer. For a change of pace in the Wildwoods, pay a visit to **Hereford Inlet Lighthouse** (Central Avenue, North Wildwood, 609-522-4520). Al-though the turret of this white-painted Victorian house is visible above the densely packed houses of its neighborhood, it comes as something of a surprise when you turn the corner and see the entire lighthouse. It is a lovely house, considered one of the Shore's better lighthouses in terms of living conditions. It has five fireplaces and pleasant living quarters for the keeper and his family, and a flower garden makes the surroundings even more inviting in summer. Here-ford Inlet Lighthouse is open year-round, but hours vary by season, so be sure to call before you go.

Stone Harbor and its northern neighbor, **Avalon**, share a barrier beach island just up from the Wildwoods along Ocean Drive; you have to pay a fifty-cent toll on the drawbridge to get to Stone Harbor. Both towns have reputations as family resorts where people stay for days if not weeks, but there's no reason you can't go there for a day trip. In fact, there are especially good reasons to visit Stone Harbor in addition to the island's beaches, restaurants, and shopping.

The **Stone Harbor Bird Sanctuary** is registered as a National Landmark by the National Park Service. The trees—cedar and holly, among others—of the sanctuary come as something of a surprise when you approach them in the midst of an otherwise open and marshy landscape. This twenty-one-acre nature area is officially a heronry, and a wide variety of herons nest there in early spring.

The **Wetlands Institute** (1075 Stone Harbor Boulevard, 609-368-1211) is much larger—6,000 acres. Its protected salt marshes are home to birds, butterflies, and other fauna. There are trails and boardwalks, as well as educational exhibits. The Institute is open year-round, and its Wings 'n' Water Festival is a popular post–Labor Day event.

Avalon, like other towns along the Shore, offers a variety of fishing opportunities. The **Avalon Sport Fishing Center**, between 15th and 16th Streets in the northern section of town, is the headquarters for a fleet of charter and head boats. Farther south, at 54th Street, is the **Bay Park Marina**, which has a municipal boat ramp and slips. You don't even need to leave dry land to do your angling: you can also fish from the surf, jetties, and piers.

If you drive through on a cool, cloudy day, **Sea Isle City** feels less like a beach resort and more like a mainland town than its neighbors to the south. It has lots of shops and restaurants and a pleasantly built-up feeling in its central area. But the impression is misleading. The key attraction in season, of course, is Sea Isle City's long stretch of sandy beach and the paved promenade that runs along the beach. Sea Isle City also has a fishing-boat fleet offering trips of varying lengths, from four hours on up.

And then there's Ocean City, one of the legendary family Shore resorts. It's a dry town, which gives it, if not exactly a peaceful quality, a different overall mood than towns where public alcohol consumption is part of the scene. It does, however, have eight miles of beaches, three miles of boardwalk, twenty public tennis courts, a twelve-hole golf course, and an arts center and historic museum.

The **Ocean City Music Pier** (609-525-9248), built in 1928, remains a center of activity. **Gillian's Wonderland Pier** at Sixth Street is a perennial Boardwalk magnet for children and others. **Corson's Inlet State Park** (Ocean Drive, 609-861-2404) is a place for boating and fishing, as well as walking along the coastal dune trail, if man-made amusements begin to pall.

The Shore in summer and the Shore in the off-season are two distinctly different places. In summer, there's a dazzling array of ice-cream places, snack shops, and restaurants at every taste and price level. The summer Shore is a constant festival, and its delights are widely announced in a variety of media. You can find everything from fireworks to historical museums. In winter, there's less to choose from, but you will not go hungry or un-entertained. (And in most towns, parking regulations are suspended after mid-September, so all those beckoning, empty parking spots are free and legal.) Be sure to call before you head for any Shore points out of season, though, to find out if your specific destination is open—whether it's Hereford Lighthouse or **Kuishimbo** (330 96th Street, Stone Harbor, 609-967-7007), the popular Japanese restaurant whose hours vary with the seasons.

Coda: "Inland" Cape May

Wait, there's more. Cape May City isn't isolated; it's part of a larger, historic, and still-attractive community, known in travel brochures as the Jersey Cape. The stretch of Route 9 between Clermont and Cape May Court House isn't dramatically beautiful, but there are dozens of quiet old houses along the road—and almost as many antique shops, as well as a smattering of farmstands. And then there is the surprise of **Leaming's Run Gardens** (1845 Route 9, Cape May Court House, 609-465-5871). The shaded, sandy parking lot just off the highway sets a peaceful mood and makes a fine transition to these lovely gardens, which are open May through October. More than thirty acres of gardens offer a variety of color and vistas. The twenty-five individually designed gardens make up the largest annual gardens in the nation. Special features include bridges, ponds, and gazebos, and the gardens are particular attraction for humming-birds in August. The Colonial Farm section illustrates seventeenth-century Cape May life. There is a vegetable garden outside a log cabin, and the surprisingly southern crops of cotton and tobacco also grow at the farm.

Cape May County Park (Route 9 and Pine Lane, Cape May Court House, 609-465-9210) offers another somewhat unexpected treat. In addition to being an especially pretty park, with lots of shade trees and a lovely white gazebo at the end of a pier visible just off Route 9, it has a very popular and well-maintained zoo, which is open daily.

Chapter Twenty-six

Wheaton Village:
Glass Old and New

Geographically speaking, Wheaton and Waterloo are almost as far apart as two places in New Jersey can be. One is in Sussex County, tucked away in the rolling Musconetcong River Valley along the remnants of the Morris Canal. The other is on the plains of Cumberland County, where the Maurice River winds its way to Delaware Bay. Their names go well together, however, and, more to the point, they both represent significant aspects of the state's economic and social past: the iron and transportation activity of the early nineteenth century in the case of the Village at Waterloo, and the glassmaking era that thrived well into the twentieth century at Wheaton Village. Even more to the point for this book, they both make terrific day trips that can be tweaked to fit many interests and age groups.

Wheaton Village (Glasstown Road, Millville, 856-825-6800; www.wheatonvillage.org) is the place in New Jersey, maybe in the whole mid-Atlantic region, to go to learn about American glassmaking. It's easily accessible via Route 55, one of those wide, flat South Jersey roads that people in the densely populated northern counties don't know about. It opens up the central part of the state's southern tier as effectively as the Parkway leads to the Shore

Photograph courtesy of Wheaton Village

A display at the Museum of American Glass at Wheaton Village

and the Turnpike leads to Camden and beyond. When you drive up to the parking lot at Wheaton Village, it doesn't look terribly imposing; the entrance is modest, and admission isn't very expensive. As soon as you walk in, however, you realize that there is a lot more than met the eye a few minutes ago. Wheaton Village is all about glassmaking, from its earliest colonial history to the present day. The Village is quite compact, and the small map in the brochure you get when you arrive will lead you reliably to all the attractions. Incidentally, this is a year-round attraction, open daily from April through December and Wednesday through Sunday from January through March; it is closed on Thanksgiving Day, Christmas Day, New Year's Day, and Easter Sunday. It is an excellent family day trip because the crafts demonstrations and the shop give all age groups something to be intrigued by; the museum alone is worth a trip from anywhere in the state.

The first major feature you see is the **Museum of American Glass**, with a mildly elegant exterior that doesn't really prepare you for the extensive and impressive exhibit inside. Its lobby is furnished like an elaborate and impressive Victorian parlor, full of sparkling glass objects and ornate furniture. After that dramatic introduction, you can tour the museum for a chronological display of all sorts of American glass. The museum has the largest collection of American glass in the country; it displays more than 6,500 items. (The wonderful glass museum in Corning, New York, is larger, but it covers the whole world, and many more centuries.) The early displays reflect the earliest stages of American glassmaking history, with very simple pitchers and bottles; it's impressive to see how many of the early pieces were made in southern New Jersey, whose sandy soil provided a key material for the industry. One of my favorite rooms is the one that displays all sorts of delicately colored, elaborate glassware from the mid-nineteenth century. They lend themselves to serving fruit compotes and punch, and the technology behind them is as intriguing as the colors and designs are appealing. Another highlight is the kitchen vignette, which displays not only the expected glass utilitarian items such as Mason jars but also such oddities as a glass washboard. The glass canes are a surprise, as well. The room full of paperweights is a special treat, not just for the Millville Roses but for the amazingly intricate flowers and historical scenes that have been created over the years by craftspeople to commemorate important events or beautiful natural objects. The room or rooms you like best will depend on what sort of glasswork and artwork you like best. For me, the later rooms, with their Art Nouveau pieces, are very impressive but not as distinctive to Wheaton Village as the earlier rooms; the contemporary exhibits at the end are often striking, but don't necessarily fit the reflective mood set by the earlier work. Other visitors may have a completely different reaction and be delighted by the unusual artwork produced by contemporary artists.

Once you have seen the museum's extraordinary offerings, it becomes even more interesting to watch present-day glassblowers at work. Especially for children, the T. C. **Wheaton Glass Factory** will probably be more appealing than the museum because it is dramatic and active. On a hot day, the fires of the glass factory ovens add to the heat of the air and give spectators a vivid idea of just what it

must have felt like to work in a glass factory day in and day out. One
June day when my daughter and I visited, people edged toward open
doors for a breeze, but didn't want to stray too far from the demonstrations, either. The work looks startlingly bright and dangerous.
Molten glass is fiercely hot, and for all its beauty, a little sinister.
There are several narrated demonstrations a day, and the glass blow-
ers make pitchers, bottles, bowls, vases and paperweights.

A special feature of the factory is the opportunity to make your
own paperweight, from one of four designs, under the guidance of
one of Wheaton Village's master glass artists. You need an advance
appointment (856-825-6800, ext. 2753). The cost in autumn of
2000 was $55 plus $5 for shipping and handling, and participants
must be twenty-one or older.

The glass factory is just the first of many opportunities to watch
craftspeople in action. **Crafts and Trades Row** highlights the skills
of potters, woodcarvers, and, perhaps most spectacularly,
flameworkers, who manipulate glass rods into brightly colored, often intricate shapes. There's a tin shop, too, but it's separated from
the rest of the crafts area by something else that children will like—
the Palermo railroad station. This restored 1897 building is the boarding point for a short ride on a half-scale model of an 1863 train.
There's also a small schoolhouse not too far away, on the way to the
row of shops. The **Centre Grove Schoolhouse** is a one-room building that dates to 1876. The **Down Jersey Folklife Center** is just across
the way from the schoolhouse; while it does not have the flash and
fire of the crafts demonstrations on the other side of the village, it is
definitely worth some time. It features the artistic and cultural traditions of the state's eight southern counties, and once you adjust to
the different pace of the exhibits, it becomes just as absorbing as the
rest of the Village.

It may seem too materialistic to focus on the shops at Wheaton

Village. After all, the point of the visit is supposed to be a trip to the museum and the crafts demonstrations, a nicely balanced combination of history and culture. But these shops reflect the activities and mission of Wheaton Village so well that it almost seems as if browsing through the shops and then buying at least a small souvenir is part of the educational and entertaining experience.

The **Arthur Gorham Paperweight Shop** has a large selection of contemporary and traditional paperweights in a wide range of prices. The shop also sells replicas of Wheaton Village paperweights, ranging from a frog and a sleeping cat (each for well under ten dollars), to more elaborate bubble weights, a delicious-looking peach (for about fifty dollars), and Tony DePalma's Millville Rose, with the traditional colored glass rose in the center. (You will probably already have admired Millville Rose paperweights at the museum and may be especially tempted to possess one of your own.) A moderately priced object with an unusual history is the glass egg, used by women in the Victorian era to cool their hands on hot days. The eggs are available in several cheerful colors.

Among the other more expensive items are the pieces by contemporary artists such as Paul J. Stankard, whose delicate botanical designs are amazingly realistic and really beautiful. Many of the more elaborate paperweights cost hundreds of dollars, and admiring them is more in the nature of a gallery visit than a shopping trip, but they're well worth admiring; the abundance of lower-priced items means there is something for almost everyone to purchase. The shop also sells vases and other tempting pieces such as kaleidoscopes. This is definitely a shop primarily for grownups, although my daughter still treasures the simple green paperweight with white swirls that we bought there several years ago, when she was still in elementary school.

On a similarly high level of artistry, the **Gallery of American Craft** sells pottery and glass items, as well as other products made by the craftworks at the Village. For slightly more practical purchases, there is the **Brownstone Emporium**, which is less an art-glass store than a great place to buy gifts and mementoes made of glass. It sells cut, pressed, and hand-blown glassware from the Village as well as from a number of well-known American manufacturers. For child-centered shopping (also fun for grownups), there is the **General Store**, which is less unusual and more like the stores at other historic sites but still very appealing. It sells old-fashioned candy, housewares, books, marbles, dry goods, and other nostalgic items that are easy for twenty-first-century visitors to relate to (and afford). There is also a **Christmas Shop**. Open year-round, it sells hand-blown glass ornaments and other items appropriate to the season.

Food

If there's shopping, can food be far behind? Fortunately, no. Wheaton Village is one of those places where you can park and not leave until you've seen everything you want to see; there's no need to go off the premises to find food. Located at the edge of the Village, at the end of a small lake, the **PaperWaiter Restaurant and Pub** (1111 Village Drive, Millville, 856-825-4000) serves lunch and dinner daily, and breakfast on Saturday and Sunday.

Chapter Twenty-seven

Sand, Space, and Sandwalks: The Delaware Bay Shore

This is a region and a trip for wandering, exploring, and discovering, whether it is a street of picture-perfect sea captains' homes in Mauricetown, a multipurpose park in Bridgeton, or a beach accessible from a dead-end road so pitted you wonder whether you were really supposed to drive your car down it quite as far as you did. Bridgeton's historic district is very large, Mauricetown's charming center is very small, and the beaches along the Delaware Bay are havens for birds more than people. Perhaps the whole is greater than the sum of its parts, and any single attraction taken by itself may not be a star, but there's a lot here that doesn't resemble anyplace else along the Atlantic Shore or in the more polished historic districts farther north, and one person's desolate beach is another person's bird-watching paradise.

Bridgeton

When you read that Bridgeton is the town with the state's largest historic district, with more than two thousand buildings, you may have a vision of a secret Williamsburg. This is not a manicured colonial treasure, however, but a small city with a diverse architectural and economic personality. Bridgeton was founded in 1686; its location, on the Cohansey River, was the key to its early prosperity. Its first settler was Richard Hancock, who built a sawmill at the head of the river. After the first bridge across the river was constructed in 1716, Bridgeton's importance increased.

Because of its relative prominence during the eighteenth and nineteenth centuries, Bridgeton has a major collection of interesting houses and commercial buildings. It is not a compact community, however, and it is easy to lose your way among the evocatively named streets. Do you want East Commerce Street? West Broad? Atlantic? Laurel? To figure out where you are and where you are going, you should stop for a map and all possible brochures at the **Bridgeton Cumberland Tourist Information Center** (856-451-4802) at the junction of Route 49 (East Broad Street) and Route 77.

For an overview of centuries-old buildings, stroll along Lake Street, West Commerce Street, and Franklin Drive, where you can feast your eyes on simple Federal-style homes and more elaborate Victorian ones. **Potter's Tavern** (49-51 West Broad Street), a mid-eighteenth-century clapboard structure, is where the first newspaper in New Jersey was published: the *Plain Dealer* appeared weekly for several months in early 1776. A few blocks east, the **George Woodruff Indian Museum** in the Bridgeton Free Public Library (150 East Commerce Street, 856-451-2620) displays Nanticoke Lenni-Lenape arrowheads, clay bowls, and other artifacts—20,000 in all.

Bridgeton has been the Cumberland County seat since 1749. In the lobby of the county courthouse on West Broad Street, you can visit Cumberland County's own Liberty Bell, an exhibit of the Cumberland County Historical Society. The bell was cast in 1763 in Bridgewater, Massachusetts, and purchased by Cumberland County citizens. On July 7, 1776, it rang to summon people to the courthouse at what was then called Cohansey Bridge to hear a formal reading of the Declaration of Independence. From 1852 to 1929, it hung in the belfry of the West Jersey Academy.

When you have seen as much architectural history as you want to, there is still more to do in Bridgeton. During the nineteenth century, the Cumberland Nail and Iron Works thrived and for a time was the town's largest employer. The company closed in the 1890s, and in 1902 the town bought the 1,100 acres that had been the nail company's site and turned it into **Bridgeton City Park** (Mayor Aitken Drive). This park, along the west bank of the Cohansey River north of downtown, is an impressive civic resource and houses a number of museums and other attractions. In addition to nature trails and facilities for picnicking, swimming, boating, and sports, it is the home of the **Cohanzick Zoo** (856-455-3230); opened in 1934, it was New Jersey's first municipal zoo and is open daily. The **New Sweden Farmstead Museum** (856-455-9785) is a relatively recent addition to the park. Built in 1988, it is a re-creation of a seventeenth-century South Jersey Scandinavian farmstead and includes barns and other outbuildings. Tours are offered May through September; be sure to call before you go if you want to visit when it is open. Nearby, in the building that was once the nail company's office, is the **Nail Mill Museum** (856-455-4100). It contains both nail-industry items and general Bridgeton artifacts.

Mauricetown

Mauricetown is a village on the banks of the Maurice River, not too many miles south of Millville along the high-speed state routes and accessible via an incongruously large and up-to-date bridge from Route 47 that deposits you in a much quieter world. Mauricetown was a fishing port, one of several villages along the river—Port Norris and Bivalve were the best-known—that served as centers for the American oyster industry. During the second half of the nineteenth century, Mauricetown was also known as the home of a surprisingly large number of trans-Atlantic and coastal ship captains. During the 1800s and early 1900s, as Port Norris and Bivalve developed as busy working ports, shipping millions of pounds of oysters a year, Mauricetown continued to have a more solidly residential appearance.

Before you drive over the bridge expecting to find a little Nantucket, you should be aware that the town center is only a few blocks square, with a nice collection of well-maintained nineteenth-century houses and one notably older house, the **Caesar Hoskins House**, at the corner of South and Second Streets. It is a cedar log cabin, probably built before 1714, with a lath-and-plaster protective coating dating to the early 1800s. A number of the houses have plaques on them, so you will learn as you walk by who lived there. The beautiful Greek Revival Mauricetown Academy on High Street is an elegant highlight of the village, and the **Mauricetown Methodist Episcopal Church**, at the corner of Noble and Second Streets, has a spire visible from Delaware Bay and the mouth of the Maurice River. The **Mauricetown Historical Society** (856-785-0457) sponsors several events throughout the year designed to give visitors and local residents a chance to learn more about the town's past.

In the 1950s, a parasite attacked the oysters of Delaware Bay, and research continues into ways to revive oystering in the area; quahog clams are now the leading industry. If you would like to learn more about the Delaware Estuary's natural resources and maritime life, you may be interested in the **Delaware Bay Schooner Project**, based in Bivalve (2800 High Street, 856-785-2060 or 800-485-3072). Founded in 1988, it owns and operates the *A. J. Meerwald,* which started life in 1928 as an oyster schooner. The schooner's homeport is Bivalve, whose shipping sheds still evoke the oyster industry when it was at its peak, but it sails from port to port, providing educational sails and programs. The **Delaware Bay Museum** (1727 Main Street, Port Norris) is another of the organization's projects; its exhibits focus on the maritime traditions of the Bay. Call the Delaware Bay Schooner Project for museum hours and the *A. J. Meerwald's* sail schedule.

The Maurice River isn't all fisheries and sea captains' houses. It is a federally designated Wild and Scenic River, and although it isn't long—about twenty miles from Millville, where it is dammed to form Union Lake, to its mouth at Bivalve—it is, indeed, scenic, and for most of its length very peaceful. In fact, four rivers make up the Wild and Scenic River system here: the Maurice, the Menantico, the

Walter Choroszewski

East Point Lighthouse, Heislerville

Manumuskin, and the Muskee Creek. The Maurice is known now primarily as a canoeing river, but there are also a number of marinas along its banks. In addition to recreational boating, income-producing crabbing and oystering still play an important part in life along the Bay and the river.

Farther east, surprisingly close to Cape May, on a dead-end road off Route 47, is an especially picturesque lighthouse. It isn't open to the public at the time of this writing because the interior is undergoing restoration, but its location is so appealing that it's worth the short detour. The **East Point Lighthouse** (856-327-3714) in Heislerville was built in 1849 to mark the mouth of the Maurice River (it's across the river from Port Norris and Bivalve). This house-shaped lighthouse—it's a rectangle with a peaked roof—is built of brick and looks as though it was whitewashed or painted once, but now it's mostly red again. The tower on the roof looks less like a traditional New England widow's walk and more like the top of a lighthouse. It served as a navigational marker to Port Norris, Millville,

Mauricetown, and Port Elizabeth and is the second-oldest lighthouse still standing in New Jersey.

One of the main features along this section of the Delaware Bay is the seemingly endless expanse of tidal marshes. Some have been virtually untouched for centuries, others were once diked to keep them from flooding so they could be used as salt-hay fields but have now reverted to tidal marshes. Many of the marshes are now nature preserves or wildlife management areas. Many are designated, though usually unstaffed, points of interest along the New Jersey Coastal Heritage Trail and are ideal for bird-watching and, in some cases, hiking.

One of the best-known of the latter is the **Heislerville Wildlife Management Area**, accessible by several roads—they are marked with signs for the area—including a narrow road just off the almost-as-narrow road that leads to East Point Lighthouse. The nearly 4,000 acres of this preserve include Moores Beach and Thompsons Beach, which are both known for their springtime populations of horseshoe crabs that have come ashore to lay their eggs. You can drive around a portion of the Heislerville Wildlife Management Area for an overview of the flora and fauna. The wildlife include wintering snow geese, mute swans who live there year-round, and, occasionally, bald eagles. It is also a good place to observe seasonal migrations of shore birds. In spring, they stop on their way back from South America to feast on horseshoe-crab eggs.

Also off Route 47, a little east of the Heislerville/East Point turnoff, is the road to Moores Beach. There's a parking lot just past the last house on this road, and then a very pitted path that may be wide enough for cars but is clearly not intended for them. You can walk from the parking area about a mile to the beach. This is essentially a walk through salt marsh, although there are some ponds, which attract shorebirds in spring and fall. If you are a bird-watcher, you will find a lot to look at, including herons, egrets, ducks, and geese (not that you can't see lots of ducks and geese in any local park pond, but these belong here and are part of a special landscape). The mudflats at the beach attract more exotic birds in May, when the horseshoe crabs lay their eggs.

Chapter Twenty-eight

Salem and Greenwich: Historic Names, Historic Places

New Jersey's Salem isn't quite as old as the one where witches were hunted, but its history does date back to the seventeenth century. Not only that, it has a generous share of wonderful old buildings. Not far from our Salem, there's a state park adjacent to a tiny national cemetery. And a winding drive away, across the salt marshes, there's Greenwich, a smaller town abundantly graced by lovely old houses; it is known, at least by some, as the town where New Jersey's own Revolutionary War tea party took place.

The southwestern corner of New Jersey, home of Salem and Greenwich, is flat and peaceful. When you look at a map you see that the Delaware River curves around it, getting wider as it gets closer to Delaware Bay. You also notice that however distant it may seem from the busier places, it is not nearly as remote as its peaceful back roads and seemingly unbounded salt marshes would suggest. Wilmington, Delaware, is slightly north across the river, and standing at the edge of New Jersey, looking out with the marshes behind you, you can see bridges, dredges, and a world of activity at odds with the beautiful backcountry a few miles inland. Whichever perspective you take, looking inland or looking out to the water, this

253

corner of the state may be a revelation to you. If you've already been there, then you know it's an acquaintance worth renewing.

For many people, the acquaintance begins at the southernmost exit of the New Jersey Turnpike. From there, Route 49 South leads to Salem. On the way to Salem, marked by an almost-too-unobtrusive sign, Salem County Route 632 runs through a cornfield toward Fort Mott State Park and Finns Point National Cemetery. Before you get to the park itself, you will drive through a lovely stretch of unspoiled (except for power lines) countryside, then suddenly see a tall black metal tower rising at the side of the road. Oddly enough, this is **Finns Point Rear Range Light** (197 Lighthouse Road, Pennsville, 856-935-1487). Set in Supawna Meadows National Wildlife Refuge, the light (there's no house attached) is on the National Register of Historic Places and is designated as a point of interest along the New Jersey Coastal Heritage Trail. It was erected in 1876 for the Lighthouse Service and restored in 1983. Because it would be exposed to high winds, it was built of wrought iron to let the wind blow through openings, rather than the more commonly used and solid cast iron. "Rear" is the key word here; its height of 115 feet was intended to make it visible at a distance from ships that were approaching Finns Point; it was never at the waterfront. There was another light—the Front Range Light—closer to the water; together, the Finns Point Range Lights served as a point of entry for ships passing between the Delaware Bay and River. After the river was deepened by dredging in 1950, the lights became obsolete. From June through September, the light is open to the public on the third Sunday of the month. Even if you cannot enter the light, it makes a short but interesting stop on the way to Fort Mott; in October, it is also a good place to look up at the hawks that float and circle high overhead.

Fort Mott State Park (454 Fort Mott Road, Pennsville, 856-935-3218) overlooks the Delaware River just where it starts to curve east. Fort Mott is the southern center for the New Jersey Coastal Heritage Trail, the driving tour that highlights maritime and local history, coastal habitats, and other natural features throughout the state's coastal areas. The entrance drive to Fort Mott is lined with tall, old maple trees and rail fences; it looks like the approach to a small country estate rather than a somewhat isolated former military post. Established by the federal government after the Civil War, Fort Mott was intended to serve, along with Fort Delaware and Fort DuPont, as one of three forts that would defend the river. The land had been purchased by the federal government in the late 1830s, and nearby, on Pea Patch Island, Fort Delaware had been in operation since the early 1820s. The Civil War delayed construction of a battery at Finns Point, however. Confederate prisoners of war were held at Fort Delaware. In recognition of the Confederate prisoners of war who were buried there, Finns Point National Cemetery was dedicated on October 3, 1873.

Work on the Finns Point fortifications began anew in 1872, and as technology developed and the perceived threat of the Spanish-American War came into view, new fortifications were built at Finns Point in 1896. A long, high concrete-and-earth embankment shielded gun emplacements from the river, and landscaping helped camouflage the fort. The fortification was renamed Fort Mott in honor of General Gershom Mott, who had served in the Mexican-American War and the Civil War. During the early twentieth century, Fort Mott was a full-fledged and self-contained community, with more than thirty buildings, including a hospital, a library, a stable, a YMCA, and a school for soldiers' children. Before World War I, construction of Fort Salisbury in Delaware rendered Fort Mott obsolete, along with its two contemporary neighboring forts, Delaware and DuPont. Although the forts were active through World War II, they were phased out soon after, and the guns that had been at Fort Mott were sent elsewhere. The state of New Jersey bought Fort Mott in 1947 and opened it to the public as a state park in 1951.

Now, Fort Mott State Park still bears many traces of its military past. A self-guided walking tour leads visitors along the embankment, past the batteries, named after officers who served during the nineteenth century, and to the room where a switchboard was installed to centralize control of weapon firing during World War I. There are also scheduled interpretive programs, and living history programs are planned. The park's welcome center has exhibits about

South Jersey history, the construction of Fort Mott, and other park and regional information. A path that goes through a break in the embankment leads to the small building where tickets are sold for the seasonal (April through September) ferry trip to Fort Delaware. A picnic area and playground on the outer side of the embankment provide the more traditional recreational facilities of a state park. Fishing and crabbing are permitted.

Just down a narrow road from Fort Mott is Finns Point National Cemetery. There is a small parking lot just outside the stone enclosure. Beyond the enclosure, a grassy area gives the uncanny first impression of looking like a well-maintained football field. Close to the entrance a graceful miniature Grecian temple, erected in 1936, commemorates the Union soldiers who died while serving at Fort Delaware. Small stone markers are arranged in rows near it. Across the field, a tall, slender column, a gesture of reconciliation, commemorates the more than two thousand Confederate soldiers who died while being held as prisoners of war at the fort.

You have to leave Fort Mott the way you came; on the road that leads back to Route 49. Route 49 leads directly to **Salem**, near the mouth of the Salem River. Salem is a place to visit if you are interested in American history and like to look at old buildings. The approach to town is somewhat industrial, and the first view entering from this direction is of the port of Salem, which in late 2000 was quiet, with empty railroad cars stationed near somewhat rusted buildings. As soon as you turn onto West Broadway, though, the view starts to change. Brick and stuccoed row houses line the streets, and their condition improves as you drive toward the Friends Burial Ground. There seems to be ample street parking along Broadway, so choose a spot anywhere from the Burial Ground on toward Market Street and start to explore. The key streets are Broadway and Market. The Market Street Historic District has been on the state and national registers since 1974, and the Broadway District has been in the registers since 1992. The brick sidewalks add to the atmosphere, though what looks like a mix of old and new brick makes some of the sidewalks look a little patchy; so many towns in New Jersey and elsewhere use new brick sidewalks in an attempt to give their downtowns a mellower, more historic look that at first it's easy to forget that in Salem's case the old brick is authentic.

The **Friends Burial Ground** (West Broadway near Oak Street) is surrounded by a brick wall; the gravestones are the small, low rectangles typical of Quaker cemeteries. Rising from this low-key background is a very old-looking tree. This is the **Salem Oak**, a white oak tree believed to be more than five hundred years old. A tablet erected by the New Jersey Society of Pennsylvania in 1925 says the tree is a survivor of the original forest that was standing here when Salem was founded in 1675 as the first English settlement on the Delaware River by John Fenwick, leader of a Quaker community. Fenwick is supposed to have sat beneath the tree when he negotiated for land with the Native Americans who lived in the area. Across from the burial ground is an impressive brick building that was once the **Orthodox Friends Meeting House** (107 Broadway); built in 1852, it is a replica of the 1772 **Friends Meeting House** at East Broadway and Walnut Street.

As you leave the burial ground and walk toward Market Street, you will pass the public library, a wonderfully ornate structure dating from 1885, featuring a combination of stone and brick, topped by green fretwork.

Market Street is where the historic buildings are most concentrated and most fixed-up. The old **Salem County Courthouse** at the corner of Broadway and Market is picture-perfect. The first courthouse was built in 1692 and replaced in 1735. The present building incorporates part of the 1735 structure, but largely reflects an 1817 expansion and renovation and a 1908 remodeling. The brass cannon in front of the courthouse is from the War of 1814. Nearby on Market Street is the county office building, designed in 1850. Walking down Market Street away from Broadway gives you a view of the very graceful white steeple of the **First Presbyterian Church**. The **Johnson House** (90 Market Street) is tucked back from the street next door to the church. Built in 1806, it is important not just because it's nice to look at but also because it was the home of local landowner Robert G. Johnson, "the champion of New Jersey tomatoes" according to the plaque in front of the house. Johnson imported tomato plants, and, in 1820, he ate one on the steps of the old courthouse to convince people that they were not poisonous. The tomato became an important component of Salem County's agricultural economy; there were more than two dozen canning factories in the county by 1900, including the Heinz ketchup factory.

Another interesting home is the **Goodwin Sisters' House** (47 Market Street), built in 1821. Abigail and Elizabeth Goodwin operated an Underground Railroad Station here.

This stretch of Market Street is the heart of the formally designated Salem Historic District. To explore the past in greater depth, a visit to the **Salem County Historical Museum and Library** (79–83 Market Street, 856-935-5004) is definitely in order. Housed in the Alexander Grant House, which dates to 1721, it is open from noon to 4 PM Tuesday through Friday and the second Saturday of each month and Sunday from 1:30 to 3:30. Even if the museum is closed when you are in Salem, you can enjoy its beautiful brick exterior. The brick **Fenwick Building** next door was built in 1891 as a hotel and converted just after World War I to a county hospital for soldiers. Renovated in 1989, it now serves as a county office building. Signs explaining the historic sites along Market Street were put up in 1998 by the 1798 Fair Committee.

Not all the storefronts look as though they are thriving, but Salem is a member of the Main Street New Jersey Program. The program, established in 1989, builds on the Main Street Approach™ developed by the National Trust for Historic Preservation's National Main Street Center to aid downtown revitalization efforts. The Main Street program provides a series of services for businesses in Salem, including preservation education, promotional activities, grant-application preparation, and marketing advice, as well as a packet of information for visitors, listing local businesses of many kinds. Although signs along the downtown sidewalks invite you to discover historic Salem, on a recent weekday morning in October, it didn't look as though too many people had found it. With luck and continued hard work, perhaps by the time you visit, the streets will be bustling, the historic buildings as beautiful as ever, and the shops prospering.

Driving out of Salem along East Broadway will lead you directly to signs for the **Hancock House** in Hancock's Bridge; here's another officially designated historic site—this one from the Revolutionary War. The drive is very pretty, and the house itself would be interesting even if nothing had happened here, because of the intricate herringbone-pattern brickwork on one end. The brickwork is highlighted by the initials HWS (for William and Sarah Hancock) and the date 1734 (the year the house was built). The event that gives the Hancock House its place in Revolutionary history is grim. In March 1778, British General Sir William Howe sent 1,500 British troops and loyalists, under the command of General Charles Mawhood, to find food, cattle, and horses in South Jersey to provide sustenance for the larger British army in Philadelphia. About a month earlier, George Washington had sent General Anthony Wayne on a similar errand to benefit the American troops at Valley Forge. Many of the people in Salem County were Quakers who opposed war but supported the American cause, and the local militia and other citizens resisted the British troops. The British were halted at Quinton's Bridge and, to punish the people of the area, General Mawhood ordered his troops to execute local citizens. About three hundred British troops, guided by local Tories and led by Major John Simcoe, attacked the Hancock House, which was known as a place where the local militia gathered. Ten Americans were killed, including Judge William Hancock of the County Court for the County of Salem, son of the William Hancock who had built the house. The British troops left Salem County a few days later.

Hancock House Historic Site is administered by the state park service and staffed by rangers from Fort Mott (Wednesday through Sunday from Memorial Day through Labor Day; first and third Saturday of each month September through May). This is another of those places worth visiting when it is open and worth a look even when it is closed. The house and setting, at Front Street and Locust Island Road overlooking the salt marshes and Alloways Creek, are still evocative of earlier times, and a display case outside the building contains a variety of helpful brochures about both the site and Salem County in general.

Going east from Hancock's Bridge, several county roads wind through the fields through small towns such as Harmersville and Canton; they present several ways to get to Greenwich. They are very narrow and have no shoulders but because they are fairly level and not heavily trafficked, they would be good for adult bicycle riding.

On the way to Greenwich from Salem, I accidentally came across an unusual point of interest along the New Jersey Coastal Heritage Trail: the **Stow Creek Bald Eagle Nest Viewing Platform**, just south of Canton on Route 623 and just north of the bridge that spans Stow Creek, separating Salem County from Cumberland County. There's room to pull over and park, then walk a few yards along a path away from the road that leads to the wooden platform. Between 1983 and 1990, the state department of fish, game, and wildlife raised and released sixty young eagles in southern New Jersey. The eagles first built a nest here in 1990, and it was productive through most of the next decade, though there were no eaglets in 1997. A new nest was built in 1998, and two eaglets were raised here in 1999. Thanks to the state program, in 1999 there were twenty-one pairs of nesting eagles in the region.

As you approach **Greenwich** from this direction on Route 623, the area becomes gently rolling rather than flat. Starting at the community of Othello, there is a stretch of historic buildings just before downtown Greenwich, including the Greenwich Presbyterian Church and the brick Hicksite Friends Meeting. A sweeping bend in **Greate Street** makes a striking approach to the center of town, where the street is lined with perfect eighteenth-century houses. The **Gibbon House** (856-451-8454), now open as the home of the Cumberland County Historical Society, is one highlight on Greate Street. Another, an officially designated Coastal Heritage Trail point of interest, is the **Teaburner Monument** at the corner of Market Lane. Erected in 1908, it honors the "patriots of Cumberland County who on the evening of December 22 1774 burned British tea" near the site. The tea had

Walter Choroszewski

Teaburner Monument, Greenwich

been taken off a British ship and stored in the basement of a local Tory because the ship's captain thought the tea would be safer in Greenwich than in Philadelphia, which was its intended final destination. The Stone Tavern (1730) and the Friends Meeting (c. 1770) are other lovely old buildings you can admire as you stroll along Greate Street.

The Gibbon House, built in 1730 by wealthy merchant Nicholas Gibbon, is a replica of a London townhouse he admired. The brick is laid in the Flemish Bond pattern using a red stretcher and blue header. The house is furnished with eighteenth- and nineteenth-century items. Open-fire cooking demonstrations are held in the kitchen, which has a walk-in fireplace. The second floor contains several exhibits, including children's toys, a craft room, and Civil War artifacts. The Barn Museum behind the house displays nineteenth-century farming, housekeeping, and shipbuilding tools. The house is open April through mid-December, Tuesday through Saturday from noon to 4 PM, and Sunday from 2 to 5 PM. It is closed in January, February, and March.

The **John Dubois Maritime Museum** (856-451-8454), also on Greate Street, contains a large collection of southern New Jersey maritime items from the nineteenth and early twentieth centuries, including tools used to carve ship ribs, planking, masts, and booms. It is open April through November on Sundays from 1 PM to 4 PM, or by appointment.

Greenwich was laid out by John Fenwick, and during the late seventeenth century it thrived as a port on the Cohansey River. When Bridgeton was named the Cumberland County seat in 1748, Greenwich started to decline, and by 1800, as road transportation improved, Greenwich's importance as a water-transportation center waned. There was little development in town over the ensuing centuries, and Greenwich's architecture and serenity are wonderfully preserved. You can follow signs to the piers and boatworks for a reminder of the waterfront that helped shape Greenwich's past.

Uncommercial and unspoiled as Greenwich is, however, you don't need to go hungry while you are there. The **Greenwich Country Store** (1016 Ye Greate Street, 856-453-3622), next door to the post office, sells sandwiches, salads, and beverages; there are tables inside if you prefer not to picnic.

At the mouth of the Cohansey River, not far from Greenwich, is one of New Jersey's more unusual lighthouses: **Ship John Shoal Lighthouse**, named for a ship that crashed on the nearby shoal and sank in 1797; fortunately, vessels from Greenwich were able to save all sixty passengers. Although the water is only about eight feet deep at this point, and therefore hazardous to ship traffic, a warning light was not established here until the middle of the nineteenth century; the existing lighthouse was first lit in 1874. The octagonal, mansard-roofed keeper's house, built in 1877, makes this light especially distinctive. It is not open to the public.

A Change of Pace

Although Salem County is still rural, it may come as something of a surprise to learn that a weekly rodeo is one of the area's best-known and most popular attractions. The **Cowtown Rodeo** (780 Route 40, just west of Sharptown, in Pilesgrove Township, 856-769-3200) has its roots in Salem County's agricultural past, when livestock and livestock auctions were a basic part of the economy. In its present Saturday-night version, the rodeo is run by Grant Harris, whose family started Cowtown Rodeo more than seventy years ago. The Rodeo is open May through September, with shows starting at 7:30 and running until about 10 PM. In 2000, admission was $10 for adults and $5 for children, and this is definitely something children will enjoy. Among the events are bareback riding, calf roping, steer wrestling, team roping, and bull roping—a cowboy movie come to life in a family-friendly setting.

About two miles east, Woodstown has a tree-lined Main Street, a variety of shops, and interesting old houses, but not the intensely historic quality of Salem and Greenwich. This pleasant place is good for a stroll or a snack. During the day, if you are heading north and don't want to get on a superhighway, you can enjoy a very pretty stretch of Route 45, which will lead you to the town of **Mullica Hill** and its very tempting collection of antique shops. They include the Grate Shop, which sells old iron heating grates and is just one of many appealing shops in the **Yellow Garage Antique Marketplace** (66 South Main Street, Mullica Hill, 609-478-0300), and **Raccoon's Tale** (6 High Street, Mullica Hill, 609-478-4488), where you can buy mid-twentieth-century American pottery. Mullica Hill is fairly compact; most of the shops and antiques centers run along Main Street, which is Route 45, with a few outlying shops on the side streets just off Main Street. Although Route 45 is a main north-south route, the overall atmosphere of Mullica Hill is still sheltered and peaceful, just right for walking and browsing.

Index

Moores Beach, 252
Moorestown, 180
Morris Canal, 44, 79–80, 84, 95, 106,
   158
Morristown, 85–96
Morristown National Historical Park,
   85–90; Cross Estate Gardens, 89;
   Ford Mansion, 86, 87; Jockey Hol-
   low, 86, 87–88; New Jersey Brigade
   Area, 89; visitor center, 88; Wick
   House, 88
Morven, 119
mountain biking, 55, 59, 61
Mount Holly, 177–179
Mount Hope Historical Park, 84
Mount Mitchell Scenic Overlook, 186
Mountain Creek, 61
Musconetcong Art Gallery, 160
museums: American Labor Museum/
   Botto House National Landmark,
   47–48; Atlantic City Historical Mu-
   seum, 221; Canal Museum, 80;
   Franklin Mineral Museum and Mine
   Replica, 64; George Woodruff In-
   dian Museum, 248; Gibbon House,
   262; John Dubois Maritime Mu-
   seum, 262; Liberty Science Center,
   4–5; Long Beach Island Museum,
   212; Macculloch Hall Historical
   Museum, 95; Monmouth Museum,
   192; Museum of American Glass,
   242–243; Nail Mill Museum, 249;
   Newark Museum, 33–35; New Jersey Children's Museum, 27; New
   Jersey Historical Society, 35–36;
   New Jersey State Museum, 169; New
   Sweden Farmstead Museum, 249;
   Noyes Museum, 224; Old Barracks
   Museum, 169; Paterson Museum,
   46; Salem County Historical Museum and Library, 258; Sea Life Education Center, 223; Sterling Hill

Mining Museum, 64; Stickley Museum at Craftsman Farms, 91–92

natural areas: Edwin B. Forsythe National Wildlife Refuge, 224–226;
   Great Swamp National Wildlife Refuge, 97–99; Heislerville Wildlife
   Management Area, 252; Island
   Beach State Park, 196–197
Newark, 29–42; baseball in, 29, 31–
   33; Branch Brook Park, 39–40; ca-
   thedral, 36–38; Loop Shuttle Bus,
   30, 35; Newark Museum, 33–35;
   New Jersey Historical Society, 35–
   36; performing arts in, 29–31
Newark Museum, 33–35; Ballantine
   Mansion, 34–35; Junior Museum,
   35; parking, 35; planetarium, 33–34;
   special programs, 35
New Bridge Landing Historic Park,
   22–24
New Jersey Cardinals, 65
New Jersey Children's Museum, 27
New Jersey Coastal Heritage Trail, 186,
   252, 254, 260
New Jersey Historical Society, 33–34
New Jersey Performing Arts Center, 29–
   31; Prudential Hall, 30; Victoria The-
   ater, 30; restaurants, 31; tours, 31
New Jersey State Aquarium, 181
New Jersey State Museum, 169
Newton, 61, 67
NJ Transit Terminal (Hoboken), 12–14
North Jersey Coast Line, 201–202
North Haledon, 47–48
Northlandz, 133
Noyes Museum, 224

Ocean City, 238–239; Music Pier, 239
Ocean Grove, 199–200; architecture,
   200; food, 200; Great Auditorium,
   200; history, 199

Old Barracks Museum, 169
Old Dutch Parsonage, 123–124
Old Mine Road, 70
Old Tennent Church, 136–137
Oxford, 150–152; Oxford Furnace, 150; Pequest Wildlife Management Area, 151–152; Shippen Manor, 151
oyster industry, 249, 250

Palisades Interstate Park, 19–22; picnicking, 20; trails, 20, 21–22
parks and forests: Allaire State Park, 202–204; Allamuchy State Park, 83; Barnegat Lighthouse State Park, 210–212; Bass River State Park, 213–214; Branch Brook Park, 39–40; Bridgeton City Park, 209; Cape May Point State Park, 232–233; Colonial Park, 129–130; Cooper Mill County Park, 108–109; Corson's Inlet State Park, 239; Deep Cut Park, 192; Delaware and Raritan Canal State Park, 120, 126–129; Fort Mott State Park, 254–256; Garrett Mountain Reservation, 49; Gateway National Recreation Area, 188–190; Hacklebarney State Park, 109–110; High Point State Park, 59–60; Holmdel Park, 191; Hopatcong State Park, 65–66; Hugh Moore Park, 157; Island Beach State Park, 194–197; Kittatinny Valley State Park, 61; Lewis Morris County Park, 88–89; Liberty State Park, 1–4; Long Pond Ironworks State Park, 54; Lord Stirling Park, 100–101; Monmouth Battlefield State Park, 135–136; Mount Hope Historical Park, 84; Palisades Interstate Park, 19–22; Park and Fifth Streets (Hoboken), 15; Patriots' Path, 109; Princeton Battlefield State Park, 114–115;

Ringwood State Park, 50–57; Round Valley Recreation Area, 153–154; Seven Presidents Oceanfront Park, 201; Spruce Run Recreation Area, 154–156; Stokes State Forest, 60–61; Swartswood State Park, 61; Washington Crossing State Park, 171, 172–173; Wawayanda State Park, 58–59; Wharton State Forest, 213–216
Paterson, 43–49; food, 49; Great Falls of the Passaic, 43, 44–46; Lambert Castle, 49; museum, 45, 46; silk industry, 44; submarines, 46; walking in, 46–47
Paterson Museum, 45, 46
Patriots' Path, 109
Paulus Hook Historic District, 7
Pequest Wildlife Management Area, 151–152; butterfly garden, 152; education center, 152; fishing area, 151; hatchery, 151–152; natural resource trail, 152
Peters Valley Craft Education Center, 75–76; Gallery Without Walls, 76
Phillipsburg, 158
picnicking, 53, 57, 82, 88, 108, 111, 120, 127, 129–130, 135, 147, 150, 151, 152, 154, 155, 157, 163, 191, 196, 201, 210, 213, 249, 256
playgrounds, 89, 130, 135, 201, 256
Point Pleasant Beach, 198–199, 202; antiques, 198; food, 199; Jenkinson's, 198
Princeton, 112–122; Battle of Princeton, 114–115; cemetery, 118; food, 121–122; Historical Society, 119; houses, 118; parks, 120; university, 112–113; walking tours, 119
Princeton Battlefield State Park, 114–115; Battle Monument, 115; Clarke House, 115; Mercer Oak, 115